REFERENCE GUIDES IN LITERATURE
NUMBER 10
Everett Emerson, *Editor*
Joseph Katz, *Consulting Editor*

EARLY PURITAN WRITERS:
A Reference Guide

William Bradford
John Cotton
Thomas Hooker
Edward Johnson
Richard Mather
Thomas Shepard

Edward J. Gallagher

Thomas Werge

G. K. HALL & CO., 70 LINCOLN STREET, BOSTON, MASS.

Library of Congress Cataloging in Publication Data

Gallagher, Edward Joseph, 1940-
    Early puritan writers.

    (Reference guides in literature ; no. 10)
    Bibliography: p.
    Includes index.
    1. American literature--Colonial period, ca.
1600-1775--Bibliography. I. Werge, Thomas, joint
author. II. Title.
Z1227.G34   016.81'08'001   76-2498
ISBN 0-8161-1196-0

This publication is printed on permanent/durable acid-free paper
MANUFACTURED IN THE UNITED STATES OF AMERICA

Contents

Introduction

New England theology...with its intense clearness, its sharp-cut
crystalline edges and needles of thought, has had in a peculiar
degree the power of lacerating the nerves of the soul.... In New
England society, where all poetic forms, all the draperies and ac-
cessories of religious ritual, have been rigidly and unsparingly
retrenched, there was nothing between the soul and these austere and
terrible problems; it was constantly and severely brought face to
face with their infinite mystery.
> —Harriet Beecher Stowe, Oldtown Folks

Our critical assumptions about, and interpretations of, the
thought and writings of the six first-generation Puritans included
in this volume have shifted considerably during the past century.
The attacks on the English Puritans in the first half of the seventeenth century by Laud and other Anglican churchmen gave way, during
the last part of that same century, to hagiographies. The originally
pejorative descriptions of "Puritan" and "Dissenter" were invested
with positive and in some places even heroic meaning. Since then,
and since the appearance in 1878 of Moses Coit Tyler's monumental A
History of American Literature, 1607-1765, our critical attitudes
toward these six figures have been characterized by three major modes:
an "antiquarian" reverence, pietistic in tone, which is nonetheless
often marked by uncertainty and ambivalence; an active hostility
based on the conviction that the Puritans were oppressive, theocratic,
and the champions of a repressive theological and political doctrine
whose tenets held democracy and liberty in check until Franklin and
Jefferson; and a sustained insistence that Puritan ideas and literature possess a depth and integrity, morally and aesthetically, that
modernity had deliberately or unconsciously chosen to ignore in order
to preserve its own self-image--and to pursue its own self-deceptions.
In the past twenty years, the criticism of Puritan thought and literature has emerged with a strength, vitality, and complexity that for
the most part eschews extreme polemics. Yet its position toward the
Puritans is clearly and consistently sympathetic.

INTRODUCTION

These general patterns may be seen in the criticism of each of the
six figures. It is especially pronounced, however, in the criticism
of John Cotton, Thomas Shepard, and Thomas Hooker. The question
whether Hooker's polity in Connecticut was "democratic," either incip-
iently or explicitly, rather than orthodox, sets him somewhat apart
from Cotton and Shepard. Similarly, Bradford's status an an especially
venerated Pilgrim in Plymouth rather than a Massachusetts Bay Puritan;
Mather's role as part of a religious and political "dynasty" as well
as a divine about whose prose very little has been written in recent
times; and Johnson's interest as a prose stylist and apologist for,
and interpreter of, the Heilegeschichte of New England, all tend to
differentiate their situations from those of Cotton and Shepard. Yet
in its broad outlines the critical interpretations of these three major
figures are valid for the others as well; and to examine the history
of the criticism of any one of the three is to examine the criticism
of the other two. As Tyler states: "Of all the great preachers who
came to New England in our first age, there were three who, according
to the universal opinion of their contemporaries, towered above all
others,--Thomas Hooker, Thomas Shepard, John Cotton. These three could
be compared with one another; but with them could be compared no one
else."[1]

Tyler's seminal study of the literature of the American Puritans
is not "antiquarian" in nature or tone. He characterizes the similarity
of Cotton, Hooker, and Shepard in language at once valid and admiring:
"They were alike in bold and energetic thinking, in massiveness of
erudition, in a certain overpowering personal persuasiveness, in the
gift of fascinating and resistless pulpit oratory."[2] Yet the ambivalence that marks the antiquarian accounts of Shepard, for example,
written during the first decades of the twentieth century, also typifies
Tyler's more searching analyses. The tone of the antiquarians seeks
constantly to vindicate the human qualities of the Puritans in the face
of their abhorrent theology. It attempts to rescue them from the
hagiography that makes them inaccessible and the condemnation that
makes them anathema. "At least these gleanings prove," goes the common refrain, "that our ancestors were human." The interpretation of
the men is often admiring; of their thought, negative. Even a cursory
examination of Tyler's language reveals similar ambivalences. The
theology of the New England Puritans is harsh, strident, terrifying;
but the men are noble, brilliant, and often generous of spirit. Ours
is an age that is "grinning and flabby, an age hating effort, and
requiring to be amused." In contrast, the age of the Puritans was an
age of faith, earnestness, "mental robustness," and the religious
writings of the early Puritans are prodigious "monuments of vast
learning, and of a stupendous intellectual energy both in the men who
produced them and in the men who listened to them." They can no longer

---

[1]*A History of American Literature, 1607-1765* (New York: G. P. Putnam's
Sons, 1878), I, p. 193.

[2]*ibid.*, p. 193.

be of any "vital human interest," and "few of them can be cited as literature." But though we may see them as relics, concludes Tyler, "they were conceived by noble minds; they are themselves noble. They are superior to our jests. We may deride them, if we will; but they are not derided."[3]

For Tyler, the language of the American Puritans, including that of Cotton, Shepard, and Hooker, comes to represent both the power of the Puritan spirit and the greatest difficulty our own historical imagination confronts in dealing with that spirit. Most Puritan writings "have long since done their work in moving the minds of men." Their theology "lingers in the memory of mankind only through certain shells of words long since emptied of their original meaning." But if the concrete words so central to Puritan experience are only abstruse "shells" to modernity, Tyler insists that there is no denying their efficacy for the Puritan mind and heart. Tyler has been roundly criticized of late for his tone toward Puritan theology. But his discussions of Shepard and Hooker emphasize the animating power and even beauty of their language. Similarly, he identifies the "central and commanding incident" which "would seem sometimes to shake the world of New England to its centre" as the sermon. Tyler's respect for the force and authenticity of the language of Shepard and Hooker, his corresponding sense that their words have become empty shells for our own time, his distaste for the "stern and haggard" oppressiveness of Puritan theology and certain of its political forms, and his sustained contrast between the "flabbiness" of modern thought and the granite-like integrity of Puritan faith, constitute the complexity of his point of view. Emerson adumbrates it when, in 1842, he comments on the "hollow" and "cunning" nature of the rhetoric, preaching, and institution of Unitarianism, and continues: "But in the days of the Pilgrims and the Puritans, the preachers were the victims of the same faith with which they whipped and persecuted other men, and their sermons are strong, imaginative, fervid, and every word a cube of stone."[4]

No such admiration for the intensity of Puritan language or thought characterizes the major commentaries on American Puritanism during the years from 1910 to 1930. For various reasons, none of them legitimate, Puritanism and prohibitionism came to be regarded as the same oppressive force. H. L. Mencken defined a Puritan as someone possessed by the haunting fear that someone, somewhere, might be happy. "Mr. Dooley" suggested that the Puritans founded Thanksgiving in gratitude for being preserved from the Indians, and we keep it to give thanks for being preserved from the Puritans. In more elaborate, sustained, and scholarly forms, Brooks Adams, James Truslow Adams, and Vernon Louis Parrington advanced the same theme.

---

[3]ibid., pp. 192-93.

[4]Bliss Perry (ed.), The Heart of Emerson's Journals (Boston: Houghton Mifflin Co., 1926), pp. 178-79.

Introduction

Parrington's <u>Main Currents in American Thought</u> was unquestionably
the most important and influential study of New England Puritanism,
in the larger framework of American economic and cultural history,
to be written during this period. Parrington explicitly stated his
point of view as that of a Jeffersonian democrat who viewed the course
of American history as a progressive movement from theocratic to democratic rule. Two of Parrington's assumptions deserve special notice.
First, he argued that men are motivated more by economic and political
concerns than by "religious ideas"; the methodologies of Tawney, Veblen,
and, more immediately, Charles Beard, are significant here. Second,
Parrington tended to consistently associate theological preoccupations
with political tyranny. The growth of freedom and democracy in
America came about despite the best efforts of the Puritans to sup-
press it.

The specific judgments and omissions of Parrington's study follow
logically from these assumptions. Jonathan Edwards was an "anachro-
nism" whose typically Puritan fascinations were morbid: hellfire, sin,
damnation, self-abasement. Had he not been "shackled" by his Calvinist
language, he might have been a great thinker. Shepard is not mentioned; Cotton is the quintessential Puritan theocrat; and while Hooker
is praised, it is for his atypical democratic and liberal ideas.
Parrington portrays only Roger Williams and Hooker with any real sympathy, and their anticipation of modern democracy is the source of
their ideological importance for him. Except for these two figures,
American thought was largely a barren and sterile landscape until the
advent of Franklin. There is no better way to see revealed the outlines of Parrington's critical vision than to read, in the juxtaposition
in which they occur, his concluding paragraph on the intolerant, morbid, and anachronistic Edwards and his introduction to the generous,
benign, and brilliantly modern Franklin. Although Parrington was
aware of the emergence of a very different and far more sympathetic
critical attitude toward the American Puritans--most explicitly in
Kenneth B. Murdock's study of Increase Mather--he interpreted it as
a form of special pleading: an apologia for the early giants of
Harvard written by Harvard professors who were their real, or would-
be, ancestors.

The work of Perry Miller--and of such others as Murdock, Samuel
Eliot Morison, and, more recently, Edmund Morgan--made Parrington's
charge of special pleading irrelevant. More than any other scholar,
Miller, in his studies of the Puritan mind, became the foremost interpreter of the Puritan rhetorical, philosophical, and theological
tradition. Michael McGiffert's description of Miller's <u>The New
England Mind, The Seventeenth Century</u>, is precisely apt: it "remains
the monumental study to which all subsequent work on the subject is
elaboration, clarification, qualification, or contradiction."[5]

---

[5]Michael McGiffert (ed.), <u>God's Plot, The Paradoxes of Puritan Piety,
Being the Autobiography and Journal of Thomas Shepard</u> ([Amherst, Massachu-
setts]: University of Massachusetts Press, 1972), p. 240.

INTRODUCTION

Miller's learned examinations of Puritan thought, rhetoric, history, social and political forms, and concern with the apocalypse have not been surpassed, nor are they likely to be.[6] Whether it is substantive, or, as it is on occasion, churlish, even the most recent criticism of Miller's studies acknowledges his preeminent place.

Two recurring themes in Miller's thought are of great importance in understanding the nature of his contribution. In interpreting the Puritan mind--and his interpretations make important and consistent use of Cotton, Shepard, and Hooker, the last of whom he insists is as thoroughly orthodox and non-democratic as Cotton and Shepard--Miller assumes that ideas, more than economic circumstances, determine events. Belief and character are far more important considerations in the workings of history than Marxist or other naturalistic commentators are willing to allow. In addition, Miller is clearly and consistently sympathetic to the distinctively religious ideas of the Puritans. If our age has no conception of the meaning of the covenant, regeneration, grace, or sin--most undergraduates, remarks Miller, believe sin to be an invention of Kafka's--the fault lies not in the Puritans but in ourselves. It would perhaps be excessive to call Miller an apologist for the Puritan vision of the world. Miller could be as ironic about Puritanism as about the modern world, and he also remarked that if the origins of American civilization had been economic rather than religious, he would have explored them with equal vigor; these origins simply happened to be religious ideas. Yet one rightly mistrusts this last assertion. Tyler's contrast between the flabby and anti-intellectual shallowness of his time and the penetrating, tough-minded clarity and faith of the Puritan world finds a strong and recurring echo in Miller's works. His sympathetic mode dominates the ironic. To Parrington's contention that American history consists in the casting off of theocracy and the growth of liberalism and democracy, Miller countered that it might more profoundly be seen as the gradual shedding of a fundamentally religious conception of the universe and of man's place in it.

During the past twenty years, important studies of Hooker, Shepard, Cotton, and the literary and theological traditions of American Puritanism have followed on the seminal studies by Miller, Murdock, and Morison. Several areas of investigation first examined by Miller have been elaborated on and clarified, as in Edmund Morgan's consideration of the "morphology of conversion" in Visible Saints and Babette May Levy's consideration of prose style in Preaching in the First Half Century of New England History. Other areas Miller did not explore with any detail, such as the Puritan tradition of meditation, have been treated more closely. The theology, hagiography, sermon form, prose style, poetry, intellectual history, autobiographies, and

---

[6]For a discussion of recent "revisionist" tendencies with respect to Miller, see Michael McGiffert, "American Puritan Studies in the 1960's," WMQ, third series, XXVII (January, 1970), 36-67.

soteriology of the American Puritans are now being accorded scholarly and sympathetic analysis. Although the bibliographical and textual problems surrounding the establishment of sound texts and editions of Puritan writings are formidable, important work is progressing in that area. There have been several first-rate considerations of individual Puritans and particular sermons in the very recent past.

Apart from the clear bibliographical and textual needs, several other areas of concern seem especially in need of scholarship: the relationships between the Puritans and the ancient philosophers, the Church Fathers, and medieval thought; the relationships between the Puritans and Luther, Calvin, Beza, and other Reformation thinkers; and the relationships between later American authors and their Puritan predecessors. Even now, caricatures of Aristotle, patristic writings, and the medieval mind creep into otherwise sane and scholarly dis-cussions of Puritan thought. In some instances, these pervasive in-fluences are not mentioned at all. It often seems as though the history of ideas is bound to begin with Peter Ramus. While some work has been done to illuminate the influences of Calvin, Luther, and others in the Reformation tradition on the American Puritans, much more remains to be explored and accomplished. Serious students of American literature have long known that the Puritan influence in later American literature and thought has been formative. As Ran-dall Stewart and others have noted, it is significant that our most important nineteenth-century authors--including Hawthorne, Emerson, and Melville--are those who have most strongly felt the Puritan tradition to be part of their own "useable past." The specific theological and literary uses they make of that tradition remain to be clarified. But Michael Colacurcio's recent study of Hawthorne's use of Puritan and antinomian ideas and images in The Scarlet Letter, as well as briefer studies by other scholars following similar lines of inquiry, are beginning to point a promising way.[7]

In an age in which modern literature, as Richard Poirier has said, is constantly in the process of telling us how little it means, it seems clear that the writings of the Puritans will continue to compel our interest and concern. The self-contained, even solipsistic aestheticism and triviality of much contemporary writing will con-tinue to prove insufficient. Faith and language, as Emerson recognized in the Divinity School Address, are mutually dependent: when religious meaning and purpose disappear, they take with them any hope for an efficacious language. When Norman Mailer lamented that modern American Protestantism, with few exceptions, had become "oriented to the machine, and lukewarm in its enthusiasm for such notions an heaven, hell, and the soul,"[8] his lament was made still more intense by the

---

[7]"Footsteps of Anne Hutchinson: The Context of The Scarlet Letter," ELH, XXXIX (September, 1972), 459-94.

[8]"Catholic and Protestant" in "The Hip and the Square," Advertisements for Myself (New York: G. P. Putnam's Sons, 1959), p. 426.

realization that the loss of this vision made inevitable the frag-
mentation of language and meaning as well as America's rejection of
its religious origins, identity, and purpose. For the Puritans,
words are referential in a sense both human and divine. They matter
and have meaning. If those words are often severe, they are often
tender. Whatever their tone and immediate point of reference, they
are meant to lead the soul to self-knowledge, solace, and ultimately
to salvation. Allen Tate has said that "the New England idea" had
"an immense, incalculable value for literature: it dramatized the
human soul."[9] The dramatizing of the soul is a perennial human need
and a perennial process. The American Puritans' ability to intensely
dramatize the individual and national soul through their theology,
literature, and faith, suggests that our own concern with their
thought and writings will be equally, and justly, perennial.

In assembling this reference guide we have tried to cite all
significant twentieth century writings about each of the six authors.
We have also included substantive material from the seventeenth,
eighteenth, and nineteenth centuries; and we have included passing
references and brief notices from these centuries when some particular
historical interest, or some clear originality in content or style
is involved. In accordance with the principles of this series,
primary material is included only when there is important editorial
or introductory apparatus.

The index contains the titles of the secondary material, the
authors of the secondary material, and, since the number of citations
for each author is relatively small, only several subject categories
such as biography, bibliography, Anne Hutchinson, democracy, and
typology. There are references for specific works by individual
authors, but in Bradford and Johnson, for instance, essentially one-
book authors, references are made only to their lesser known work
(e.g. Bradford's poetry and Johnson's Good News).

We also recommend the following basic and general books on the
colonial period for a broader understanding of the context within
which these six authors lived and wrote: William Haller's The Rise
of Puritanism, W. Fraser Mitchell's English Pulpit Oratory from
Andrewes to Tillotson, Perry Miller's New England Mind: The Seven-
teenth Century and Errand into the Wilderness, Moses Coit Tyler's
History of American Literature, 1607-1765, Edmund S. Morgan's Visible
Saints, Michael Walzer's Revolution of the Saints, Herbert W.
Schneider's, The Puritan Mind, Vernon Louis Parrington's The Colonial
Mind, 1620-1800, Kenneth B. Murdock's Literature and Theology in
Colonial New England, Babette M. Levy's Preaching in the First Half
Century of New England History, and Alan Heimert's Religion and the
American Mind.

---

[9]Collected Essays (Denver, Colorado: Alan Swallow, 1959), p. 199.

Introduction

Finally, we would like to thank Prof. Jackson R. Bryer, Joan Bischoff, Kevin Cole, Joel Kehler, Steven Grohovsky, Rita Bonventre, Ann Harson, and Noelle Werge for generously assisting in the research and proofreading; Prof. George Jenkins of Lehigh University's Office of Research for a grant; Mary Jo Carlen for typing the final copy; and the library staffs of the University of Notre Dame, Lehigh University (especially William J. Fincke, Jr.), Rutgers University in New Brunswick, New Brunswick Theological Seminary of the Reformed Church in America, New York Public Library, Historical Society of Pennsylvania, and the American Philosophical Society.

List of Abbreviations

AHR   American Historical Review
AL   American Literature
AN&Q   American Notes and Queries
AQ   American Quarterly
ArQ   Arizona Quarterly
BNYPL   Bulletin of the New York Public Library
BPLQ   Boston Public Library Quarterly
BRMMLA   Bulletin of the Rocky Mountain Modern Language Association
BuR   Bucknell Review
CE   College English
CH   Church History
CHR   Catholic Historical Review
CJ   Classical Journal
CMHS   Collections of the Massachusetts Historical Society
DA   Dissertation Abstracts
DAI   Dissertation Abstracts International
DD   Doctoral Dissertations in America
EAL   Early American Literature
EALN   Early American Literature Newsletter
EHR   English Historical Review
EIHC   Essex Institute Historical Collections
ELH   Journal of English Literary History
ESQ   Emerson Society Quarterly
HLB   Harvard Library Bulletin
HLQ   Huntington Library Quarterly
HTR   Harvard Theological Review
JA   Jahrbuch fur Amerikastudien
JAH   Journal of American History
JEGP   Journal of English and Germanic Philology
JHI   Journal of the History of Ideas
JMH   Journal of Modern History
JSH   Journal of Southern History
LQ   Library Quarterly
MLN   Modern Language Notes
MP   Modern Philology
MVHR   Mississippi Valley Historical Review
NEHGR   New England Historical and Genealogical Register

LIST OF ABBREVIATIONS

NEQ	New England Quarterly
PAAS	Proceedings of the American Antiquarian Society
PBSA	Papers of the Bibliographical Society of America
PCSM	Publications of the Colonial Society of Massachusetts
PMHS	Proceedings of the Massachusetts Historical Society
PULC	Princeton University Library Chronicle
QQ	Queen's Quarterly
RALS	Resources for American Literary Study
SCN	Seventeenth-Century News
SELit	Studies in English Literature (Tokyo)
TLS	Times Literary Supplement
WMQ	William and Mary Quarterly
YR	Yale Review

Writings About William Bradford, 1669 - 1973

1669 A   BOOKS - NONE

1669 B   SHORTER WRITINGS

1   MORTON, NATHANIEL. <u>New Englands Memoriall</u>. Cambridge, Massachusetts: Printed by S. G. and M. J. for John Usher of Boston.
Much of this work, which contains two poems on Bradford's
death, was taken from Bradford's manuscript.

1702 A   BOOKS - NONE

1702 B   SHORTER WRITINGS

1   MATHER, COTTON. "Galeacius Secundus. The Life of William
Bradford, Esq.; Governor of Plymouth Colony," in <u>Magnalia
Christi Americana</u>, Book II. London: Thomas Parkhurst,
pp. 2-5.
    Bradford's association with the Puritans is developed
through emphasis on a long sickness, reading of scripture,
the illuminating ministry of Richard Clifton, many dis-
tresses of the mind, and a resolve in the face of the rage
of his friends which is soon ratified by a remarkable providence. The "Consumption of his Estate" while in Holland
comes to prevent a "Consumption in his Virtue," and his role
as governor in Plymouth (exemplified in the well known
Christmas game, personal property, and Weston episodes)
mark a "well-temper'd spirit," a man of more than ordinary
piety, wisdom, and courage. Bradford is a Moses, and
Mather, finally, takes special notice of his unselfishness,
learning, and time of death.

1747 A   BOOKS - NONE

1747 B   SHORTER WRITINGS

1   NEAL, DANIEL. <u>The History of New-England</u>, Vol. I. London:
A. Ward, pp. 316-17.

1747

> (NEAL, DANIEL)
> Bradford "was a Gentleman of a very noble and generous
> Spirit, laying aside all private Views, when they stood
> in competition with the publick Good.... a Person of
> excellent Temper, as appeared by his admirable Management
> of the peevish and froward Humours of the People, under
> the inexpressible Hardships they suffered."

1793 A BOOKS - NONE

1793 B SHORTER WRITINGS

> 1 ANON. PMHS, I (July), 52-53.
> Records the donation of Bradford's letter book, found
> in a grocer's shop in Halifax, and prints the letter by
> James Clarke which accompanied it. Speculates that it
> left Boston at the time of the evacuation in March, 1776.

1798 A BOOKS - NONE

1798 B SHORTER WRITINGS

> 1 BELKNAP, JEREMY. American Biography, Vol. II. Boston:
> Isaiah Thomas and E. T. Andrews, pp. 217-51.
> "He had read much of history and philosophy, but theology
> was his favorite study. He was able to manage the polemic
> part of it, with much dexterity; and was particularly
> vigilant against the sectaries which infected the Colonies;
> though by no means severe or intolerant, as long as they
> continued peaceable; wishing rather to foil them by argu-
> ment, and guard the people against receiving their tenets,
> than to suppress them by violence or cut them off by the
> sword of the magistracy."

1822 A BOOKS - NONE

1822 B SHORTER WRITINGS

> 1 ANON. "Mourt's Relation," CMHS, second series, IX, 26-73.
> A note at the end, presumably by J. Davis, suggests
> that the first part of this work was written by Bradford
> or copied from his manuscript.

WILLIAM BRADFORD: A REFERENCE GUIDE

1826 A   BOOKS - NONE

1826 B   SHORTER WRITINGS

1   ANON. "Memoir of William Bradford, Esq., Governor of the
    Colony of Plymouth, North America," The Congregational
    Magazine, IX (July, August), 337-40, 393-96.
       Biographical sketch intended to indicate that noncon-
    formity has been the cause of private persons, and not, as
    it has often been represented, solely as the cause of a too
    scrupulous ministry.

1830 A   BOOKS - NONE

1830 B   SHORTER WRITINGS

1   BAYLIES, FRANCIS. An Historical Memoir of the Colony of New
    Plymouth. Boston: Hilliard, Gray, Little, and Wilkins,
    Part I, pp. 315-16; Part IV, pp. 160-62.
       "His prose writings are above mediocrity, and the anti-
    quarian will never cease to regret the loss of his
    precious manuscript history.... He attempted poetry, but
    the muses were woo'd in vain:--his verses are prosaic,
    rough, and inelegant." Also included is a section of
    Bradford's manuscript, then thought irretrievably lost,
    from Hutchinson's history.

1835 A   BOOKS - NONE

1835 B   SHORTER WRITINGS

1   THACHER, JAMES. History of the Town of Plymouth from Its
    First Settlement in 1620, to the Present Time (2nd
    edition). Boston: Marsh, Capen, and Lyon, pp. 106-9.
       "As a chief magistrate, he was compelled to deal with
    many turbulent spirits, yet he seldom failed to enforce
    respect both to the laws and the magistrates, rather by
    appealing to the sense of shame and fear of self-degradation,
    than by the exercise of the penal authority of the govern-
    ment." Contains an illustration (facing p. 24) entitled
    "Landing of the Pilgrims at Plimouth" by G. L. Brown and
    S. Schoff in which Bradford might be presumed to be among
    the central figures.

1836

1836 A BOOKS - NONE

1836 B SHORTER WRITINGS

1   CLARK, MARY. <u>Biographical Sketches of the Fathers of New
     England</u>. Concord, New Hampshire: Marsh, Capen and Lyon,
     pp. 91-106.
         Intended to acquaint youth with the lives, character, and
     sufferings of the chief early settlers. If one follows
     Bradford's life from the beginning among the vicious and
     uninstructed people of Austerfield, through his progress in
     virtue, learning, usefulness, and respectability, to the
     highest office in his land, we shall find an instance of
     the scriptural truth, "The Lord doeth good to the upright
     in heart."

1841 A BOOKS - NONE

1841 B SHORTER WRITINGS

1   MOORE, JACOB B. "Sketches of the Governors and Chief Magis-
     trates of New England, from 1620 to 1820," <u>American Quar-
     terly Register</u>, XIV (November), 155-59.
         Bradford allowed no one to trample the laws, but he de-
     sired to mingle clemency with justice.

1843 A BOOKS - NONE

1843 B SHORTER WRITINGS

1   SAVAGE, JAMES. "Gleanings for New England History," <u>CMHS</u>,
     third series, VIII, 298-99.
         Reprints a letter from Joseph Hunter in which Ansterfield
     mentioned by Mather as Bradford's birthplace is corrected
     to Austerfield, an important step in the search for mate-
     rials about Bradford.

1844 A BOOKS - NONE

1844 B SHORTER WRITINGS

1   YOUNG, ALEXANDER. <u>Chronicles of the Pilgrim Fathers of the
     Colony of Plymouth from 1602 to 1625</u> (2nd edition). Boston:
     Charles C. Little and James Brown.
         Young here is the first to recognize that a manuscript in
     the handwriting of Nathaniel Morton found in the records
     of the First Church of Plymouth is part of Bradford's "lost"
     work; Bradford's manuscript was not discovered until 1855.
     Copious footnotes to the selection from the history include
     interesting references to Hubbard's use of Bradford. This
     anthology also contains "Mourt's Relation," Bradford's first
     "Dialogue," and some of his letters.

William Bradford: A Reference Guide

1848 A BOOKS - NONE

1848 B SHORTER WRITINGS

1 ANDERSON, JAMES S. M. The History of the Church of England in the Colonies and Foreign Dependencies of the British Empire, Vol. II. London: Francis and John Rivington, p. 371.
   Scholars missed this obvious footnote reference to the Bradford manuscript, then long believed lost, which indicates that there are "few passages to be found in which this hatred of Puritans against the Episcopal Order is expressed in more awful terms, than in Bradford's MS. history." Thus, this work has gained considerable historical notice.

2 ANON. "Incidents on Board the Mayflower, 1620," NEHGR, II (April), 186-88.
   Prints the John Howland episode, from a manuscript by Thomas Prince, for the first time.

3 CHEEVER, GEORGE B. The Journal of the Pilgrims at Plymouth in New England, in 1620. New York: John Wiley.
   Reprints "Mourt's Relation," and contains a chapter on "The Life, Character, and Administration of Governor Bradford" (pp. 219-38), based largely on Mather, and a chapter on "Governor Bradford's Letter Book," with selections from some of the letters and commentary which places them in a contemporary context. Like Washington, Bradford guided the ship of state through the breakers with self-possession, prudence, and piety. "He was a man whose natural stamp of character was very much like Franklin's; but in him a calm and noble nature was early renewed and enriched by grace," not left to exhibit the qualities of a sage in the wisdom of mere mortal humanity.

4 MOORE, JACOB BAILEY. Lives of the Governors of New Plymouth and Massachusetts Bay. New York: Gates and Stedman, pp. 49-92.
   Bradford was eminently a practical man, with a strong mind, sound judgment, and an inclination toward study; and in his office as Governor he was prudent, temperate, and firm, suffering no person to trample on the laws or disturb the peace.

1849 A BOOKS - NONE

1849 B SHORTER WRITINGS

1 SAMUEL [WILBERFORCE], Lord Bishop of Oxford. A History of the Protestant Episcopal Church in America. New York: Stanford and Swords, p. 53.
   Contains a footnote reference to the lost Bradford manuscript which was overlooked by American scholars, giving the book historical significance.

1850

1850 A   BOOKS

   1   FESSENDEN, GUY MANNERING. A Genealogical Memoir of the Descendants of William Bradford, Second Governor of New Plymouth, in New England. Boston: Coolidge and Wiley.
        414 entries.

1850 B   SHORTER WRITINGS - NONE

1851 A   BOOKS - NONE

1851 B   SHORTER WRITINGS

   1   ANON. "The Will of Gov. William Bradford," NEHGR, V (October), 385-86.
        Prints it without comment.

1853 A   BOOKS - NONE

1853 B   SHORTER WRITINGS

   1   BARTLETT, W. H. The Pilgrim Fathers, or, The Founders of New England. London: Arthur Hall, Virtue and Co., pp. 30, 205-7.
        "Besides his active services to the colony while living, Bradford rendered it one more imperishable by his writings.... their style is frequently almost scriptural in simplicity and expressiveness."

1854 A   BOOKS - NONE

1854 B   SHORTER WRITINGS

   1   HUNTER, JOSEPH. Collections concerning the Church or Congregation of Protestant Separatists Formed at Scrooby in North Nottinghamshire in the Time of King James I: The Founders of New-Plymouth. London: John Russell Smith, pp. 99-120.
        Contains the first factual information on Bradford's life and social condition in England. It appears that the Bradfords associated with the best of the slender population which surrounded them. There was a previous edition of this book in 1849 (See CMHS, fourth series, I [1852], 75-81).

   2   WEBSTER, DANIEL. "First Settlement of New England," in The Works of Daniel Webster, Vol. I, edited by Edward Everett. Boston: Little, Brown and Co., pp. 1-50.
        Remembrance of the "mild dignity" of Bradford is included in this oration delivered at the Plymouth bicentennial.

1855 A   BOOKS - NONE

1855 B   SHORTER WRITINGS

1   ANON. PMHS, II (January), 601-3.
      Letter from Charles Deane to Joseph Hunter, dated Feb. 17,
    1855, asking him to visit the Fulham Library in London and
    to determine if the Bradford manuscript is there.

2   ANON. "Discovery of Gov. Bradford's Manuscript History,"
    NEHGR, IX (July), 231-32. Reprints an article from the
    Boston Evening Transcript for April 16, 1855 (See 1856.B1
    and 1866.B1).

3   BARRY, JOHN STETSON. The History of Massachusetts, Vol. I.
    Boston: Phillips, Sampson and Company, pp. 61-62, Appendix,
    and passim.
      Short biographical description of Bradford taken from
    Mather, but interesting because this history was written
    just at the time of the discovery of the manuscript by one
    of the men involved in the discovery.

4   DEANE, CHARLES F. PMHS, III (April), 19-24.
      Brief account of the Bradford manuscript; prints the
    Joseph Hunter letters of March 12 and March 19, 1855, verify-
    ing the existence of the manuscript.

5   SHURTLEFF, NATHANIEL B. Records of the Colony of New Plymouth
    in New England. Boston: William White, passim.
      Many brief references.

1856 A   BOOKS - NONE

1856 B   SHORTER WRITINGS

1   ANON. Review of the History of Plymouth Plantation by William
    Bradford, NEHGR, X (July), 286-87.
      Review of the Deane edition (1856.B3) which indicates that
    it will do for the present, but not for the future, and
    which laments that it was not published "independently of
    the trammels of any historical society."

2   ANON. "Letter to the Editor," NEHGR, X (October), 354. Re-
    plies to the previous Boston Evening Transcript article
    (1855.B1), giving less credit to Mr. Barry in the discovery
    of the manuscript.

3   BRADFORD, WILLIAM. History of Plymouth Plantation. Edited by
    Charles Deane. Boston: Published for the Society [The
    Massachusetts Historical Society] by Little, Brown, and
    Company.
      This is the first edition of Bradford's history published
    after the discovery of the manuscript in 1855. There is an

1856

(BRADFORD, WILLIAM)
    editorial preface, the complete text with notes, and appen-
    dices which contain "Passengers of the Mayflower," "Commis-
    sion for Regulating Plantations," and a poem on Mrs. Bradford
    possibly written by Nathaniel Morton. Deane's preface con-
    tains remarks on the discovery and transcription of the manu-
    script, on the use of the manuscript by other historians, and
    brief biographical details.

1857 A   BOOKS - NONE

1857 B   SHORTER WRITINGS

1   ANON. "Discovery of Gov. Bradford's History," NEHGR, XI
     (January), 44.
          Reprints an article from the New York Daily Times for Oct.
     11, 1856, which gives brief factual details.

1865 A   BOOKS - NONE

1865 B   SHORTER WRITINGS

1   DEXTER, HENRY MARTYN, ed. Mourt's Relation or Journal of the
     Plantation at Plymouth. Boston: John Kimball Wiggin.
          Argues for Bradford's authorship of the section entitled
     "A Relation or Journall of the Proceedings of the Plantation
     Settled at Plimoth in New England."

2   MORSE, ABNER. "A Precious Relic," NEHGR, XIX (January), 12.
          Reports the location and condition of Bradford's Bible.

1866 A   BOOKS - NONE

1866 B   SHORTER WRITINGS

1   DRAKE, SAMUEL G. An Historical Memoir of the Colony of New
     Plymouth...by Francis Baylies with Some Corrections, Addi-
     tions, and a Copious Index. Boston: Wiggin and Lunt, pp.
     9-14.
          Reprints a piece from the Boston Evening Transcript dated
     April 16, 1855, on the discovery and significance of the
     Bradford manuscript, particularly the genealogical matter
     the history can supply (See 1855.B1 and 1856.B1).

2   DUYCKINCK, EVERT A. and GEORGE L. Cyclopaedia of American
     Literature, Vol. I. New York: Charles Scribner, pp. 30-31.
          Brief biographical details with selections from Bradford's
     poetry.

1871 A   BOOKS - NONE

WILLIAM BRADFORD: A REFERENCE GUIDE

1871 B SHORTER WRITINGS

1 BRADFORD, WILLIAM. "A Dialogue, Or Third Conference betweene some Yonge-men borne in New-England, and some Ancient-men, which came out of Holand and Old England, concerning the Church, and the Governmente thereof." Edited by Charles Deane. PMHS, XI (October), 396–464.
   The full text with notes and introduction. In this work Bradford defends Congregationalism, and we can see what he felt concerning the religious sects of his day.

2 DEANE, CHARLES. "Verses by Governor Bradford," PMHS, XI (October), 465–82.
   Here printed, with a few notes, are Bradford's "Some observations of God's merciful dealing with us in this wilderness," and "A Word to New Plymouth." The former poem is the full text of the poem entitled "A Descriptive and Historical account of New England in verse" which was published in 1794 (CMHS, III, 77–84).

1873 A BOOKS - NONE

1873 B SHORTER WRITINGS

1 SMITH, CHARLES C. "Memoir of Rev. John Stetson Barry, A. M.," PMHS, XIII (December), 136–39.
   Calls attention to the "fortunate discovery" by Barry which led to the identification of Bradford's manuscript.

1876 A BOOKS - NONE

1876 B SHORTER WRITINGS

1 BANCROFT, GEORGE. History of the United States of America from the Discovery of the Continent, Vol. I. Boston: Little, Brown, and Company, pp. 252–53.
   The fathers of Plymouth, such as Bradford, merit gratitude as guides and pioneers. "Through scenes of gloom and misery, the pilgrims showed the way to an asylum for those who would go to the wilderness for the liberty of conscience." In world histories many pages are devoted to men who have beseiged cities, subdued provinces, overthrown empires; a colony is a better offering than a victory.

2 PALFREY, JOHN GORHAM. History of New England, Vol. II. Boston: Little, Brown, and Company, pp. 405–6.
   Bradford was unselfish, courageous, impartial, diligent, versatile, tender, firm, wise, conscientious, pious, calm, tolerant, independent, intrepid, and without rancor or rashness.

1878

1878 A   BOOKS - NONE

1878 B   SHORTER WRITINGS

1   TYLER, MOSES COIT. A History of American Literature, 1607–
      1765, Vol. I.   New York: G. P. Putnam's Sons, pp. 115–26.
          Because of an assurance that what it was doing the future
      would desire to know about, New England wrote contemporaneous
      history or historical diarizing rather than reviews of the
      past. Bradford deserves to be called "the father of American
      history." His manliness shines through his writings, and he
      possessed every qualification of a trustworthy narrator.
      His mind was placid, grave, and well-poised; he wrote in an
      orderly, lucid, instructive, reserved, and simple manner.
      His history, relieved by flashes of sarcastic humor and
      marked by realistic glimpses of the Pilgrim Fathers, is dis-
      tinguished by its thoroughness and its evocation of the lofty
      motives of our first settlers.

1879 A   BOOKS - NONE

1879 B   SHORTER WRITINGS

1   DEANE, CHARLES. "Remarks by Charles Deane," PMHS, XVII
      (April), 64–66.
          Because of Thomas Prince's deletion of the "John Howland"
      episode in Bradford from the finished copy of his history,
      it is clear that Prince was more interested in "brief ex-
      tracts" than in this episode of fortunate and providential
      deliverance.

1880 A   BOOKS - NONE

1880 B   SHORTER WRITINGS

1   RAE, W. FRASER. "Founders of New England: William Bradford,"
      Good Words, XXI, 337–43. Biographical sketch. However un-
      attractive the early New England leaders appear as a body,
      they improve when singled out for study, particularly
      Bradford.

1881 A   BOOKS - NONE

1881 B   SHORTER WRITINGS

1   ANON. "Remarks by the Vice-President," PMHS, XIX (October),
      64–67.
          Takes note of the recent proposal by the Chamberlain of
      London to return the Bradford manuscript to America and dis-
      cusses the various claims to ownership.

2   WINSOR, JUSTIN. "Paper on the Manuscript of Governor Brad-
      ford's History," PMHS, XIX (November), 106-22.
        Extremely detailed account, occasioned by renewed interest
      in regaining Bradford's manuscript from London, of the use
      of Bradford's manuscript by early historians, of the strange
      way in which obvious clues to the presence of the manuscript
      were overlooked, of the controversy between John Wingate
      Thornton and John S. Barry over discovery of the manuscript's
      existence, and of subsequent attempts to have the manuscript
      returned.

1883 A   BOOKS - NONE

1883 B   SHORTER WRITINGS

1   ADAMS, CHARLES FRANCIS. "Account of Sir Christopher Gardiner,"
      PMHS, XX (January), 60-88.
        Bradford "is a writer on whose simple, sinewy English it
      is scarcely less dangerous to try to improve than it would
      be to try to improve on the English of John Bunyan" (p. 71).

2   _____. "The Printing of Old Manuscripts," PMHS, XX (April),
      175-85.
        Bradford's English "is unsurpassed for simplicity, purity,
      and that strength which is so near allied to pathos."

3   DAVIS, WILLIAM T. Ancient Landmarks of Plymouth. Boston: A.
      Williams and Co., passim.
        Contains abstracts of titles of estates and a Genealogical
      register.

4   MORTON, THOMAS. The New English Canaan, edited by Charles
      Francis Adams, Jr. Boston: The Prince Society.
        Bradford's account of Morton is mentioned throughout the
      introduction; Morton's "Sterne Radamant" is a clear refer-
      ence to Bradford (p. 291).

1884 A   BOOKS - NONE

1884 B   SHORTER WRITINGS

1   DEXTER, FRANKLIN B. "The Pilgrim Church and Plymouth Colony,"
      in Narrative and Critical History of America, Vol. III, ed-
      ited by Justin Winsor. Boston and New York: Houghton,
      Mifflin and Company, pp. 257-94.
        Between Bradford's style and that of Winthrop, there is
      something of the same difference that existed between the
      two emigrations. Contains an excellent "Critical Essay on
      the Sources of Information" which provides a full, detailed,
      chronological survey of material on the colony.

1885

<u>1885 A BOOKS - NONE</u>

<u>1885 B SHORTER WRITINGS</u>

1   DAVIS, WILLIAM T. <u>History of the Town of Plymouth</u>. Philadel-
     phia: J. W. Lewis and Co., <u>passim</u>.
        With the deaths of Bradford and Standish the original
     leaders disappeared and with them much of the sweetness,
     moderation, and liberality which had characterized Plymouth.
     Within three months of Bradford's death the narrower spirit
     of Massachusetts began to make itself felt where Bradford
     had always exercised a restraining hand (p. 65).

<u>1888 A BOOKS - NONE</u>

<u>1888 B SHORTER WRITINGS</u>

1   GOODWIN, JOHN A. <u>The Pilgrim Republic: An Historical Review
     of the Colony of New Plymouth</u>. Boston: Houghton, Mifflin
     Co., pp. 454-59.
        Bradford was remarkably free from the prevalent supersti-
     tion of his times. "He never renounced the names of the
     days and months; he declined to express an opinion that the
     great eclipse of 1635 had any connection with the preceding
     storm; he never mentioned the comets which so generally
     alarmed even the educated people of that century nor has he
     even alluded to witchcraft." He sowed the seed of liberality.

2   RICHARDSON, CHARLES F. <u>American Literature, 1607-1885</u>, Vol. I.
     New York: G. P. Putnam's Sons, pp. 72-81.
        Bradford is not an historian, an early Palfrey or Bancroft,
     but a forerunner of literature. He describes Plymouth as a
     human community, with the imperfections of humanity, and his
     best prose captures something of the spirit and style of
     Milton.

<u>1889 A BOOKS - NONE</u>

<u>1889 B SHORTER WRITINGS</u>

1   ANON. "Round About Scrooby," <u>New England Magazine</u>, I (Septem-
     ber), 31-40.
        An account of Bradford's birthplace.

2   DOYLE, J. A. <u>English Colonies in America</u>, Vol. II. New York:
     Henry Holt & Co., pp. 32-34.
        Bradford's simple, vigorous, and picturesque history is
     much superior to the tedious and pedantic writing character-
     istic of the later period, though at times there is a disap-
     pointing lack of detail and precision. The language is like
     the language of Bunyan, that of a man who trained himself

(DOYLE, J. A.)
not merely to speak but to think in the words of Scripture.
"Occasionally we feel that in the aims ,and hopes which Bradford assigns to himself and his fellow workers at the outset
of their enterprise, he is unconsciously winning the easy
success of a retrospective prophecy."

1890 A BOOKS - NONE

1890 B SHORTER WRITINGS

1 DREW, THOMAS BRADFORD. "Celebrating the Birth of William
Bradford," Magazine of American History, XXIII (March),
227-31.
    Concludes with the hope that a fitting memorial will soon
be erected in Bradford's honor.

2 WEEDEN, WILLIAM B. Economic and Social History of New England,
1620-1789. Boston: Houghton, Mifflin and Co., pp. 867-68.
"The Pilgrim was greater in the home; the Puritan was
greater in the state. Robinson and Bradford well may be
studied as house fathers,--men of the family,--while Winthrop and Hooker were essentially men of the state; citizens
succeeding to a political system developed from a union
of homes."

1891 A BOOKS - NONE

1891 B SHORTER WRITINGS   .

1 JAMESON, J. FRANKLIN. The History of Historical Writing in
America. Boston and New York: Houghton, Mifflin and
Company, pp. 3-4, 13-22.
    There were two classes of historians in the seventeenth
century. Those like Smith and Johnson were interested in
stimulating immigration, and those like Bradford and Winthrop wrote permanent memorials for posterity. Bradford's
qualifications for writing history were great. He had a
thoughtful mind, a high degree of intelligence, and some
scholarship, though he was not pedantic. He writes a plain,
sober, straightforward, accurate account, in language often
revealing the beauty of expression which bespeaks a close
familiarity with the English translation of the Bible
(See also New England Magazine, III [September, 1891],
645-55).

1892

1892 A BOOKS - NONE

1892 B SHORTER WRITINGS

   1   KINGMAN, BRADFORD. <u>Epitaphs from Burial Hill, Plymouth,
       Massachusetts, from 1657 to 1892</u>. <u>With Biographical and
       Historical Notes</u>. Brookline, Massachusetts: New England
       Illustrated Historical Publishing Co., pp. 1-3.
         Copy of the inscription on Bradford's tombstone with
       notes.

1894 A BOOKS - NONE

1894 B SHORTER WRITINGS

   1   DEXTER, MORTON. <u>The Story of the Pilgrims</u>. Boston and Chicago:
       Congregational Sunday School and Publishing Society, pp.
       79-82.
         Bradford had the "tastes of a student and became some-
       what accomplished as a linguist, philosopher, and theologian.
       He seems to have been a man of grave and modest demeanor,
       but of unusual versatility, good judgment, and executive
       capacity, and, especially in view of the conditions of his
       early life, of exceptional culture."

1895 A BOOKS - NONE

1895 B SHORTER WRITINGS

   1   BEERS, HENRY A. <u>Studies in American Letters</u>. Philadelphia:
       George W. Jacobs and Company, p. 20.
         The impression one gets from reading Bradford, Winthrop,
       and Mather is that the sun shone but dimly in New England,
       that the landscape was always dark and wintry, an impression
       of gloom, of night and cold, of mysterious fears besieging
       infant settlements.

   2   BROWN, JOHN. <u>The Pilgrim Fathers of New England and Their
       Puritan Successors</u>. New York: Fleming H. Revell Co.,
       pp. 65-70.
         Bradford was "trained by Him who leads men in a way they
       know not, for service the issues of which they see not.
       The honor of helping humanity forward towards its great
       consummation can only thus be won by those who are willing
       to bear the cross to the steep of Calvary, to go through
       sorrow and self-sacrifice with meekness and magnanimous
       patience."

1896 A   BOOKS - NONE

1896 B   SHORTER WRITINGS

1   BLAXLAND, G. CUTHBERT. "Mayflower" Essays on the Story of the
Pilgrim Fathers. Philadelphia: J. B. Lippincott.
      Without implying conscious selection and arrangement of
materials for artistic effect, it may be said that Bradford's history is a prose epic, an epic of the way of God
with man, of the vindication of His faithfulness to those
who trust in Him. The English in which it is written is
that of the Bible or Pilgrim's Progress; it is terse,
vigorous, and expressive, flowing usually with a transpar-
ent clearness. Bradford chooses words with felicity,
whether "wielding them with terrible emphasis like blows
of a hammer in indignant denunciation, or pouring them out
in lucid narrative or in the eloquent expression of deep
and tender pathos." Also contains a chronological summary
of Bradford's history.

2   BRADFORD, WILLIAM. History of the Plimoth Plantation. Edited by John A. Doyle. London: Ward and Downey Ltd.
      Facsimile edition with introduction. Bradford was tol-
erant precisely because he was an idealist. Like Winthrop,
he avoids turning history into hagiography.

1897 A   BOOKS - NONE

1897 B   SHORTER WRITINGS

1   ARBER, EDWARD. The Story of the Pilgrim Fathers, 1606-1623
A.D., as told by Themselves, their Friends, and their
Enemies. Boston and New York: Houghton, Mifflin and Co.
      Ascribes sections of "Mourt's Relation" to Bradford·(pp.
427, 432).

2   BRADFORD, WILLIAM. Bradford's History "Of Plimoth Plantation."
Boston: Wright and Potter Printing Co., State Printers.
      An edition, without notes, done from the original manuscript
after its return to America in 1897. The introduction contains a brief description of the manuscript and a "Report
of the Proceedings incident to the Return of the Manuscript
to Massachusetts": selections from the Senate journal; the
decree of the London Consistorial Court; receipts by Bayard
and Wolcott; addresses by Hoar, Bayard, and Wolcott; and an
acknowledgement by the Bishop of London. Hoar refers to
the manuscript as "the most precious manuscript on earth,

1897

(BRADFORD, WILLIAM)
> unless we could recover one of the four gospels as it came in the beginning from the pen of the evangelist....there is nothing like it in human annals since the story of Bethlehem." Appendices contain "Passengers of the Mayflower" and "Commission for Regulating Plantations."

3   DREW, THOMAS BRADFORD. The Ancient Estate of Governor William Bradford. Boston: Thomas P. Smith Printing Co.
> A brief history of the estate with Bradford's will.

4   EAMES, WILBERFORCE. "The Return of Bradford's History," Nation, LXIV (8 April), 259.
> Notice of the return with a brief sketch of the history and discovery of the manuscript.

5   HAXTUN, ANNIE ARNOUX. Signers of the Mayflower Compact, Part I. New York: The Mail and Express, pp. 5-7.
> Reprinted newspaper article at the time of the return of the Bradford manuscript to America.

6   WINSOR, JUSTIN. "The Bradford Manuscript," PMHS, second series, XI (April), 299-304.
> After briefly tracing the history of the manuscript and efforts to retrieve it, Winsor concludes that if the manuscript is given to the government at Washington the petition might have been a mistake: "it is notorious in what a loose way important historical documents are sometimes cared for in the governmental departments."

1898 A   BOOKS

1   American Antiquarian Society. The Bradford Manuscript. Account of the Part Taken by the American Antiquarian Society in the Return of the Bradford Manuscript to America. Worcester, Massachusetts: Press of Charles Hamilton.
> Reprints many relevant documents.

1898 B   SHORTER WRITINGS - NONE

1899 A BOOKS - NONE

1899 B SHORTER WRITINGS

1   ANON. "Governor Bradford's List of The Mayflower Passengers,"
    The Mayflower Descendant, I (January), 9-16.
       Prints it.

2   BOWMAN, GEORGE ERNEST. "The Date of Governor Bradford's
    Passenger List," The Mayflower Descendant, I (July), 161-63.
       Written between March 6, 1651 and April 3, 1651.

3   EGGLESTON, EDWARD. The Beginners of a Nation. New York: D.
    Appleton and Co., p. 306.
       Distinguishes Roger Williams, the prophet, from Bradford,
    the reformer. The union of moral aspiration with a certain
    disengagedness constitutes the prophetic temperament, but
    Bradford, though a man of high aspiration, was restrained
    by practical wisdom, compelled to take into account the
    limits of the attainable, turned aside by the logic of the
    impossible.

4   PIERCE, JAMES OSCAR. "Historical Treasure Trove," Dial, XXVI
    (March), 197-98.
       Article on the recovery of the manuscript.

1900 A BOOKS

1   SHEPARD, JAMES. Governor William Bradford, and His Son Major
    William Bradford. New Britain, Connecticut: James
    Shepard.
       This "biography" is meant to honor a worthy ancestor by
    bringing together in a single book the substance of what
    has been written about him. In form, then, the book is a
    chain of sentences or paragraphs from about thirty
    "authorities" under such headings as "The Name," "Bradford's
    Character," and "In Holland." There are photographs of the
    Bradford house, tombstone, and chapel in Austerfield, as
    well as a photograph of a painting by Charles Lucy entitled
    "The Departure of the Pilgrims," in which a relaxed Brad-
    ford calmly contemplates the future among a group of
    fainting and downcast Pilgrims. Bradford's will and an in-
    ventory of his estate are included.

1900

1900 B   SHORTER WRITINGS

1   BOWMAN, GEORGE ERNEST. "Governor William Bradford's Will and
    Inventory," The Mayflower Descendant, II (October), 228-34.
    Prints them in full.

1901 A   BOOKS - NONE

1901 B   SHORTER WRITINGS

1   BOWMAN, GEORGE ERNEST. "Alice (Carpenter) (Southworth) Brad-
    ford's Will and Inventory," The Mayflower Descendant, III
    (July), 144-49.
    Prints them in full.

2   WALKER, WILLISTON. Ten New England Leaders. New York: Silver,
    Burdett and Co., pp. 3-45.
    In this book which contains a series of biographical
    sketches of men prominent in the various epochs of Congrega-
    tional history, Bradford typifies and epitomizes the initial
    epoch. There is significant emphasis on the religious con-
    text in which Bradford matured, on the way in which the re-
    ligious controversies of the day were felt in the hamlet of
    Austerfield. The sketch of his life in America focuses on
    the four or five most important services he rendered to the
    Plymouth colony: easing the colony through periods of fam-
    ine, Indian attack, internal dissension, church building,
    and the writing of his history. Bradford's character
    emerges as quietly heroic. His simple, direct, dignified
    prose style reflects a man who is modest, sober, sweet,
    strong, noble, straight-forward and forceful.

1902 A   BOOKS - NONE

1902 B   SHORTER WRITINGS

1   ROGERS, HALLIDAY. "A Bit of American Lost Property," Chamber's
    Journal, LXXIX (28 June), 465-66.
    An account of the discovery and return of Bradford's
    manuscript, "America's certificate of birth" and "patent of
    nobility," a document that Englishmen, too, should be proud
    of.

1903 A BOOKS - NONE

1903 B SHORTER WRITINGS

1   CARRUTH, FRANCES W. "Governor Bradford's 'Breeches' Bible,"
     The Bibliographer: A Journal of Bibliography and Rare
     Book News, II (June), 400-4.
         Account of the discovery of the Geneva Bible once owned
     by Bradford and the efforts by William T. Davis to secure
     it for the Pilgrim Society.

2   HOAR, GEORGE F. Autobiography of Seventy Years, Vol. II.
     New York: Charles Scribner's Sons, pp. 234-41.
         The personal account of the man instrumental in having
     the Bradford manuscript returned to America.

1905 A BOOKS - NONE

1905 B SHORTER WRITINGS

1   BOWMAN, GEORGE ERNEST. "The Record of Governor Bradford's
     Baptism, on the Parish Register at Austerfield," The
     Mayflower Descendant, VII (April), 65-66.
         Facsimile of the record too.

2   CHANNING, EDWARD. A History of the United States, Vol. I.
     New York: Macmillan, p. 295.
         "Besides being a scholar, Bradford was a born leader of
     men; he had great common sense and an extraordinary capacity
     for bringing difficult business transactions to prosperous
     endings. The key to his success lay in the fact that in his
     own character he realized the sense of his declaration that
     'all great undertakings must be both enterprised and over-
     come by answerable courages.'"

3   DEXTER, HENRY MARTYN. The England and Holland of the Pilgrims.
     Boston and New York: Houghton, Mifflin, and Co., pp. 387-91.
         Brief factual details regarding Bradford's family in
     Austerfield.

1906 A BOOKS - NONE

1906 B SHORTER WRITINGS

1   ANON. "Governor Bradford's Journal," The Gentleman's Magazine,
     LXXVII, 586-602.

1906

    (ANON.)
        Summary of the early sections of Bradford's history governed by the idea that "the record of sufferings endured in the assertion of the right is worthy of our careful attention." Bradford seems inclined more to the life of a student than a governor.

2   THOREAU, HENRY DAVID. The Writings of Henry David Thoreau, Vol. IX, edited by Bradford Torrey. Boston: Houghton, Mifflin and Co., pp. 164, 169, 170, 177.
        Evidence that Thoreau knew Bradford's history, finding there, as F. O. Matthiessen points out (American Renaissance, pp. 116, 163), that he could get nearer to primitive times, and that Thoreau's characteristic mood toward nature is that of the Sunday morning worshipper.

1908 A BOOKS - NONE

1908 B SHORTER WRITINGS

1   BRADFORD, WILLIAM. Bradford's History of Plymouth Plantation, 1606-1646, edited by William T. Davis. New York: Charles Scribner's Sons.
        Edition, with notes, which differs from the previous ones by "giving to these manuscript marks the form which, we may presume, they would have borne in print if Bradford's manuscript had been printed in his lifetime." The introduction is predominantly a biographical sketch, though there is a section which attempts to "clear up some of the mystery" surrounding Mourt's Relation. "Passengers of the Mayflower" and "Commission for Regulating Plantations" are included.

2   HENDERSON, T. F. "William Bradford," in Dictionary of National Biography, Vol. II, edited by Leslie Stephen and Sidney Lee. New York: The Macmillan Company, pp. 1069-72.
        Biographical sketch with much bibliographical information.

3   HOSMER, JAMES KENDALL. Winthrop's Journal: "History of New England," 1630-1649, Vol. I. New York: Charles Scribner's Sons, pp. 92-93.
        Recounts Winthrop's visit to Plymouth, October 25, 1632, in which he met Bradford, "a very discreet and grave man."

1909 A BOOKS - NONE

1909 B   SHORTER WRITINGS

  1   BRADFORD, WILLIAM. <u>Bradford's History of the Plymouth Settle-</u>
<u>ment, 1608-1650</u>, edited by Valerian Paget. London:
Alston Rivers, Ltd.
      Enthusiastic introduction places Bradford's history in
the "irresistible course of the stream of Freedom."

  2   OTIS, WILLIAM BRADLEY. <u>American Verse, 1625-1807</u>. New York:
Moffatt & Yard, pp. 4-5.
      The characteristic Puritan belief that the present age
is more wicked than any in the past, which is evident in
Bradford's poetry, stimulates love of the battle with the
forces of evil and emotional excitement caused by the
impending day of doom.

1911 A   BOOKS - NONE

1911 B   SHORTER WRITINGS

  1   POOL, REV. D. DE SOLA. "Hebrew Learning Among the Puritans of
New England Prior to 1700," <u>Publications of the American</u>
<u>Jewish Historical Society</u>, XX, 31-83.
      "To Bradford, the Old Testament was never truly itself
in a translation, and his quotations from it are made
by preference from the original Hebrew," but in most cases
the printers have obscured the Hebraic coloring by omitting
the Hebrew quotations.

1912 A   BOOKS - NONE

1912 B   SHORTER WRITINGS

  1   BRADFORD, WILLIAM. <u>History of Plymouth Plantation, 1620-1647,</u>
2 Vols, edited by Worthington C. Ford. Boston: Published
for the Massachusetts Historical Society by Houghton,
Mifflin Co.
      This edition, which was the standard edition before Mor-
ison, claims to be the first in which "the text is printed
in its entirety." There is no editorial introduction,
but there are copious notes and illustrations, and an ap-
pendix on "The Bradford Manuscripts." "Passengers of the
Mayflower" is also included.

  2   FORD [SKEEL], EMILY ELLSWORTH FOWLER. <u>Notes on the Life of</u>
<u>Noah Webster</u>. New York: privately printed, pp. 7-9.
      Prints a letter indicating that Bradford is an ancestor
of Webster.

1914

1914 A BOOKS - NONE

1914 B SHORTER WRITINGS

   1   PHILIPSON, DAVID. "The Hebrew Words on the Tombstone of William
          Bradford," Publications of the American Jewish Historical
          Society, XXII, 186-87.
            The Hebrew inscription on the tombstone probably means
         "The Lord is the strength of my life." This is further
         indication of Bradford's love and esteem for the language
         in which the books of the Bible were written.

1917 A BOOKS - NONE

1917 B SHORTER WRITINGS

   1   TRENT, WILLIAM PETERFIELD, et al. The Cambridge History of
          American Literature, Vol I. New York: G. P. Putnam's Sons,
          pp. 19-21.
            Bradford's history is a "Puritan book in the best sense;"
         a sincere faith in Puritanism gives purity to the whole
         book.

1918 A BOOKS - NONE

1918 B SHORTER WRITINGS

   1   PERRY, BLISS. The American Spirit in Literature. New Haven,
          Connecticut: Yale University Press, pp. 28-29.
            Bradford's sketch of Brewster will bear comparison with
         the best English biographical writing of the century.

   2   Usher, Roland G. The Pilgrims and their History. New York:
          Macmillan, pp. 203-6.
            The government of Plymouth was an extraordinary tribute
         to the rectitude, impartiality, diligence, energy, dis-
         cretion, and ability of Bradford; but, at the same time,
         Bradford's ascendancy rendered the colony unattractive to
         those energetic leaders who emigrated from England after
         1630. "While he occupied the stage there could be no space
         on it for men who also felt themselves capable of directing
         large affairs and who were conscious of great ambitions."

1919 A BOOKS - NONE

1919 B SHORTER WRITINGS

1 ANDREWS, CHARLES M. The Fathers of New England. New Haven,
    Connecticut: Yale University Press, pp. 19-20.
       Plymouth is conspicuous in history because of the faith,
    courage, and suffering of those who engaged in it, "and be-
    cause of the ever alluring charm of William Bradford's
    History of Plymouth Plantation." Otherwise, Plymouth was
    overshadowed by her more vigorous neighbors, and the
    Pilgrim Fathers "stand rather as am emblem of virtue than
    a moulding force in the life of the nation."

2 BOYNTON, PERCY H. A History of American Literature. Boston:
    Ginn and Company, pp. 7-8.
       Bradford was a brave, sober, devout leader with an abid-
    ing sense of the holy cause in which he was enlisted; un-
    happily, this heroic trait of Puritanism was coupled with
    a desperate religious bigotry which the world is yet slow
    to forgive.

1920 A BOOKS

1 PLUMB, ALBERT H. William Bradford of Plymouth. Boston: Richard
    C. Badger, The Gorham Press.
       A biography of about 100 pages which seems to be drawn
    mostly from Bradford's history. Bradford is characterized
    as one of those "unconscious heroes," and his administration
    of Plymouth was "unpretentious but wise and kind." Brad-
    ford was unfailingly humble, rarely speaking in the first
    person, and the language of his history is that "of a
    careful recorder, plain and unaffected, having a lucid sim-
    plicity combined with the replete vocabulary of a reflective
    literary mind." He combined immovable fidelity with marked
    ability, though, like Washington, he was not brilliant.
    "To Bradford also belongs the singular honor of being the
    first ruler to demonstrate...true Christian democracy
    not exaggerated into Communism, as a successful principle
    of government."

1920 B SHORTER WRITINGS

1 *DESPREZ, MAY McCLELLAN. "William Bradford, Puritain," La
    Revue Hebdomadaire, XXIX (September), 407-22.
       Not seen.

2 GRIFFIS, WILLIAM ELLIOT. Young People's History of the
    Pilgrims. Boston and New York: Houghton, Mifflin Company,
    pp. 115-23.

1920

(GRIFFIS, WILLIAM ELLIOT)
   On the voyage to America, Bradford stands out as the
practical, all-around business man. "View and appraise
Jesus as we may...we shall appreciate Him all the more
if we can also enter into Bradford's experiences."

3   PLOOIJ, D. and J. RENDEL HARRIS. <u>Leyden Documents Relating</u>
      <u>to the Pilgrim Fathers.</u> Leyden, Holland: E. J. Brill, Ltd.,
      p. xvii.
         Facsimile of the banns notation for Bradford and Dorothy
      May.

4   WRIGHT, THOMAS G. <u>Literary Culture in Early New England, 1620-</u>
      <u>1730.</u> New Haven, Connecticut: Yale University Press, pp.
      27, 58-59.
         Partial listing of the books in Bradford's library, and
      a partial listing of books cited by Bradford in his own
      writing.

<u>1921 A   BOOKS - NONE</u>

<u>1921 B   SHORTER WRITINGS</u>

1   ADAMS, JAMES TRUSLOW. <u>The Founding of New England.</u> Boston:
      The Atlantic Monthly Press, pp. 86-87.
         Bradford, a leader in church affairs when very young,
      developed into a man of sound judgment and morals, whose
      counsel was invaluable to the young colony.

2   BAKER, GEORGE P. <u>The Pilgrim Spirit: A Pageant in Celebration</u>
      <u>of the Tercentenary of the Landing of the Pilgrims at</u>
      <u>Plymouth, Massachusetts, December 21, 1620.</u> Boston: Mar-
      shall Jones Company.
         Bradford's role in the expulsion of John Lyford and John
      Oldham is particularly emphasized, and in the end he is
      flanked by the figures of Washington and Lincoln.

3   LODGE, HENRY CABOT. <u>The Pilgrims of Plymouth: An Address at</u>
      <u>Plymouth, Massachusetts, December 21, 1920.</u> Washington,
      D. C.: Government Printing Office, pp. 7-8.
         "As told in Bradford's truly wonderful journal and in
      Winslow's Relation it is an epic poem written in seventeenth
      century English, in the language of Shakespeare and Milton,
      because the authors had no other."

4   THAYER, WILLIAM ROSCOE. "Pen Portraiture in Seventeenth
     Century Colonial Historians," PAAS, XXXI (April),
     61-69.
        We seek in vain for pen portraits in the histories of
     Bradford, Winthrop, and Mather. "Many men and women are
     mentioned, but I do not recall a single vivid outline of
     the face or figure of any of them." They represent generic
     types, not individuals, each of whom has definite features
     unlike those of his neighbors.

1927 A   BOOKS - NONE

1927 B   SHORTER WRITINGS

1   HART, ALBERT BUSHNELL. Commonwealth History of Massachusetts,
     Vol. I. New York: The States History Company, pp. 365-66.
        "No one can deny that Bradford's history is literature;
     unless we deny that distinction to Caesar's Commentaries."
     The founders were all Elizabethan and wrote well; when
     we come to the born New Englanders the sands run dry.

2   HAZARD, LUCY LOCKWOOD. The Frontier in American Literature.
     New York: Thomas Y. Crowell Co., pp. 6, 34.
        The Puritan's justifiable pride in his own fortitude,
     and his less justifiable contempt of individuals who were
     less thick-skinned can be seen in Bradford's answer to anti-
     cipated objections about life in America. The end result
     of Bradford's spiritual pioneering was an established church,
     and it takes a Chesterton to find orthodoxy exciting. "We
     need a perennial rebirth of the spiritual as of the geo-
     graphical frontier."

1928 A   BOOKS - NONE

1928 B   SHORTER WRITINGS

1   BANKS, CHARLES EDWARD. "Bradford's Portrayal of a Religious
     Rival," PMHS, LXII (December), 34-53. The treatment of
     John Lyford shows Bradford in his most malevolent mood.
     Bradford regarded Lyford as a challenge to the supremacy
     of his sect at Plymouth, and his motives in dealing with
     Lyford were no higher than common religious enmity. Brad-
     ford "missed no scornful adjective or sarcastic noun to
     pillory the hapless clergyman for the judgment of posterity,"
     just as he blasted the reputations of several other indi-
     viduals who did not agree with him. The treatment of
     Lyford is unfair, for we have only the unsupported word
     of a hostile writer motivated by bitterness of the spirit.

1928

2   BRADFORD, E. F. "Conscious Art in Bradford's History of Plymouth
      Plantation," NEQ, I (April) 133-57.
         This is the first study which attempts to deal with Brad-
      ford as a conscious stylist. It moves beyond obvious
      comparisons of Bradford's style with the Bible and
      Pilgrim's Progress to focus on his use of balance, anti-
      thesis, alliteration, couplings, metaphor, simile, analogy,
      personification, punning, and organizational devices. It
      stresses that the plain style which Bradford attains is
      by no means the plain style of a writer blind and deaf
      to the effects of language as a fine instrument. Brad-
      ford's style was conscious and intentional, a style
      purposefully reached.

3   MURDOCK, KENNETH B. "The Puritan Tradition," in The Reinter-
      pretation of American Literature, edited by Norman Foerster.
      New York: Harcourt, Brace and Co., p. 312.
         Great literature, in the strictest sense, would not
      suffer if the works of Mather, Bradford, Winthrop, Ward,
      and Bradstreet were lost; "but the reader who has learned
      to find more than one source of enjoyment in books, ap-
      preciates the good as well as the great, and can discover
      the best even when it is half buried by the less worthy,
      would have real cause to mourn."

1929 A   BOOKS - NONE

1929 B   SHORTER WRITINGS

1   BANKS, CHARLES EDWARD. The English Ancestry and Homes of the
      Pilgrim Fathers. New York: The Grafton Press, passim.
         Many facts about Bradford in this study of the origin
      and family connections of the Pilgrims.

2   MORISON, SAMUEL ELIOT. "William Bradford," in Dictionary
      of American Biography, Vol. II, edited by Allen Johnson.
      New York: Charles Scribners' Sons, pp. 559-63.
         Repeatedly referred to as "the" best short biographical
      account. Bradford took a responsible part in the prepara-
      tions for removal to the new world, and his life is
      inseparable from the history of the Pilgrim colony, which
      he ruled as an overseas Congregational Church. Bradford
      dealt with troublemakers as a genuine Christian and a
      consummate politician; though he never professed toleration,
      his temper was distinctly liberal for the period. Bradford
      had the common sense to see that the colony would never
      prosper until its members were given a stake in its

1929

(MORISON, SAMUEL ELIOT)
 prosperity, and he always held out the hand of fellowship
to other colonies. The peculiar quality of his history
is imparted by the beauty, simplicity, and sincerity of
his character.

1930 A BOOKS - NONE

1930 B SHORTER WRITINGS

1 SCHNEIDER, HERBERT W. The Puritan Mind. New York: Henry
  Holt & Co., pp. 29-30.
   Prints a letter from Charles Gott to Bradford on the
  choice of a pastor and teacher in Massachusetts Bay.

1931 A BOOKS - NONE

1931 B SHORTER WRITINGS

1 ANGOFF, CHARLES. A Literary History of the American People,
  Vol. I. New York: Alfred A. Knopf, pp. 69-76.
   Bradford's history is unquestionably a document of
  the greatest historical value, but historians have also
  professed to see it as a great piece of literature. These
  judgments are gross exaggerations. Bradford was a dull
  personality and his writing was of a like character. "He
  remained the dreary Puritan, constantly in fear of his
  soul, throughout his life and throughout everything he did
  or wrote." Bradford was a kindly, pious man and an able
  administrator, "but the gift of writing was simply not in
  him. He was almost always dull, and frequently very con-
  fused. He did possess vigor of a sort, but it was not
  the vigor of a clear, sharp mind, but rather that of a
  merciful and sincere heart."

2 MURDOCK, KENNETH B. "Colonial Historians," in American Writers
  on American Literature, edited by John Macy. New York:
  Tudor Publishing Co., pp. 3-12.
   Bradford's work, motivated by his Puritanism and seasoned
  by his worldliness, is art that conceals art. Bradford
  chose to emphasize by rigid pruning of style, by restrained
  diction, by ordered simplicity.

3 NICKERSON, W. SEARS. Land Ho! -- 1620: A Seaman's Story of
  the Mayflower, Her Construction, Her Navigation and Her
  First Landfall. Boston: Houghton, Mifflin Co.

1931

    (NICKERSON W. SEARS)
        Use of details in Bradford to chart the exact movement
    of the Mayflower on November 9-11, 1620.

4   ROURKE, CONSTANCE. <u>American Humor: A Study of the National
      Character</u>. New York: Harcourt, Brace, and Co., p. 21.
        In a primitive world the mask had been a safeguard,
      preventing revelations of surprise, anger, or dismay. The
      mask had become habitual among the older Puritans, and
      Governor Bradford encouraged its use on a considerable
      scale. The mask would prove useful in a country where
      the Puritan was still a pioneer, and the Yankee retained
      it.

1932 A BOOKS - NONE

1932 B SHORTER WRITINGS

1   PLOOIJ, D. <u>The Pilgrim Fathers from a Dutch Point of View</u>.
      New York: New York University Press, pp. 83-85.
        Reprints a letter from Bradford to Christopher Ellis in
      Leyden, dated December 11, 1649.

1936 A BOOKS - NONE

1936 B SHORTER WRITINGS

1   TAYLOR, WALTER FULLER. <u>A History of American Letters</u>. New
      York: American Book Company, pp. 5-7.
        There is no hell-fire, bigotry, posing, self-conscious
      heroics, or spectacular scenes in Bradford, but his work
      comes near being the literary classic of the seventeenth
      century because the situation of civilized people
      struggling with a savage environment has proved perennially
      attractive in our literature. Reprinted in 1956 as <u>The
      Story of American Letters</u>.

1937 A BOOKS - NONE

1937 B SHORTER WRITINGS

1   GEE, C. S. "The Bradford Manuscript," <u>CH</u>, VI (June), 136-44.
        This article brings together material on the history
      of Bradford's manuscript of <u>Plymouth Plantation</u> from his
      death in 1657 through its return to America in 1897 by
      the efforts of Senator Hoar.

2   KRAUS, MICHAEL. A History of American History. New York:
      Farrar and Rinehart, pp. 3, 21, 29-30, 33-39.
      (See 1953.B3).

3   NIEBUHR, H. RICHARD. The Kingdom of God in America. New York:
      Harper and Row, pp. 46-48.
         Doubtless there is some virtue in Parrington's idealistic
      interpretation of the early American kindgom of God, but
      someone who goes to Bradford, for instance, will be dis-
      appointed. The strain of the early writers is realistic
      rather than idealistic; the leaders do not speak so much
      of high flown plans as of given necessities.

1938 A   BOOKS - NONE

1938 B   SHORTER WRITINGS

1   HALLER, WILLIAM. The Rise of Puritanism. New York: Columbia
      University Press, pp. 189-91.
         When Bradford first stepped ashore at Plymouth he still
      saw and expressed life as war with Satan and as a journey
      from this world to the next, but once arrived in America
      he was compelled to become a pioneer, a man of business,
      a ruler, in short, a Yankee. As he goes on, he writes
      less and less like the Puritan preacher and more and more
      like the author of Robinson Crusoe.

2   MILLER, PERRY and THOMAS H. JOHNSON. The Puritans: A Source-
      book of their Writings. New York: American Book Co.,
      pp. 87-89.
         Very influential anthology. "Of all the writings by
      New England Puritans in the seventeenth century Bradford's
      History is the pre-eminent work of art. No other doc-
      ument so perfectly incarnates the Puritan ideal of the
      simple and plain style, is so filled with the deep feeling
      of religious dedication, so perfectly masters the rhythms
      of Biblical prose, so fluently handles the imagery of the
      devotional life, or so reveals the solid, broad, and gen-
      erous aspects of the Puritan character."

3   ORIANS, G. HARRISON. "Hawthorne and 'The Maypole of Merry-
      Mount,'" MLN, LIII (March), 159-67.
         "The unpublished account of Bradford, through the
      redactions of at least four annalists, provided the cen-
      tral feature of Hawthorne's story."

1939

1939 A BOOKS - NONE

1939 B SHORTER WRITINGS

   1   MEYER, ISIDORE S. "America's First Thanksgiving," <u>Contemporary</u>
       <u>Jewish Record</u>, II (#6), 9-15.
          The beginnings of Thanksgiving after the harvest, as
       described by Bradford, are derived from festivals still
       celebrated by Jews according to the Hebrew scriptures.

   2   PIERCY, JOSEPHINE K. <u>Studies in Literary Types in Seventeenth</u>
       <u>Century America (1607-1710)</u>. New Haven, Connecticut:
       Yale University Press, pp. 171-75.
          In Bradford's depiction of John Smith as neither god
       nor devil, but as human being, and in Bradford's sketch
       of the hypocrite John Lyford, the Uriah Heep of New
       England, we can see the use of "character" as it moves
       toward real biography.

1942 A BOOKS - NONE

1942 B SHORTER WRITINGS

   1   MURDOCK, KENNETH B. "William Hubbard and the Providential
       Interpretation of History," <u>PAAS</u>, LII (April), 15-37.
          Bradford obviously treats facts only as part of the
       eternal struggle between God and the devil, and Morton's
       <u>Memoriall</u>, one of Hubbard's chief sources, though following
       Bradford almost word for word, goes farther in stressing
       the providential. "Any reader who compares the two texts
       will find places where Morton's adds to Bradford's by
       supplying explicit comments on this or that as an example
       of God's direct action." But Hubbard is less concerned
       with the providential interpretation of history than some
       of his contemporaries may have wished.

1943 A BOOKS - NONE

1943 B SHORTER WRITINGS

   1   ADAMS, JAMES TRUSLOW. <u>The American: The Making of a New Man</u>.
       New York: Charles Scribner's Sons, pp. 56-59.
          Bradford's simply told story of the early settlement
       strikes many American notes: the empty and unknown con-
       tinent, savage inhabitants and danger, loneliness, idealism,
       the ocean barrier, and the strength of the English
       tradition.

1943

2   BENET, STEPHEN VINCENT. Western Star. New York: Farrar and
     Rinehart, Inc., pp. 121, 138, 143, 144.
          Several references to Bradford in this unfinished narra-
     tive poem about western migration.

1944 A BOOKS- NONE

1944 B SHORTER WRITINGS

1   JANTZ, HAROLD S. The First Century of New England Verse.
     Worcester, Massachusetts: American Antiquarian Society,
     pp. 15-17, 182.
          Bibliography plus brief mention of the poems. In "Word
     to New Plymouth," for example, Bradford exhibits the deep
     pride in community which opened up a new land for the
     exiled and distressed when persecution engulfed Europe
     (See also PAAS, LIII [October, 1943], 219-508).

1945 A BOOKS - NONE

1945 B SHORTER WRITINGS

1   WILLISON, GEORGE F. Saints and Strangers: Being the Lives
     of the Pilgrim Fathers and Their Families, with Their
     Friends and Foes. New York: Reynal and Hitchcock, pp.
     3-5.
          This is a history, a "group biography," of the Plymouth
     colony which naturally is partially based on Bradford,
     which contains many references to him, and which attempts
     to rescue the Pilgrims from their image as "anemic Victor-
     ians." Bradford is seen as a man who "had an eye for
     character and color, a sense of dramatic situation, ap-
     parently boundless energy, and a gifted hand at writing
     prose--a fine, full-bodied Elizabethan prose, strong and
     supple, studded with many brilliant turns of phrase."
     However, he was not above "politic distortion" of facts
     or misrepresentation of events in order to justify some
     dubious action, and his remarks about those who opposed
     him are often unreliable and always savage.

1946 A BOOKS - NONE

1946

1946 B   SHORTER WRITINGS

   1   STEWART, RANDALL. "Puritan Literature and the Flowering of
        New England," WMQ, third series, III (July), 319-42.
          Bradford's history is largely a record of difficulties
        overcome, and it has been justly praised for its biblical
        style.

1947 A   BOOKS - NONE

1947 B   SHORTER WRITINGS

   1   WERTENBAKER, THOMAS J. The Puritan Oligarchy: The Founding
        of American Civilization. New York: Charles Scribner's
        Sons, pp. 87-89.
          "Bradford and Winthrop, even when describing controversies
        in which they themselves were involved, obviously though
        not always entirely successfully, attempt to be impartial."

1948 A   BOOKS - NONE

1948 B   SHORTER WRITINGS

   1   BRADFORD, WILLIAM. The History of Plymouth Colony, edited by
        George F. Willison. New York: Published for the Classical
        Club by Walter J. Black.
          This edition contains the full text, a few footnotes, and
        about 25 pages on Bradford's biography, and his religious
        and cultural context. The pilgrims were not the pale
        plaster saints uninspired mythmakers have made them out
        to be; Bradford shows them to be red-blooded, self-assert-
        ive rebels, in conscious and deliberate revolt against
        the existing order. Though Bradford is usually praised
        for his truth, he is disingenuous about the move to
        Leyden; shameful contention with the Ancient Bretheren was
        the real reason. Also, "for political reasons," he tells
        nothing of the Pilgrim press in Leyden. Bradford is at
        his best in describing the first years at Plymouth, when
        men staggered from hunger, scarcely able to get the food
        on which their lives depended.

   2   SPILLER, ROBERT E., et al. Literary History of the United
        States, Vol. I. New York: Macmillan, pp. 34-35.
          Bradford's literary style is simple and sincere; he
        reveals the Puritan at his best. Winthrop's character was
        more complex, and he did not always display Bradford's
        Christian charity. Both men were well-educated, and, within

1948

(SPILLER, ROBERT E.)
the narrow limits of their religious beliefs, "they were able to discern and to think clearly." Their language was the language of the day, contemporaneous with the publication of the King James Bible.

3   . Literary History of the United States. Vol. III. New York: Macmillan, pp. 412-14.
This bibliography is best for locating primary material (the citation for "A Word to New Plymouth" should be PMHS, XI [1871], 478-82) and biographical writing, but less helpful on other secondary material. Other poems attributed to Bradford are cited in Runyan (1970.A1). (See also the Bibliography Supplement, 1959, and the Bibliography Supplement II, 1972, edited by Richard M. Ludwig).

1949 A   BOOKS - NONE

1949 B   SHORTER WRITINGS

1   MEYER, ISIDORE S. "The Hebrew Preface to Bradford's History of the Plymouth Plantation," Publications of the American Jewish Historical Society, XXXVIII, pp. 289-303.
Facsimile reproduction, followed by annotations, of the eight pages of Hebrew writing introducing Plymouth Plantation.

2   MURDOCK, KENNETH B. Literature and Theology in Colonial New England. Cambridge, Massachusetts: Harvard University Press, pp. 78-84.
Bradford demonstrates that his facts are not simply significant in themselves, but are parts of an age-old struggle between God and the devil, and formed a special stage in Protestantism's triumphant progress. He shows the Puritan conception of history as a record of God's providential management of the world; his work is a memorial to the pious, a testimony to God's providential power, and a useful lesson for present and future. Bradford has an untutored sense for a good story; a vein of humor; and his phrasing is not that of the imaginative artist, wide-ranging in metaphor and simile, nor that of the scholar, ransacking books for illustrations and parallels, but that of the man whose ears were full of the plain speech of English farmers and who was bred to relish simple rhythms and words rich with the sense of familiar life.

1950

1950 A   BOOKS - NONE

1950 B   SHORTER WRITINGS

   1   GEBLER, ERNEST. The Plymouth Adventure: A Chronicle Novel of
        the Voyage of the Mayflower. Garden City, New York:
        Doubleday and Co.
          A novel about the Plymouth group from just before depar-
        ture to the departure of the Mayflower from New England.
        Bradford's role is not emphasized all that much. He is
        stern, bluff, hard, irascible. Interestingly, Gebler posits
        an interview between Captain Jones and Bradford in which
        Bradford agrees to speak with the colonists about staying
        in New England, and in which Jones agrees not to return
        Brewster to England for imprisonment. A movie entitled
        "Plymouth Adventure" was made from the book in 1952,
        starring Spencer Tracy and Gene Tierney.

1951 A   BOOKS

   1   *HALL, RUTH GARDINER.   The Descendants of William Bradford.   Ann
        Arbor, Michigan: Edwards Bros.
          A genealogy containing 11,000 descendants of the first
        seven generations from the Governor (cited by Bradford Smith
        in Bradford of Plymouth, p. 328. (See 1951.B2.)

   2   SMITH, BRADFORD.   Bradford of Plymouth.   Philadelphia: J. B.
        Lippincott.
          This is a "popular" biography of Bradford, and, in effect,
        a history of the Plymouth colony. Since little was recorded
        of Bradford's personal life, this is an attempt to recapture
        his personality from his works and acts, and then to pro-
        ject his influence upon American life. It contains recon-
        structions of contemporary manners, customs, physical envi-
        ronments, and culture as well as Bradford's feelings and
        character. Bradford emerges as a practical, self-made man,
        the first American, who entered church affairs because he
        was seeking a father, and who ruled successfully because
        he became a father/brother to his people. Bradford's vision
        of a small, self-managed community of believers, a voluntary
        family of the faithful, is the essence of democracy, and,
        though swallowed up by the Massachusetts Colony, Plymouth
        ultimately triumphed in American life. It is the myth
        which guides our best efforts, which tells us what we ought
        to be. Modern urban civilization must somehow find ways
        to tie its people to such small community units, where they
        can recapture the deep satisfaction of being responsible,
        contributing members of a responsive, useful community.

1951

3   TAYLOR, ELLERY KIRKE. "Welcome Englishmen": A 330 Year History
       of the Bradford Family. Haddonfield, New Jersey: privately
       printed.
          A Bradford genealogy.

1951 B   SHORTER WRITINGS

1   LABAREE, L. W. Review of Bradford of Plymouth by Bradford
       Smith, New York Times, (18 November), p. 16.
          A good many passages are compounded of a small proportion
       of known fact and a large dose of imaginative reconstruction.
       While this can hardly be called valid history in a proper
       sense, Bradford becomes a real human being.

2   MORISON, SAMUEL ELIOT. Review of Bradford of Plymouth by Brad-
       ford Smith, New York Herald Tribune Book Review, (4 Novem-
       ber), p. 3.
          "So much sentimental slop and (of late) disparaging
       nonsense has been written about the Plymouth Colony, that
       this sober, competent biography by Mr. Smith is thrice
       welcome."

3   MURDOCK, KENNETH B. "The Colonial and Revolutionary Period,"
       in The Literature of the American People, edited by
       Arthur Hobson Quinn. New York: Appleton-Century-Crofts,
       pp. 72-73.
          Bradford's work is a classic because it tells a heroic
       story in dignified and beautiful prose. His clumsy pages
       are overshadowed by his narrative skill, humor, robust
       phrasing, and "genius for making restrained diction com-
       municate an exalted spiritual fervor."

1952 A   BOOKS - NONE

1952 B   SHORTER WRITINGS

1   BRADFORD, WILLIAM. Of Plymouth Plantation, 1620-1647, edited
       by Samuel Eliot Morison. New York: Knopf.
          The standard edition, rendered in modern English "to
       introduce a very great book to a much wider public." The
       introduction contains a short biography, a history of the
       manuscript, and a description of previous editions. Many
       letters and official documents are contained in the thirteen
       appendices.

1952

2   JONES, HOWARD MUMFORD. O Strange New World. New York: The
     Viking Press, pp. 117, 240, 253-54.
        Doubtless the spirit of Sir Thomas Elyot rather than
     Castiglione reigns in the careers of Bradford and Winthrop,
     yet each exemplifies in decent measure the universalism
     of the ideal. Bradford's history may owe something to the
     annales formula of historians of antiquity. Since first
     settlers are more concerned with keeping alive than with
     aesthetic response, there is little excellent descriptive
     writing in the 17th century; Bradford is scarcely more
     specific than Columbus and his topographical passages can-
     not compare to William Byrd's.

3   MILLER, PERRY. Review of Bradford of Plymouth by Bradford
     Smith, Saturday Review of Literature, XXXV (12 January),
     17.
        Although his imaginative recreations sometimes verge on
     the sentimental, and although his grasp of seventeenth
     century theology is sketchy, Smith does give the reader a
     sense of how truly monumental a figure Bradford was.
     Blurring and confusing the true issues between Separatist
     and Non-Separatist independency does Bradford more harm
     than good, and Smith's embellishments and interjections
     are often tasteless.

4   _____. Review of Of Plymouth Plantation, edited by Samuel
     Eliot Morison, The New Republic, (17 November), pp. 28-29.
        Miller takes issue with Morison's suggestion that some
     readers might want to skip over the first four chapters
     of Bradford's history and get at once into the "story."

5   MORSE, JARVIS M. American Beginnings: Highlights and Side-
     lights of the Birth of the New World. Washington, D. C.:
     Public Affairs Press, pp. 58-61.
        Bradford's style is not as simple as he proclaimed, but
     he seldom departed from the first function of a Puritan
     historian, to tell exactly what happened. Bradford is
     less prone than other Puritan historians to burden his
     work with special providences; the later sections of
     Plymouth Plantation, in fact, read "like entries in a
     wholesale merchant's register." Bradford condemned the
     evil and took the virtuous for granted, indulging in per-
     sonality only for censure.

6   MURDOCK, KENNETH B. Review of Of Plymouth Plantation, edited
     by Samuel Eliot Morison, New York Times, (28 September),
     p. 14.
        "Because of Mr. Morison's contributions, this edition
     will be treasured by those who already know Bradford's work."

1953 A BOOKS - NONE

1953 B SHORTER WRITINGS

1   FEIDELSON, CHARLES, JR. Symbolism and American Literature.
       Chicago: University of Chicago Press, pp. 78-79.
         The symbolizing process was constantly at work in the
       Puritan mind. In his use of "wilderness," for instance,
       Bradford is not merely narrating the facts; he is invoking
       an image which colored that history as it was experienced.

2   HEIMERT, ALAN. "Puritanism, The Wilderness, and The Frontier,"
       NEQ, XXVI (September), 361-82.
         The conception that society was an organism and not an
       aggregate of individuals and that the public good was to
       be achieved by cohesiveness and cooperation dominated the
       Puritan attitude toward expansion and the frontier. Ply-
       mouth was especially embarrassed by removals from the
       original settlement into adjacent areas, and Bradford saw
       this as quite ominous, as the ruin of New England. Until
       1640, "the orthodox mind was unable to equate even tentative
       penetration of the inerior with the purposes of the Lord."

3   KRAUS, MICHAEL. The Writing of American History. Norman,
       Oklahoma: University of Oklahoma Press, pp. 14, 17-18,
       20-24.
         The historians of the first settlements were less con-
       cerned with past events than with history in the making,
       and their works have the freshness which comes from first
       discovery. They felt a need to render God a statement of
       their accounts and to thank Him for help. Their task was
       not to entertain, but to discover their place in God's
       plan for the universe. Bradford's history is not only the
       most important of the founders' narratives, but it also has
       a singular charm as literature. It reveals the ideal
       Pilgrim: thoughtful, simple, forthright, and tolerant.

4   MILLER, PERRY. The New England Mind: From Colony to Province.
       Cambridge, Massachusetts: Harvard University Press, p. 31.
         Historians have failed to see the difference between
       Bradford's serene movement from point to point, morally
       improving each incident, and Increase Mather's conscious
       organization, the imposition of the dialectic of decline
       and recovery on history.

1953

5   MORISON, SAMUEL ELIOT. <u>By Land and By Sea</u>. New York: Knopf,
        pp. 235-49.
        Almost all American historians agree that the Plymouth
        Colony was insignificant, but it bulks large in our histor-
        ical consciousness because of Bradford's history: "a story
        of simple people impelled by an ardent faith in God to a
        dauntless courage in danger, a boundless resourcefulness in
        face of difficulty, an impregnable fortitude in adversity.
        It strengthens and inspires us still, after more than
        three centuries, in this age of change and uncertainty."

1955 A BOOKS - NONE

1955 B SHORTER WRITINGS

1   MURDOCK, KENNETH B. "Clio in the Wilderness: History and
        Biography in Puritan New England," <u>CH</u>, XXIV (September),
        221-38.
        History and biography were means of making loneliness,
        doubts about identity, homesickness, and uncertainties
        about the American enterprise more bearable for the
        colonial Puritan. Thus, it is not surprising that authors
        dignify the colonists by portraying them as actors in a
        crucially important chapter of Christian history. Bradford,
        for example, portrays the Pilgrims, not as reckless rebels
        and subverters of order, but as saints dedicated to the
        conservation of principles Christ established for his
        church, and saints who had been able to triumph over the
        wars, oppositions, and strategems of Satan. Reprinted in
        <u>EAL</u>, VI (Winter, 1972), 201-19.

2   SIMPSON, ALAN. <u>Puritanism in Old and New England</u>. Chicago:
        University of Chicago Press, pp. 32-34.
        The key element of Puritanism is the conversion experience,
        a new birth, and the history of the New England Way is the
        losing struggle to preserve this experience and authority
        over society. Decay is the theme of almost all the founders
        as they survey the community in their declining years.

1956 A BOOKS - NONE

1956 B   SHORTER WRITINGS

1   MILLER, PERRY. Errand Into the Wilderness. Cambridge, Massachusetts: Harvard University Press, pp. 3-4.
    The Plymouth colonists did not leave England on an
"errand," with a sense of mission. "The great hymn that
Bradford, looking back in his old age, chanted about the
landfall is one of the greatest passages, if not the very
greatest, in all New England literature; yet is does not
resound with the sense of a mission accomplished--instead,
it vibrates with the sorrow and exultation of suffering,
the sheer endurance, the pain and the anguish, with the
somberness of death faced unflinchingly." We see in
Bradford's account the prototype of what Oscar Handlin
calls "the Uprooted." The story of Massachusetts is quite
different.

2   MORISON, SAMUEL ELIOT. The Story of the "Old Colony" of New
Plymouth. New York: Knopf, pp. 218-19.
    Of America's colonial founders, only John Winthrop,
William Penn, John Smith, and Lord Baltimore can be men-
tioned in the same breath as Bradford.

1957 A   BOOKS - NONE

1957 B   SHORTER WRITINGS

1   WRIGHT, LOUIS B. The Cultural Life of the American Colonies,
1607-1763. New York: Harper & Row, pp. 157-60.
    Bradford's work has the simplicity and sincerity of John
Bunyan and the dignity of John Milton. His history is
realistic, without effort to disguise the fact that not
all the settlers of Plymouth were saints.

1959 A   BOOKS - NONE

1959 B   SHORTER WRITINGS

1   DUNN, RICHARD S. "Seventeenth-Century English Historians
of America," in Seventeenth-Century America: Essays in
Colonial History, edited by James Morton Smith. Chapel
Hill, North Carolina: University of North Carolina Press,
pp. 195-225.
    The contrast between the histories of John Smith and
Bradford is extraordinary. Smith dramatized his personal
prowess, pictured Virginia as a paradise, and linked the
plantation with the Mother Country. Bradford submerged

1959

(DUNN, RICHARD S.)
    his identity in the sufferings of the community, pictured
    New England as a wilderness, and made a sharp differentia-
    tion between the plantation and the Mother Country. In
    Bradford we see the Puritans take the first step toward
    creating a distinct American society.

1960 A   BOOKS - NONE

1960 B   SHORTER WRITINGS

1   JONES, JOSEPH, et al. American Literary Manuscripts: A Check-
        list of Holdings. Austin, Texas: University of Texas
        Press, p. 46.

2   VAN TASSEL, DAVID D. Recording America's Past: An Interpreta-
        tion of the Development of Historical Studies in America,
        1607-1884. Chicago: University of Chicago Press, pp.
        12-13.
            "Although Bradford never completed his work, it was in-
        tended for publication as a major effort to stem the dis-
        persion and decline of the Plymouth settlement."

3   WISH, HARVEY. "From Bradford to Mather: The Puritan Mission
        in History," in The American Historian: A Social-Intellec-
        tual History of the Writing of the American Past. New
        York: Oxford University Press, pp. 3-21.
            The Puritans had inherited the Christian interpretation
        of history which saw God's design in the whole story of
        mankind, and they saw themselves as the Chosen People being
        guided to Plymouth by Bradford, a new Moses. History,
        then, was proof that their policies reflected the divine
        purpose, and it ranked next to the Bible as a revelation
        of God's will, though Bradford seldom allowed his concerns
        for supernatural causes to conceal natural reasons for
        surprising events. Bradford, more than other Puritans,
        practiced the scientific ideal set down by Thucydides,
        and his Puritanism, evident in his savage condemnation
        of Morton, is often tempered by native kindliness.

1961 A   BOOKS - NONE

1961 B SHORTER WRITINGS

1   BOWDEN, EDWIN T. "Sweet and Delightful Society: William
    Bradford, Of Plymouth Plantation," in The Dungeon of the
    Heart: Human Isolation and the American Novel. New York:
    Macmillan, pp. 1-19.
       This book is a discussion of twelve American novels that
    reflect the continuing concern in American life with the
    problem of human isolation. Bradford's history is an apt
    introduction to this study because it gives something of
    the effect of a novel itself, and because it makes clear
    that isolation was one of the great and troublesome
    problems in early American life. The Pilgrims suffered
    not only from the physical isolation of the wilderness,
    but also from the rejection and betrayal by those in
    England. The isolation was from without, however, never
    from within, and could be overcome, for the group was
    united by a covenant derived from faith in God and directed
    toward his service. This unity could not last, but its
    memory lingers, and the American novel picks up the search
    again and again.

2   *GERSON, NOEL B. The Land is Bright. Garden City, New York:
    Doubleday.
       Cited in A. T. Dickinson, American Historical Fiction
    (3rd edition), Metuchen, New Jersey: Scarecrow Press,
    1971, p. 24, as a "portrait of William Bradford and the
    hardships of the first years of the Massachusetts Bay
    Colony."

3   PERRY, THOMAS W. "New Plymouth and Old England: A Suggestion,"
    WMQ, XVIII (April), 251-65.
       The interesting fact about the removal to Holland is the
    utterly non-political view the Pilgrims took of the causes
    that drove them there. Bradford, who in other matters is
    quite outspoken, refers to Elizabeth as "gracious" and has
    no harsh words for James. "Though radical in religion,
    they remained loyal and conservative in their political
    outlook."

4   SANFORD, CHARLES L. The Quest for Paradise: Europe and the
    American Moral Imagination. Urbana, Illinois: University
    of Illinois Press, p. 107.
       The American as "new man" was conceived of as primitive
    in relation to civilized Europe, to the increasing associa-
    tion of vice with the centers of authoritarian civilization.
    Bradford, for instance, attributes the difficulties in
    Holland to an avaricious city culture.

1962

1962 A BOOKS - NONE

1962 B SHORTER WRITINGS

1   BRADFORD, GERSHOM. "The 'Speedwell'--Another Look," American
       Neptune, XXII (April), 136-41.
          Bradford charged Captain Reynolds with "cunning and
       deceit," but Bradford was not a seaman, and, after con-
       sidering every word recorded relating to the Speedwell,
       "there is some doubt as to the extent of the deceit."

2   BRADFORD, WILLIAM. Of Plymouth Plantation, edited by Harvey
       Wish. New York: Capricorn Books.
          This paperback edition abridges the original by half,
       "largely at the expense of formal materials, routine
       affairs, lengthy theological disquisitions, and repetitive
       records," and there is a 22 page introduction which sets
       Bradford and his work in historical context.

3   COWIE, ALEXANDER. Review of The Dungeon of the Heart by
       Edwin T. Bowden, AL, XXXIV (November), 439-40.
          Bradford's experiment in Christian community is the
       chief inspiration for this study of the problem of isolation
       in American literature.

4   MORISON, SAMUEL ELIOT. "William Bradford, 1590-1657," in
       Major Writers of America, Vol. I, edited by Perry Miller.
       New York: Harcourt, Brace, and World, Inc., pp. 3-11.
          A substantial anthology introduction to selections from
       Bradford's history which provides information on editions,
       the history of the manuscript, Bradford's life and religious
       context, the purpose and style of the history. "But the
       story is the thing.... Here is an absorbing story of a
       humble people, impelled by their ardent faith to courage
       in danger, perserverance through every sort of discom-
       fort and discouragement, and resourcefulness in dealing
       with new and unexpected problems."

1963 A BOOKS - NONE

1963 B SHORTER WRITINGS

1   GUMMERE, RICHARD M. The American Colonial Mind and the
       Classical Tradition. Cambridge, Massachusetts: Harvard
       University Press, p. 50.
          Bradford, "a far more learned scholar than he has been
       given credit for," supported his belief that the perse-
       cutions of the Christians by the heathen were not greater

William Bradford: A Reference Guide

1963

(GUMMERE, RICHARD M.)
> than those of other Christians with reference to Socrates
> of Constantinople, a fifth-century historian.

2   HEATH, DWIGHT, ed. <u>A Journal of the Pilgrims at Plymouth:</u>
     <u>Mourt's Relation</u>. New York: Corinth, p. xiii.
     This is an edition of the earliest published account
     of the Plymouth colony, parts of which Bradford may have
     written. <u>Plymouth Plantation</u> is a curious combination of
     passages from Mourt's Relation, discursive classical al-
     lusions, and philosophic ruminations. Bradford's style
     generally tends to be more analytic than descriptive, and
     the specificity of detail which makes <u>Mourt's Relation</u>
     such a rich source of material rarely occurs elsewhere
     in his work. "It is entirely within the realm of possibil-
     ity that he may have incorporated in his manuscript the
     work of others as it had appeared in <u>Mourt's Relation;</u>
     he freely adapted material from other sources."

3   JAMES, SYDNEY V., JR. <u>Three Visitors to Early Plymouth</u>.
     Plymouth: Plimoth Plantation, Inc., pp. 29-30.
     Contains Emmanuel Altham's account of Bradford's second
     marriage: "We had about twelve pasty venisons, besides
     others, pieces of roasted venison and other such good
     cheer in such quantity that I could wish you some of our
     share. For here we have the best grapes that ever you
     [saw]--and the biggest, and divers sorts of plums and
     nuts which our business will not suffer us to look for."

4   KAUL, A. N. <u>The American Vision: Actual and Ideal Society</u>
     <u>in Nineteenth-Century Fiction</u>. New Haven, Connecticut:
     Yale University Press, pp. 9-17.
     Cooper, Hawthorne, Melville, and Twain are related to
     an underlying cultural tradition handed down from early
     Puritan times. Bradford's history, in its epic reference
     to the solemn exodus of a band of people from a corrupt
     world and their journey across the ocean to build a New
     Jerusalem upon a virgin land, is the imaginative arche-
     type of American experience, the first statement of the
     American myth. In Bradford we have the metaphysical di-
     mension in the theme of spearation from an established
     society in search of a more satisfying community life
     which finds recurrent expression in American literature.

5   MORGAN, EDMUND S. <u>Visible Saints: The History of a Puritan</u>
     <u>Idea</u>. New York: New York University Press, pp. 59-61.
     Evidence from Bradford concerning the procedures for
     church membership.

1963

6   PLUMSTEAD, A. W.   "Puritanism and Nineteenth Century American
         Literature," QQ, LXX (Summer), 209-222.
         The tension that has haunted American life like a
     national guilt complex, the challenge and despair of main-
     taining a constant growth towards an ideal future, which
     Bradford describes in the image of the ancient mother for-
     saken of her children, is likewise dramatized as a parent-
     child situation in Irving, Melville, Hawthorne, Twain, and
     Faulkner.

1964 A   BOOKS - NONE

1964 B   SHORTER WRITINGS

1   AKIYAMA, KEN.   "William Bradford and Cotton Mather: A
         Stylistic Analysis of the New England Mind," SELIT, XLI
         (August), 59-71.
         This article is written in Japanese.

2   GAER, JOSEPH and BEN SIEGEL.   The Puritan Heritage: America's
         Roots in the Bible. New York: Mentor, pp. 19-20, 161-62.
         Bradford avoided the melodramatic posturings of Renais-
     sance exploration literature and the fire and brimstone
     of traditional Puritan writings.

3   *GALINSKY, HANS.   "Die Ankunft in der neuen Welt: Epische und
         lyrische Gestaltung einer kolonialen Grundsituation bei
         William Bradford und Thomas Tillam," in Festschrift für
         Walther Hubner. Berlin, pp. 203-26.
         Not seen. Cited in Astrid A. von Muhlenfels "A Bibli-
     ography of German Scholarship on Early American Litera-
     ture: 1850--." EALN, II (Fall, 1967), 33 (See 1968.B3).

4   MARX, LEO.   The Machine in the Garden: Technology and the
         Pastoral Ideal in America. New York: Oxford University
         Press, 41-42.
         There are two sharply constrasting images of American
     landscape in colonial writing, the garden and the wilder-
     ness, and Bradford's description off Cape Cod in 1620 is
     the best known example of the latter. "This grim sight
     provoked one of the first of what has been an interminable
     series of melancholy inventories of the desirable--not to
     say indispensable--items of civilization absent from the
     raw continent....instead of abundance and joy, Bradford
     saw deprivation and suffering in American nature."

WILLIAM BRADFORD: A REFERENCE GUIDE

1965 A BOOKS - NONE

1965 B SHORTER WRITINGS

1 FUSSELL, EDWIN. Frontier: American Literature and the
    American West. Princeton, New Jersey: Princeton Univer-
    sity Press, pp. 92-93.
       Bradford's community perches on the brink of the ocean;
    Hawthorne's community in The Scarlet Letter crouches on
    the verge of the forest. For Bradford, the West is prac-
    tically unimaginable; for Hawthorne, the West is the mean-
    ing of America and must necessarily be imagined. Haw-
    thorne's setting engenders extensions which a man in Brad-
    ford's position could not envisage.

2 VAUGHAN, ALDEN T. New England Frontier: Puritans and Indians,
    1620-1675. Boston: Little, Brown and Co., p. 62 and
    passim.
       Winthrop, Bradford, and their contemporaries treated en-
    counters with Indians as though they were determined by all
    the complexities of human behavior, not as determined by
    any fundamental distinction of race.

1966 A BOOKS - NONE

1966 B SHORTER WRITINGS

1 GAY, PETER. "William Bradford: Caesar in the Wilderness,"
    in A Loss of Mastery: Puritan Historians in Colonial
    America. Berkeley, California: University of California
    Press, pp. 26-52.
       In 1630 the craft of history, a mixture of Medieval
    (mythic) and Renaissance (critical) traits, was delicately
    poised on the edge of modernity, but the Puritan his-
    torical writings looked to the past for style as well as
    subject, and in this we may read the ultimate failure of
    Puritan historiography. Bradford's history is comprehen-
    sive, but it offers few surprises; it is unmistakably in
    the Augustinian tradition, reflecting a parochial version
    of the Protestant theology of history, believing nature
    and history were not autonomous realms. Bradford was like
    Caesar, writing contemporary history which he had both
    witnessed and shaped, but his vision was that of a par-
    tisan. History, however, is an art as well as a science,
    and Bradford at least wrote a work of historical art, "an
    authentic masterpiece." Bradford was a born writer, with
    an exquisite ear and superb taste, and his depiction of .the
    Pilgrim enterprise is highlighted by the movement from
    gravity through sadness, melancholy, and nostalgia to the
    elegiac.

1966

2   HOUSE, KAY S. Reality and Myth in American Literature.
         Greenwich, Connecticut: Fawcett, pp. 21-22.
         Compares Donne and Bradford to show the discrepancy
     between imagination and experience about America.

3   MORGAN, EDMUND S. "The Historians of Early New England,"
         in The Reinterpretation of Early Ameican History, edited
         by Ray Allen Billington. San Marino, California: The
         Huntington Library, p. 42.
         Bradford's history "remains the outstanding piece of
     historical writing produced in the United States before
     Francis Parkman."

1967 A   BOOKS - NONE

1967 B   SHORTER WRITINGS

1   BARITZ, LOREN. Review of A Loss of Mastery by Peter Gay,
         Nation, (29 May), pp. 699-700.
             "Ignoring some of the finer distinctions between Puritan-
         ism and Calvinism," Gay's conclusions illustrate the look
         of Puritanism through essentially European lenses. In this
         context what does it mean to talk about "liberals" and
         "conservatives"?

2   BROGAN, D. W. "Hellenes, Hebrews, and Americans," Encounter,
         XXIX (August), 75-78.
             A review of Peter Gay's A Loss of Mastery. Gay is a
         Hellene and the historians he discusses were, ideologically,
         Hebrews. Gay thinks it time to show that the claims made
         in the past generation for New England as being as much
         a part of the Enlightenment as Old England are exaggerated
         and are fruits of a misguided patriotism. His job is too
         easy.

3   ENGDAHL, BONNIE T. "Paradise in the New World: A Study of
         the Image of the Garden in the Literature of Colonial
         America." Unpublished Ph.D. dissertation, University of
         California at Los Angeles, pp. 79-84.
             Bradford's use of the Canaan-Wilderness theme in his
         poetry.

4   JAMES, SYDNEY V. Review of A Loss of Mastery by Peter Gay,
         JSH, XXXIII (November), 549-50.
             Gay's category of Puritan Historians, including only
         those devoted to the Puritan version of the traditional
         Christian interpretation, builds in the conclusions by
         setting them up to be criticized for a static point of view.

5   KRAUS, MICHAEL. Review of A Loss of Mastery by Peter Gay,
      JAH, LIV (June), 102-3.
         Gay is concerned with the Europeanness of the early
      American experience, a concern which lifts us out of the
      parochialism too common in American historical writing.

6   NASH, RODERICK. Wilderness and the American Mind. New Haven,
      Connecticut: Yale University Press, pp. 23-26.
         When Bradford stepped into a "hideous and desolate
      wilderness" he started a tradition of repugnance. With
      few exceptions, later pioneers continued to regard wilder-
      ness with defiant hatred; under any circumstances the
      necessity of living close to wild country engendered strong
      antipathy.

7   PERSONS, STOW. Review of A Loss of Mastery by Peter Gay, AHR,
      LXXII (July), 1479-80.
         The chief virtue of this book is that Gay approaches his
      subject neither as a debunker or a pious celebrant. He is
      less concerned with the substance of Puritan historiography,
      than with a general analysis of Puritan historical thought
      as a function of the mythic mentality. Still unanswered
      is the question why the historians were so conservative
      when other Puritan writers were busy modifying the original
      objectives.

8   TOLLES, FREDERICK B. Review of A Loss of Mastery by Peter Gay,
      AL, XXXIX (November), 400-2.
         Taking an unfashionable perspective, Gay makes it clear
      that Puritanism was a failure, forecasting, perhaps, the
      next trend in the study of this period.

1968 A   BOOKS - NONE

1968 B   SHORTER WRITINGS

1   BERCOVITCH, SACVAN. Review of A Loss of Mastery by Peter Gay,
      EALN, III (Spring), 51-54.
         Gay's failure to master the myth of American special-
      ness decisively narrows his understanding of the histories.
      The emigrants saw themselves as part of a worldwide Re-
      formation which would end in the descent of the New Je-
      rusalem, but it is a mistake to infer from this that
      America meant to them only a place like any other place.
      "The inference may hold for the separatist Pilgrims and
      Bradford's Plymouth Plantation, though not without serious
      qualifications. It is clearly inappropriate to the
      Massachusetts histories."

1968

2   FIEDLER, LESLIE A. and ARTHUR ZEIGER. O Brave New World:
    American Literature from 1600 to 1840. New York: Dell,
    pp. 380-81.
        Interesting brief mention of the Morton episode as the
    archetypal conflict of Cavalier and Puritan.

3   *GALINSKY, HANS. "Die Ankunft in der neuen Welt: Epische und
    lyrische Gestaltung einer kolonialen Grundsituation bei
    William Bradford und Thomas Tillam," in Amerika und Europa.
    Berlin, pp. 113-37.
        Not seen. Cited in EAL, IV (Spring, 1969), 72.
    (See 1964.B3).

4   LEVIN, DAVID. Review of A Loss of Mastery by Peter Gay,
    History and Theory, VII (#3), 385-93.
        In studying Puritan history, Gay is shackled by his own
    skepticism; "on the subject of Puritan piety William Brad-
    ford is a better historian than Peter Gay." Gay's method
    of ascribing the merits of Plymouth Plantation to Bradford
    himself and its limitations to the Puritan culture excludes
    new questions about the nature of Puritanism and its liter-
    ary works. "If we assume that Bradford was a Puritan even
    when he was acting meritoriously, we may come closer to
    understanding the value of his history, his achievement as
    an historian, and perhaps even the nature of Puritanism."
    Gay treats Bradford only as an example of piety, without
    stressing his achievement in portraying that piety.

5   TICHI, CECELIA HALBERT. Review of A Loss of Mastery by Peter
    Gay, SCN, XXVII (Autumn), 61-62.
        Gay contradicts himself, confusing narrative tone with
    the essential quality of history, when he commends Brad-
    ford for his modest tone and criticizes Mather for his
    outright conviction of rectitude. Gay's conclusion is
    that Puritan History at its best in Bradford is static,
    and at its most ambitiously expansive in Edwards is
    anachronistic.

6   WAGER, WILLIS. American Literature: A World View. New York:
    New York University Press, pp. 6-7.
        Plymouth Plantation is simple, direct, vivid, and trans-
    parent; Bradford does not attempt "to achieve a stained-
    glass-window gorgeousness."

1969 A   BOOKS - NONE

1969 B SHORTER WRITINGS

1   COHEN, HENNIG. "The American as Involved and Dropout: An
    Afterword," in <u>Landmarks of American Writing</u>. New York:
    Basic Books, pp. 381-83.
       Franklin was Bradford's secular godchild and their books
    are examples of the involved, committed life, though both
    men broke with the British establishment.

2   CONNORS, DONALD F. <u>Thomas Morton</u>. New York: Twayne
    Publishers, pp. 89-102.
       The passage in Bradford about Morton's activities clearly
    reveals the official view of Plymouth, and it marks the
    turning point in Morton's activities in New England.

3   DAVIS, RICHARD BEALE. <u>American Literature Through Bryant,
    1585-1830</u>. New York: Appleton, Century, Crofts, p. 22.
       This volume is part of the Goldentree Bibliography
    series, but adds nothing to the <u>LHUS</u> bibliography (1948.B3).
    Contains a convenient list of primary material, but only
    two secondary works.

4   FRITSCHER, JOHN J. "The Sensibility and Conscious Style of
    William Bradford," <u>BUR</u>, XVII (December), 80-90.
       Bradford soothes the inherent tension between an un-
    adjustable Calvinistic theology and a democraticizing
    wilderness where adjustment was survival by laying all
    under the "smooth duress" of Providence. Thus, he con-
    dones as "creative" the modifications in Calvinism de-
    manded by the exigencies of the Pilgrim experience.
    Mutating the traditional five points of Calvinism to a
    different emphasis, he believes in "the absolute sover-
    eignty of a providential God directly intervening in the
    world to raise the elect from their natural depravity
    into the best possible New Eden." Bradford created a
    style of his own by infusing elements of "the high into
    the spare." He employed theological analogy, classical
    references, the format of scholastic disputations, a
    patrological literary temperament, humorous and pathetic
    anecdotes with moral lessons, clinical realism, and the
    shifting of tenses to heighten effect.

5   GRABO, NORMAN S. "William Bradford: <u>Of Plymouth Plantation</u>,"
    in <u>Landmarks of American Writing</u>, edited by Hennig Cohen.
    New York: Basic Books, pp. 3-19.
       A volume of essays originally prepared for Voice of
    America presentation. In addition to mercantile and
    spiritual motives, Bradford wrote out of a sense of the
    unique history that was being made. Over and over again
    he emphasizes trial and travail in order to magnify the

1969

(GRABO, NORMAN S.)
significance of the accomplishment. Over and over again,
too, he is consciously literary. He lets his tone betray
his emotional response, and he constructs his descriptions
to involve the reader emotionally in his experience. He
wants the reader's appreciation, not mere knowledge, of
the Pilgrim's plight, and he seeks to evoke pity, sympathy,
sorrow. Bradford was a great sentimentalist. The cor-
ruption of mankind and the instability of all worldly things
lie behind his view of events, but in this fallen world
Bradford is a man who cares and his history is a book of
love.

6 HOWARD, ALAN B. "The Web in the Loom: An Introduction to the
Puritan Histories of New England." Unpublished Ph.D. dissertation, Stanford University.
Contains a lengthy examination of Bradford and Winthrop
to show how the Pilgrim and Puritan philosophies of history
differed, and how these philosophies helped shape two
different interpretations of the Puritan experience.

7 LANGDON, GEORGE D., JR. "Bibliographic Essay," Occasional
Papers in Old Colony Studies, I (July), 41-50.
A selection of published and manuscript sources for the
study of Plymouth Colony in the 17th century. Useful for
wider study of the context in which Bradford lived.

8 LYNEN, JOHN F. The Design of the Present: Essays on Time and
Form in American Literature. New Haven, Connecticut: Yale
University Press, pp. 51-55.
The most significant influence of Puritanism upon the
American mind has been its effect upon the sense of time,
accustoming the imagination to conceive experience in terms
of the present in relation to a total history or conspectus
of all times (pp. 35-36). "Puritan histories are, in fact,
notably static. In Bradford's Of Plymouth Plantation, for
example, the story of cause and effect relations is much
less important than the isolated episode." What happened
at Merrymount, for instance, seems much less dependent on
necessary human preconditions than upon the immediate influence of the divine will. "The historian considers each
event as a unique point of view, a juncture at which the
divine plan can be seen from a new angle."

9 QUINN, D. B. Review of A Loss of Mastery by Peter Gay, EHR,
LXXXIV (April), 394.
"To lambast historians in this way because they do not
fit into the arbitrary frame of an inappropriate ideology
seems a pointless activity."

10   [TICHI], CECELIA L. HALBERT. "The Art of the Lord's Remem-
      brancers: A Study of New England Puritan Histories." Un-
      published Ph.D. dissertation, University of California at
      Davis.
         (See 1971.B3).

1970 A BOOKS

1   RUNYAN, MICHAEL G. "The Poetry of William Bradford: An An-
      notated Edition with Essays Introductory to the Poems."
      Unpublished Ph.D. dissertation, University of California
      at Los Angeles.
         "This dissertation is the first work to collect the entire
      body of Bradford's verse, evaluate the manuscripts, adhere
      to the best available seventeenth-century texts, and provide
      full annotation. There is also a general introduction and
      introductions to each of the poems emphasizing the most
      significant textual, biographical, historical or literary
      aspects of each." Some of the products of this study are
      Bradford's relatively conservative religious position, his
      marked antipathy toward the Dutch, his fondness for puns,
      his skillful use of Biblical allusion, and his use of
      physical threat as symbolic of spiritual threat.

1970 B SHORTER WRITINGS

1   BAYM, NINA. Review of Design of the Present by John F. Lynen,
      JEGP, LXIX (January), 183-85.
         The book's chief contribution is probably in its dis-
      cussion of the Puritans and their relations, formal and
      thematic, to the other writers discussed. Lynen develops
      an interesting set of relationships for the Puritan history:
      the Puritan does not believe in causality, nor does he see
      a purpose in sequential arrangements; he sees emblems and
      symbols, not events.

2   GARRISON, JOSEPH M., JR. "Teaching Early American Literature:
      Some Suggestions," CE, XXXI (February), 487-97.
         Bradford, Taylor, and Edwards are discussed with a view
      toward establishing a procedural model which will encour-
      age students to study colonial American literature as
      literature. A comparison of Bradford with Xenophon, for
      example, might show that he tends to insulate people from
      felt contact with the temporal world, that he reports
      things synoptically, that he views the world from a dis-
      tance and does not particularize, that he sees the world
      in categories and his language does not admit complexities,
      that he insists on a radical distinction between his voice
      as a citizen and his voice as an historian.

1970

3   ISRAEL, CALVIN. "American Puritan Literary Theory: 1620-
        1660." Unpublished Ph.D. dissertation, University of
        California at Davis, p. 67.
            Finds implications of the baroque literary theory in
        Bradford's description of the Pequot Indians.

4   MAJOR, MINOR W. "William Bradford Versus Thomas Morton,"
        EAL, V (Fall), 1-13.
            Though scholars generally speak of the accuracy of Brad-
        ford's history, he was certainly disingenuous in his treat-
        ment of Morton's career in New England. Bradford's charge
        that Morton was selling guns and ammunition to the Indians
        was never proven and probably had no basis. Bradford was
        most upset by Morton's relations with Indian women. One
        of the reasons why Bradford's partisanship here has not
        been recognized is, as Peter Gay pointed out, his ability
        to make his case persuasive, that is, to make it sound not
        like a case, but history.

5   STEELE, THOMAS S. J. "The Biblical Meaning of Mather's Brad-
        ford," BRMMLA, XXIV (December), 147-54.
            Bradford deliberately constructed his version of the storm
        which hit the Grimsby group to resemble Paul's "peril by
        sea" in Acts. Mather used this version in a praeteritio
        to begin his biography of Bradford, but, contrary to fact,
        he places Bradford on the ship. For both Bradford and
        Mather, then, "the Pilgrims, bearers of the newly purified
        truth of the Gospel, stopped off in Holland on a journey
        into the pagan West just as Paul's party had stopped off
        in Malta on their way to the pagan wilderness of Rome."
        For Mather, the reason for placing Bradford on the voyage
        is typological not historical. Mather's purpose was to
        remind his readers "that the reasons for founding New
        England were the same reasons for the founding of the Jew-
        ish nation," and he uses antonomasia, the metaphorical
        equation of a real person with a Biblical person. Bradford
        is Adam, Abraham, Moses, Job, and Josiah, but, most of all,
        Paul.

1971 A   BOOKS - NONE

1971 B   SHORTER WRITINGS

1   HOWARD, ALAN B. "Art and History in Bradford's Of Plymouth
        Plantation," WMQ, XXVIII (April), 237-66.
            Howard begins with a review of criticism governed by the
        notion that Bradford's history has been severely distorted
        by the arguments it has served (by the psychological

(HOWARD, ALAN B.)

approach of Miller/Murdock, by a progressive historian like Gay, by the distinction between history and historical narrative). Bradford's history, in contrast to Johnson's Wonder-Working Providence, is not history seen through a systematic structure of revealed theology, but an elaboration of that feeling called "the Augustinian strain of piety." Bradford realizes completely the absolute sovereignty of God and the absolute depravity of man, that God could not be contained in the federal theology. Inverting Johnson, Bradford begins in man's capacity for confusion ("Complexity, not Satan, is the real antagonist"), and moves toward an affirmation of God's sovereignty. Over and over again he warns that man, relying on his own strength, must fail, but in that failure lies the basis for success, the acknowledgement that real strength rests in God. In this sense the history has neither plot nor direction, but a rhythmic coherence of incident and meaning: it describes the continued awakening to the essential reality that God's power and man's weakness underlie the whole range of human experience. Bradford never allows the available paradigm of the Jews wandering in the desert to divert his attention from the problems which confront man in time; the best and the worst times are always linked with human infirmity. This conception of history informs his role as candid, humble, charitable narrator; his use of letters to let characters speak for themselves; his emphasis on realistic detail over providences; his "inductive" rhetorical strategy; and his framing use of scriptural analogues.

2   MEYER, ISIDORE S. "The Hebrew Exercises of Governor William Bradford," in Studies in Jewish Bibliography, History, and Literature: In Honor of I. Edward Kiev, edited by Charles Berlin. New York: KTAV Publishing House, pp. 237-88.

Facsimile reproductions of the Hebrew exercises in Bradford's third Dialogue and a discussion of the Dialogues in relation to their contemporary context which shows that Bradford's continuing concern was to further the Congregational Way. Bradford saw Plymouth, typologically, as a new Israel, and the selection and presentation of Hebrew exercises towards the end of his life "supported his theory that that Way was based upon the 'primitive sources' of the Hebrew Scriptures" (Peter Gomes mentions a "newly expanded" version of Meyer's essay by the Pilgrim Society, 1973; See 1975.B1).

1971

3   TICHI, CECELIA. "Spiritual Biography and the 'Lord's Remem-
       brancers,'" WMQ, XXVIII (January), 64-85.
          Puritan history writers expanded the genre of spiritual
       biography to include not only the individual but the tribal
       society. The journey-wayfaring motif pervades the histories.
       Bradford's metaphorical use of the ocean, for example,
       reveals the profound impact of the Atlantic voyage; viewing
       the world as a vast ocean, he depicts the colonists as
       travelers or pilgrims whose every step is marked with
       danger. (Reprinted in Sacvan Bercovitch, The American
       Puritan Imagination: Essays in Revaluation [New York:
       Cambridge University Press, 1974], pp. 56-73).

4   WHITE, B. R. The English Separatist Tradition: From the
       Marian Martyrs to the Pilgrim Fathers. London: Oxford
       University Press, pp. 1-2, passim.
          In this book which attempts to show that Robert Browne's
       influence, while greater than has been usually allowed,
       was not decisive, Bradford's first Dialogue is seen as
       "a deliberate attempt to pass on to a new generation know-
       ledge of that Separatist tradition which had shaped their
       fathers' convictions and had eventually led to the settle-
       ment of New Plymouth."

1972 B   BOOKS - NONE

1972 A   SHORTER WRITINGS

1   GRIFFITH, JOHN. "Of Plymouth Plantation as a Mercantile Epic,"
       ArQ, XXVIII (Autumn), 231-42.
          Bradford's history is epic in subject and manner; it is
       a tragic story of real men told in a style which reflects
       communal expression. It is mercantile because there is
       a money mentality at work throughout the narrative. Though
       Bradford strives to keep economic concerns subsidiary to
       spiritual ones, the value of things tends to be expressed
       as commodity value, dramatic meaning is often rendered in
       quantitative terms, and obstacles are often translated into
       economic matters. The structure of the history is that
       of the American success story, the movement from early
       wretchedness to later prosperity, and the climax is the
       moment the colony finally stands cleared of its debt. The
       ceremonial value of wealth-getting for Bradford is similar
       to the ceremonial value of fishing for Hemingway, and in
       this sense the history is closer to the story of Jacob than
       Exodus.

WILLIAM BRADFORD: A REFERENCE GUIDE

2   LEVIN, DAVID. "William Bradford: The Value of Puritan
        Historiography," in Major Writers of Early American Liter-
        ature, edited by Everett Emerson. Madison, Wisconsin:
        University of Wisconsin Press, pp. 11-31.
        The great value of the Puritan historian is to show piety
    functioning uncertainly but faithfully in the world, along
    with other motives. The common mistake has been to treat
    Bradford as an example of Puritan piety rather than to
    stress the achievement of Bradford in portraying that piety.
    This piety, rather than relying on providential causation,
    motivates a strict inquiry into historical complexity
    through worldly causes. The end result is often ambiguity
    and perplexity, the difficulty in knowing circumstances and
    characters. The letters which Bradford includes not only
    give essential information, but convey the genuine plight
    and the vivid feelings of men caught in their historical
    situation. The succession of confidence men which plague
    the colony require us to observe the Pilgrim passion for
    justice and confrontation. There is a wondrous ambiguity
    even to prosperity, for the history is a dual story of
    flourishing material growth and spiritual decline.

3   ROSENMEIER, JESPER. "'With My Owne Eyes': William Bradford's
        Of Plymouth Plantation," in Typology and Early American
        Literature, edited by Sacvan Bercovitch. Amherst,
        Massachusetts: University of Massachusetts Press, pp. 69-
        105.
        The Separatist vision of a New Jerusalem which Bradford
    shared is developed through a discussion of Henry Ainsworth
    and John Robinson. Bradford probably wrote Book One of
    Plymouth Plantation in 1630 and Book Two in 1645-46, both
    times when he was particuarly dissatisfied with Plymouth's
    role in the history of Redemption. Bradford wanted to
    resurrect a bygone holiness, to mirror past glory, to
    impress and exhort the younger generation. He tried to
    make the past live in the present through his use of letters,
    biographies, and a framework of threat and damnation.
    Bradford uses affliction to typify the vision of promise
    by concentrating on the relation between present suffering
    and future freedom, between crucifixion and resurrection.
    Christ's passion, moreover, is the key, typologically, to
    the future; the past lives again in the present as the
    Pilgrims re-enact and fulfill the wanderings of Israel.
    Bradford's purposes are the same after 1650, but the in-
    creased intensity of his concern for Plymouth's future
    leads him to abandon the role of objective narrator and
    seek in the dialogue of ancient and young men a more im-
    mediate confrontation of the generations, and finally, in
    the poems, he drops the mask altogether and pleads personally

55

1972

(ROSENMEIER, JESPER)
with his people to repent before the rod is lowered. (Reprinted in The American Puritan Imagination: Essays in Revaluation, edited by Sacvan Bercovitch [New York: Cambridge University Press, 1974], pp. 77-106).

4   STEIN, ROGER B.   "Seascape and the American Imagination: The Puritan Seventeenth Century," EAL, VII (Spring), 17-37.
    For the Puritan "the experience of the voyage itself was by its very nature dislocating, alienating man from the familiar and projecting him into a hazardous unknown.... Yet what gives imaginative shape to the Puritan voyages is the ideational context and construct which can accommodate the new and the strange to the known and the secure. The study of Puritan seascape illuminates the particular ways in which men and women came to terms imaginatively with the various psychological and social pressures upon them." The famous passages when the group lands make explicit the typological significance implicit in the selectively realistic description of the voyage itself.

1973 A   BOOKS - NONE

1973 B   SHORTER WRITINGS

1   BROOKS, CLEANTH, R. W. B. LEWIS, and ROBERT PENN WARREN. American Literature: The Makers and the Making, Vol. I. New York: St. Martin's Press, p. 17.
    Bradford announces one of the richest themes in American literature, the testing of the ideal by the actual, of the idea by experience, a theme found in Adams and in Faulkner and beyond them in the legends of Camelot, "of the rise, triumphs, troubles, and dissolution of the model community."

2   DALY, ROBERT. "William Bradford's Vision of History," AL, XLIV (January), 557-69.
    The movement of Bradford's history from a selective, coherent, and confident beginning, through a chaotic central section, to a truncated, elegiac ending is explained by his adherence to the Deuteronomic Formula, a vision of history from Eusebius, Socrates Scholasticus, and John Foxe, rather than Augustine. Bradford's history moves through three psychological moments, each based on the principle that God works through history to assure the triumph of his people and the overthrow of their enemies. In the first, from 1630-1632, Bradford is confident, for he could see that his Pilgrims were the elect of God, and thus he records only those events which affect or clarify

1973

(DALY, ROBERT)
>the progress of the colony. With signs of declension in
>1632, however, he begins to record both positive and negative
>signs of God's providence in an attempt to determine whether
>the pilgrimage was indeed a part of the second Exodus.
>Then, when he could no longer see positive signs, rather
>than denouncing his people or altering his evidence, he
>simply ended his account, "as mute testimony to a vision
>of human and divine purpose that had not been realized."

3   IRVIN, WILLIAM J.   Review of <u>Typology and Early American Liter-
ature</u> by Sacvan Bercovitch, <u>EAL</u>, VIII (Spring), 83-87.
>Rosenmeier's discussion of Bradford places a typological
>grounding under Miller's thesis that the development of the
>jeremiad was a psychological reinforcement of the sense
>of loss felt by New England leaders. An implication of his
>essay, however, "is that the extension of the typological
>exegesis beyond the limits of the Bible results in an alter-
>ation of the exegetical method." The typological pattern
>of death and resurrection emphasizes the present as crisis
>between past suffering and future fulfillment. This sense
>of crisis can be found in the conversion experience, in
>millennial attitudes, and could be tested in other doc-
>trines such as the covenant. Thus, one might "speculate
>on the assumptions about experience when experience is
>conceived of as proceeding by crises rather than by slow
>incrementation."

4   KELLER, KARL.   Review of <u>Major Writers of Early American
Literature</u> by Everett Emerson, <u>EAL</u>, VIII (Spring),
80-83.
>Levin's Bradford is a complex man whose simple piety
>demanded the dramatizing of great events. Though Levin
>argues for literature as history, he does so with a vague
>critical term, "dramatize," which makes out of a fresh
>approach an easy and overworn argument for including the
>historian as writer.

5   LANIER, STERLING.   Review of <u>Major Writers of Early American
Literature</u> by Everett Emerson, <u>WMQ</u>, XXX (October),
667-68.
>The quality of High Seriousness (a sense of mission,
>the messianic complex) is a cornerstone of our Puritan
>legacy, and, as Levin shows in regard to Bradford, in the
>early writers this stems from innate pessimism.

<u>1974 A   BOOKS - NONE</u>

1974

1974 B   SHORTER WRITINGS

   1   SCHEICK, WILLIAM J. "The Theme of Necessity in Bradford's
       Of Plymouth Plantation," SCN, XXXII (Winter), 88-90.
         Bradford initially considered necessity chiefly in terms
       of God's manipulation of the external world, as a taxing
       but ultimately benign instrument of God's providence; but,
       after the dispute over land ownership in 1623, he saw
       necessity as the human justification for indulging pride,
       as the corrupt necessity of the innately depraved heart.

1975 A   BOOKS

   1 *RUNYAN, MICHAEL G. William Bradford: the Complete Verse.
       St. Paul, Minnesota: The John Colet Press (Box 80101,
       Como Station, St. Paul, Minnesota 55108).
        Not seen, but Prof. Runyan tells us that this is a sub-
       stantial revision of his dissertation (1970.A1), particu-
       larly in "imposing standard English spelling and punctua-
       tion on the verse."

1975 B   SHORTER WRITINGS

   1   BERCOVITCH, SACVAN. The Puritan Origins of the American Self.
       New Haven, Connecticut: Yale University Press, pp. 44-46.
        "The difference between Bradford and Mather as histo-
       rians lies in their different concepts of 'Americanus.'
       For Bradford, the Plymouth settlement was part of a secu-
       lar experience from which he tried to infer the meaning of
       providence. For Mather, the New World errand was part of
       church history; he deduced its providential meanings from
       the preordained scheme of redemption."

   2   GOMES, PETER J. Review of Typology and Early American Litera-
       ture by Sacvan Bercovitch, NEQ, XLVIII (March), 127.
        "Of particular interest here for its treatment of the
       woefully neglected Henry Ainsworth is the discussion of
       Bradford, whose repute as a typologist pales beside his
       colleagues of the Bay," but Rosenmeier unfortunately was
       not able to employ the studies by Howard and Meyer.

   3   HOVEY, KENNETH ALAN. "The Theology of History in Of Plymouth
       Plantation and Its Predecessors," EAL, X (Spring), 47-66.
        Examines "A Brief Relation," "Mourt's Relation," and
       "Good News from New England" to determine the purposes for
       which they were written, to isolate their relatively simple
       theological theme, and to show how this theme forms a part
       of the more complex theology of history in Bradford's
       work. Bradford creates a single impression of God and man,
       showing "how man works under, yet also with, the Sovereign
       of history in all that he does.

Writings About John Cotton, 1658 - 1975

1658 A   BOOKS

  1   NORTON, JOHN. <u>Abel being dead, yet speaketh</u>. London: Tho.
      Newcomb for Lodowick Lloyd.
        A pious biography based, Norton tells us, on writings
     and information from John Davenport, Samuel Whiting,
     Cotton's widow, and others: "To preserve the memory of
     the blessed with the spices and sweet odors of their excel-
     lencies and wel-doing, recorded to posterity, is a <u>super-</u>
     <u>Aegyptian</u> embalming"; we must "not suffer such a light
     to be hid under a bushel." Emphasis is given to Cotton's
     life in England and to his scholarship and skill in
     polemics. Cotton's death, and the comet which appeared
     shortly before it, are seen as admonitory signs of ominous
     future events.

1658 B   SHORTER WRITINGS - NONE

1662 A   BOOKS - NONE

1662 B   SHORTER WRITINGS

  1   *CLARKE, SAMUEL. <u>A Collection of the Lives of Ten Eminent</u>
      <u>Divines</u>. London: W. Miller, pp. 55-84.
        Not seen. Cited by Etulain (1969.B2) as both largely
     taken from Norton. Emerson (1965.A1, p. 167) says that
     Norton's work is "abstracted" by Clarke. <u>See also</u> Clarke's
     <u>The Lives of Thirty-Two English Divines</u>. London, 1677,
     pp. 217-29.

1702 A   BOOKS - NONE

1702

1702 B SHORTER WRITINGS

   1   MATHER, COTTON. "Cottonus Redivivus: Or, The Life of Mr. John
       Cotton," in Magnalia Christi Americana, Book III. London:
       Thomas Parkhurst, pp. 14-32.
         This biographical sketch emhasizes Cotton's indefatigable
       and influential preaching in England and the ecclesiastical
       trouble he was involved with in New England. Particular
       attention is given to his "Treasure of Learning" in Latin,
       Greek, Hebrew, and Logic; his desire and success in
       preaching plainly, so "as to be understood by the meanest
       Capacity"; his scholarly character, humility, hospitality,
       and his role as husband and father. "This Cotton was in-
       deed the Cato of his Age, for his Gravity; but had a glory
       with it which Cato had not."

1798 A BOOKS - NONE

1798 B SHORTER WRITINGS

   1   HOLLIS, T. "Abstract of the Laws of New-England," CMHS, first
       series, V, 171-72.
         Suggests that Sir Henry Vane assisted Cotton in the prep-
       aration of this document.

1809 A BOOKS - NONE

1809 B SHORTER WRITINGS

   1   ELIOT, JOHN. Biographical Dictionary, Containing a Brief
       Account of the First Settlers and other Eminent Characters.
       Published by Cushing and Appleton, Salem, and Edward
       Oliver, No. 70, State Street, Boston, pp. 133-38.
         "In those instances where he discovered intolerance and
       the spirit of bigotry, a zeal for ecclesiastical power,
       he only manifested the inconsistency of human nature."
       Such inconsistencies are common among all Christians, so,
       instead of disturbing the ashes of our ancestors by
       repeating that the "very men who had fled from persecution
       became persecutors," we had better imitate their virtues.

1812 A BOOKS - NONE

JOHN COTTON: A REFERENCE GUIDE

1812 B SHORTER WRITINGS

1   EMERSON, Rev. WILLIAM. An Historical Sketch of the First
       Church in Boston, from Its Formation to the Present Period.
       Boston: Munroe and Francis, pp. 18-86.
          The history of the Church from 1634 to 1652 is seen
       through Cotton's activities. "It was an uncommonly inter-
       esting epoch to the Church. A fraternity was to be
       formed of discordant materials." Many were Episcopalians
       and many were simply adventurers, but "the sagacity
       and everwatchful discipline of Mr. Cotton was astonishingly
       efficacious toward conforming all descriptions of characters
       to habits of obedience and order."

1815 A BOOKS - NONE

1815 B SHORTER WRITINGS

1   HUBBARD, WILLIAM. "A General History of New England From the
       Discovery to MDCLXXX," CMHS, second series, V-VI, 175.
          "Mr. Cotton had such an insinuating and melting way
       in his preaching, that he would usually carry his very
       adversary captive after the triumphant chariot of his
       rhetoric, and, as Solomon saith, the soft tongue breaketh
       the bone."

1822 A BOOKS - NONE

1822 B SHORTER WRITINGS

1   ANON. "Memoirs of the Life of the Rev. John Cotton, formerly
       of Boston, in New England," The Investigator, V (July),
       1-21, and V (October), 239-59.
          Reprints Norton's biography (1658.A1).

1834 A BOOKS

1   NORTON, JOHN. Memoir of John Cotton, edited by Enoch Pond.
       Boston: Perkins and Marvin.
          Norton's biography is reprinted with a few notes,
       mostly biographical in nature, and the preface contains a
       short sketch of Norton.

1834

1834 B   SHORTER WRITINGS

1   PARKMAN, FRANCIS. Review of A Memoir of John Cotton, by John
       Norton, with a Preface and Notes by Enoch Pond, North
       American Review, LXXXIII (April), 486-501.
          This review also contains a biographical sketch of
       Cotton and remarks on the relation between clergy and con-
       temporary political issues. The only value of Norton's
       biography was its scarceness, and that it has now lost.
       "It is a little monument of olden times in a comely dress,
       and reveals to us for our comfort how wretchedly some
       learned men, skilled in theology, can write biography."
       Norton continually wanders after obscure allusions and
       quaint resemblances, leaving the reader to guess such things
       as the year of Cotton's birth.

1843 A   BOOKS - NONE

1843 B   SHORTER WRITINGS

1   GRAY, F. C. "Remarks on the Early Laws of Massachusetts Bay,"
          CMHS, third series, VIII, 191-215.
             Discusses and distinguishes Cotton's "Moses his Judicials"
          from Ward's "Body of Liberties."

1846 A   BOOKS

1   McCLURE, A. W. The Life of John Cotton. Boston: Massachusetts
          Sabbath School Society.
             This volume is in a series designed to find noble examples
          in the "Lives of the Chief Fathers of New England" which
          will strengthen the minds, enrich the memories, and set the
          principles of the young. Cotton's life is drawn mainly
          from earlier published accounts, joined with a discussion
          of the origin of Puritanism and the nature of Congregation-
          alism, and is certainly filio-pietistic in nature: "Mr.
          Cotton knew how to touch the keys of the human heart, so
          as to draw out responsive and accordant notes. He played
          this complicated organ with a master's hand: and though
          he found it sometimes sadly out of tune, his skill would
          often blend the jarring sounds in surprising harmony."
          "That star rose brightly on the older England, and rode
          through stormy skies. But it sweetly shed its parting
          rays on the newer England, at its serene and unclouded
          setting."

John Cotton: A Reference Guide

1846 B SHORTER WRITINGS

1 WHITING, SAMUEL. "Concerning the Life of the Famous Mr.
Cotton, Teacher to the Church of Christ at Boston, in
New-England," in <u>Chronicles of the First Planters of the
Colony of Massachusetts Bay, from 1623 to 1636</u>, edited
by Alexander Young. Boston: Charles C. Little and James
Brown, pp. 419-31.
Brief biographical sketch which provided the foundation
for the works by Norton and Mather. Attention is given,
for example, to the remarkable increase in the law practice
of Cotton's father which enabled him to stay in the
university, his indefatigable preaching, and his unique
position in New England.

1847 A BOOKS - NONE

1847 B SHORTER WRITINGS

1 THORNTON, JOHN WINGATE. "The Cotton Family," <u>NEHGR</u>, I (April),
164-66. Genealogical chart.
For a correction, see <u>NEHGR</u>, XLIX (April, 1895), 180-82.

1848 A BOOKS - NONE

1848 B SHORTER WRITINGS

1 ANON. "God's Promise to His Plantation," <u>NEHGR</u>, II (April,
July), 151, 318.
Brief note on Cotton's sermon and evidence that it was
preached at Southampton.

1850 A BOOKS - NONE

1850 B SHORTER WRITINGS

1 ANON. "John Cotton," <u>The New Englander</u>, VIII (August), 388-418.
Review article on A. W. McClure's <u>Life of John Cotton</u>
which contains a detailed biographical sketch prefaced by
remarks regarding the difficulty of writing a biography
which must be panegyric rather than impartial and critical.

1851 A BOOKS - NONE

1851 B SHORTER WRITINGS

1 ANON. "Abstracts of the Earliest Wills upon Record in the
County of Suffolk, Mass.," <u>NEHGR</u>, V (April), 240-41.
Prints Cotton's will.

1855

1855 A   BOOKS - NONE

1855 B   SHORTER WRITINGS

   1   BARRY, JOHN STETSON. The History of Massachusetts, Vol. I.
       Boston: Phillips, Sampson and Company, pp. 200-1.
        Cotton's "prudent counsels, humble deportment, and rare
      powers of conciliation harmonized conflicting opinions,
      moderated the violence of the spirit of controversy, and
      guarded safely the interests of the colony amidst the
      storms and perils which it subsequently encountered."

1856 A   BOOKS - NONE

1856 B   SHORTER WRITINGS

   1   DRAKE, SAMUEL G. The History and Antiquities of Boston,
       Pt. I. Boston: Luther Stevens, pp. 157-63.
        Portrait and a brief biographical sketch which contains
      information about Cotton's English ancestors.

   2   *THOMPSON, PISHEY. The History and Antiquities of Boston.
       Boston: S. G. Drake, pp. 412 ff.
        Not seen. Cited by Gordon in the Dictionary of National
      Biography sketch (1909.B1).

1857 A   BOOKS - NONE

1857 B   SHORTER WRITINGS

   1   SPRAGUE, WILLIAM B. Annals of the American Pulpit, Vol. I.
       New York: Robert Carter and Brothers, pp. 25-30.
        Biographical sketch and bibliography.

1861 A   BOOKS - NONE

1861 B   SHORTER WRITINGS

   1   CLARK, JOSEPH S. "John Cotton," The Congregational Quarterly,
       III (April), 133-48.
        Very full biographical sketch which, for instance,
      stresses that Cotton's move to America was not taken to
      escape suffering: "What a contraction of one's life
      sphere! What a shrinkage of human greatness, when meas-
      ured by the scale which man applies in such matters!"
      Also contains a list of Cotton's writings and an exchange
      of letters between Cotton and Cromwell in 1651.

1862 A   BOOKS - NONE

1862 B   SHORTER WRITINGS

1   HOPPIN, NICHOLAS. "The Rev. John Cotton A.M., Vicar of Old
      Boston," The Church Monthly, IV, V (December, January),
      161-67, 40-54.
         Substantial account of Cotton's career in England through
      1633. Though it is common to speak of persecution for the
      sake of conscience and banishment for mere ceremonial
      non-conformity, Cotton could hardly complain of being
      harshly treated.

1866 A   BOOKS - NONE

1866 B   SHORTER WRITINGS

1   DUYCKINCK, EVERT A. and GEORGE L. Cyclopaedia of American
      Literature, Vol. I. New York: Charles Scribner, pp. 20-24.
         Brief biographical sketch with substantial quoting from
      Cotton's poetry.

2   GUILD, REUBEN ALDRIDGE. "Introductory Remarks" to "A Letter
      of John Cotton," in Publications of the Narragansett
      Club, I, 1-10.
         In this letter, written during the Williams controversy,
      "Mr. Cotton's defense of his own course of conduct appears
      to us unworthy of his usual candor, betraying a mind
      ill at ease, and painfully conscious of unjust and unkind
      dealings toward a former friend and companion in tribu-
      lation."

1867 A   BOOKS - NONE

1867 B   SHORTER WRITINGS

1   DIMAN, REV. J. LEWIS. "Editor's Preface" to "Master John
      Cotton's Answer to Master Roger Williams," in Publications
      of the Narragansett Club, II, 1-8.
         While the main subject discussed in this reply is the
      dispute between Nonconformist and Separatist, the chief
      historical values arise from its incidental discussion
      of the reasons for Williams's banishment and from Cotton's
      vindication of his conduct in the Antinomian controversy.

1867

2. WATERSTON, ROBERT C. "George Herbert and John Cotton," PMHS, IX (January), 457-61.
    Herbert probably heard Cotton preach while they were both at Cambridge, and Herbert no doubt had people like Cotton in mind when he wrote his famous lines: "Religion stands a tiptoe in our land/Ready to pass to the American strand."

1868 A   BOOKS

1. SOMERBY, H. G.   The English Ancestry of Rev. John Cotton of Boston.   Boston: Henry W. Dutton & Son.
    Short genealogy reprinted from The Heraldic Journal, XXII (April, 1868), 49-58.

1868 B   SHORTER WRITINGS - NONE

1873 A   BOOKS - NONE

1873 B   SHORTER WRITINGS

1. WATERSTON, ROBERT C. "Early History of Our Public Schools," PMHS, XII (February), 386-91.
    Evidence for Cotton's role in the establishment of the Free School in Boston.

1874 A   BOOKS - NONE

1874 B   SHORTER WRITINGS

1. BLENKIN, G. B. "Boston, England, and John Cotton in 1621," NEHGR, XXVIII (April), 125-39.
    A series of documents relating to a supposed act of treason and disloyalty to the throne, cutting off the crosses from the king's arms, which shows that Cotton was by no means a rigid non-conformist at this time.

1876 A   BOOKS - NONE

1876 B   SHORTER WRITINGS

1. PALFREY, JOHN GORHAM.   History of New England During the Stuart Dynasty, Vol. II. Boston: Little, Brown, and Co., pp. 409-11.

(PALFREY, JOHN GORHAM)
 The personal estimation in which Cotton was held was
high, but his influence over public affairs was controlled
by men of superior qualifications for governing. He was
far from the ruling spirit of the colony, and probably
did not influence its destiny as much as he supposed.
Faith in things unseen was his steady principle of action.

1878 A BOOKS - NONE

1878 B SHORTER WRITINGS

1 HOLMES, OLIVER WENDELL. Holmes's Works, Vol. XI. Boston:
  Houghton, Mifflin and Co., p. 220.
  "If our learned and excellent John Cotton used to
sweeten his mouth before going to bed with a bit of Calvin,
we may as wisely sweeten and strengthen our sense of
existence with a morsel or two from Emerson's essay on
Resources."

2 TYLER, MOSES COIT. A History of American Literature, 1607-
  1765, Vol. 1. New York: G. P. Putnam's Sons, pp. 210-14.
  Cotton was the unmitred pope of a pope-hating commonwealth, but his writings, though clear and cogent, contain
almost no remarkable merits in thought and style. The
reader is not rewarded "by a single passage of eminent
force or beauty," or cheered "by the felicity of a new
epithet in the objurgation of sinners, or a new tint in
the landscape-painting of hell."

1880 A BOOKS - NONE

1880 B SHORTER WRITINGS

1 ELLIS, GEORGE E. "John Cotton in Church and State," International Review, IX, 370-87.
  Biographical sketch on the occasion of the 250th
anniversary of settlement which stresses the positive
forces motivating the non-conforming settlers and the
basis for strong theological influence in political affairs, concluding that Cotton's pre-eminent position was
the result simply and solely of his consummate skill in
opening the scriptures.

1884

1884 A   BOOKS - NONE

1884 B   SHORTER WRITINGS

   1   WINSOR, JUSTIN. Narrative and Critical History of America,
           Vol. III. Boston: Houghton, Mifflin and Company, p. 351.
           "Cotton was like a strong man struggling in the mire."

1887 A   BOOKS - NONE

1887 B   SHORTER WRITINGS

   1   BROOKS, WILLIAM GRAY. "The Father of Boston," New England
           Magazine, V (February), 299-308.
             Biographical sketch on the occasion of the tercenten-
           ary of Cotton's birth.

1889 A   BOOKS - NONE

1889 B   SHORTER WRITINGS

   1   FISKE, JOHN. The Beginnings of New England. Boston: Houghton,
           Mifflin and Company, p. 226.
             Neither Cotton nor Winthrop approved of toleration upon
           principle, but neither had a temperament which persecutes.
           Under their guidance, the tragic persecution of the Quakers
           would not have occurred.

1891 A   BOOKS - NONE

1891 B   SHORTER WRITINGS

   1   HIGGINSON, THOMAS WENTWORTH. The Works of Thomas Wentworth
           Higginson, Vol. VII. Cambridge, Massachusetts: The
           Riverside Press, pp. 105, 119, 126.
             Several anecdotal remarks about Cotton, for instance,
           "Holy Mr. Cotton used to say that nothing was cheap in
           New England but milk and ministers."

1892 A   BOOKS - NONE

1892 B   SHORTER WRITINGS

1   ADAMS, CHARLES F.   Three Episodes of Massachusetts History.
     Boston: Houghton, Mifflin and Company.
        Contains a basic study of the Antinomian controversy.

1893 A   BOOKS - NONE

1893 B   SHORTER WRITINGS

1   ADAMS, CHARLES FRANCIS.   Massachusetts: Its Historians and
     Its History. Boston: Houghton, Mifflin and Company,
     pp. 27-30.
        Cotton does not stand on the same pedestal as Williams,
     but "all men cannot be martyrs; nor would it be good that
     all men should be martyrs, or yet the stuff of which martyrs
     are made."

1895 A   BOOKS - NONE

1895 B   SHORTER WRITINGS

1   BROWN, JOHN.   The Pilgrim Fathers of New England and their
     Puritan Successors. New York: Fleming H. Revell Company,
     pp. 307-13.
        Excerpts from an interesting British manuscript describ-
     ing Cotton as seen by those carrying out an official
     visitation of his church in England in 1614.

1897 A   BOOKS - NONE

1897 B   SHORTER WRITINGS

1   EAMES, WILBERFORCE.   "Early New England Catechisms," PAAS,
     XII (October), 76-182.
        Contains bibliographical information on Milk for Babes.

1901 A   BOOKS - NONE

1901 B   SHORTER WRITINGS

1   ONDERDONK, JAMES L.   History of American Verse (1610-1897).
     Chicago: A. C. McClurg and Co., p. 30.
        Cotton was an intellectual giant, but his poetry was
     puerile; his elegy on Hooker was even worse than that
     written by Bulkeley.

1901

2   WALKER, WILLISTON. Ten New England Leaders. New York: Silver,
Burdett and Company, pp. 49-94.
A biographical sketch which sets Cotton's English career
in its religious context and then focuses on three special
features of his life in America: the Antinomian controversy, the debates with Roger Williams, and the series of
treatises between 1640 and 1650 which consolidated the
polity of the churches.

1902 A BOOKS - NONE

1902 B SHORTER WRITINGS

1   FORD, WORTHINGTON C. "Cotton's 'Moses his Judicials,'" PMHS,
second series, XVI (October), 274-84.
The Cotton manuscript entitled "How far Moses Judicialls
bind Mass." is a brief record of a discussion upon the
"Judicialls," and should be dated earlier than the 1643
placed on it by previous investigators. In An Abstract
on the Lawes of New England (1641) we have the text of
"Moses his Judicials," the earliest body of laws framed
in English America.

2   *TACCHELLA, B. The Derby School Register, 1570-1901. London.
Listed in Welles (1948.A1).
See also B. Tacchella, John Cotton, B.D.: An Old
Derbeian, n.p., n.d. cited in Etulain (1969.B2).

3   WEEDEN, WILLIAM B. "Three Commonwealths," PAAS, new series,
XV (October), p. 136.
The extraordinary tenacity of the sociopolitical bar-
nacle of political election for life shows that Cotton
and Winthrop did not easily part with the hope of bringing
some of the ragged offshoots of feudalism across the
Atlantic.

1907 A BOOKS - NONE

1907 B SHORTER WRITINGS

1   MEAD, EDWIN D. "John Cotton's Farewell Sermon to Winthrop's
Company at Southampton," PMHS, third series, I (June),
101-15.
Summary of the sermon plus some historiographical facts.

JOHN COTTON: A REFERENCE GUIDE

1909 A BOOKS - NONE

1909 B SHORTER WRITINGS

1   GORDON, ALEXANDER. "John Cotton," in <u>Dictionary of National</u>
       <u>Biography</u>, Vol. XXII, edited by Sidney Lee. New York:
       The Macmillan Company, pp. 492-95.
           Biographical sketch. In the controversy with Williams,
       Williams rose above the confused ideas of his age, while
       Cotton, little understanding the claims of conscience,
       fell back upon the very principles whose application to
       his own case had driven him from England.

2   KING, HENRY M. "John Cotton and Sir Henry Vane," <u>Nation</u>,
       LXXXVIII (8 April), 357-58.
           The claim that Cotton was the preceptor of Vane cannot
       be justified. "It looks very much as if Cotton's momentary
       liberalism in joining hands with Vane in the defense of
       Mrs. Hutchinson was the effect of the young Governor's
       presence and influence upon him, and that after Vane had
       departed he fell back in a most humiliating manner, and
       with ostentatious penitence...into his former
       narrowness."

3   _____. "Was John Cotton the Preceptor of Sir Henry
       Vane, Jr.?", <u>Nation</u>, LXXXVIII (10 June), 577-78.
           "Vane was an independent in sentiment when he reached
       New England, and his experience here simply confirmed him
       in views already accepted"; Vane had a thousand better
       qualified teachers at home.

4   MEAD, EDWIN D. "John Cotton's Influence on Vane," <u>Nation</u>,
       LXXXVIII (13 May), 484.
           References showing Cotton as the influence on Vane, who
       was the primary channel for the impact of New England in-
       dependency on England.

1910 A BOOKS - NONE

1910 B SHORTER WRITINGS

1   HOSMER, JAMES K. "Was John Cotton the Preceptor of Sir Henry
       Vane?" <u>Nation</u>, LXXXIX (8 July), 32-33.
           There are good historical grounds for saying that certain
       ideas were formed in Cotton's study, where Vane underwent
       useful training.

1917

<u>1917 A   BOOKS - NONE</u>

<u>1917 B   SHORTER WRITINGS</u>

1   TRENT, WILLIAM PETERFIELD, et al. <u>The Cambridge History of</u>
    <u>American Literature</u>, Vol. I. New York: G. P. Putnam's
    Sons, pp. 35-38.
       Cotton is the most authoritative representative of the
    ideals of the middle period of Puritanism--its aristocratic
    conservatism in the guise of theocratic polities. In a
    mildly persistent way, Cotton was a revolutionist, haunted
    by utopian dreams of a Christian theocracy.

<u>1918 A   BOOKS - NONE</u>

<u>1918 B   SHORTER WRITINGS</u>

1   GREENOUGH, CHESTER N. "On the Authorship of Singing of Psalms
    A Gospel Ordinance," <u>PCSM</u>, XX (April), 239-47.
       Cites some evidence which indicates that Thomas Shepard,
    not Cotton, may have been the author of this work.

2   PERRY, BLISS. <u>The American Spirit in Literature</u>. New Haven,
    Connecticut: Yale University Press, p. 32.
       Cotton became the Pope of the theocracy, a clever Pope
    and not an unkindly one.

<u>1919 A   BOOKS - NONE</u>

<u>1919 B   SHORTER WRITINGS</u>

1   ADAMS, BROOKS. <u>The Emancipation of Massachusetts: The Dream</u>
    <u>and the Reality</u>. Boston: Houghton, Mifflin Company,
    pp. 269-71.
       Cotton committed the error of his life in undertaking
    to preach a religious reformation without having the
    resolution to face a martyrdom.

<u>1921 A   BOOKS - NONE</u>

<u>1921 B   SHORTER WRITINGS</u>

1   ADAMS, JAMES TRUSLOW. <u>The Founding of New England</u>. Boston:
    The Atlantic Monthly Press, p. 170.
       Assessment of his role in the Hutchinson matter: "Mr.
    Cotton, who had no taste for that banishment which he

1921

(ADAMS, JAMES TRUSLOW)
claimed was no hardship, now went over to what was
evidently the winning side. With a broader mind and
wider vision than any of the other clergy of the colony,
he had not the courage to stand alone, beyond a certain
point, against their unanimity in intolerance. The higher
promptings of his nature were crushed by the united voice
of the priesthood."

1924 A BOOKS - NONE

1924 B SHORTER WRITINGS

1   TUTTLE, JULIUS H. "Writings of Rev. John Cotton," in
     Bibliographical Essays: A Tribute to Wilberforce Eames.
     Cambridge, Massachusetts: Harvard University Press,
     pp. 363-80.
       A bibliography of primary material with location of
     copies. Does not list poems or letters.

1927 A BOOKS - NONE

1927 B SHORTER WRITINGS

1   FROTHINGHAM, PAUL REVERE. All These. Cambridge, Massachusetts:
     Harvard University Press, pp. 17-41.
       An address on the unveiling of a statue of Cotton in
     1907, mostly biographical in nature, with emphasis on the
     Williams and Hutchinson episodes. Though many view Cotton's
     sermons as dry, there are certain aspects which cannot be
     captured in print: "the tones of a voice, the flash of a
     radiant eye, the expression of a rapt and pious counte-
     nance, the magnetic personality, which oftentimes exert
     hypnotic influence."

2   PARRINGTON, VERNON LOUIS. Main Currents in American Thought:
     The Colonial Mind, 1620-1800. New York: Harcourt, Brace
     and World, Inc., pp. 27-37.
       Cotton, who dreamed of a utopia of the saints, is the
     most authoritative representative of the ideal of priestly
     stewardship. He was more open minded than his bigoted
     associates and not one to persecute; but he was also not
     one to stand alone, and in the Hutchinson matter, for
     example, he allowed himself to be coerced by narrower-
     minded men. Cotton was both a Calvinist and a Carolinian
     gentleman, resulting in a unique political theory of an
     ethical aristocracy; he was also a social revolutionary

1927

    (PARRINGTON, VERNON LOUIS)
        who would substitute an aristocracy of saints for the
        landed aristocracy, and fashion society upon ethical rather
        than economic lines.

1929 A BOOKS

  1 *WARREN, ALICE F. "John Cotton: The Father of Boston."
         Unpublished Ph.D. dissertation, University of Wisconsin.
         See Etulain (1969.B2).

1929 B SHORTER WRITINGS

  1   PLACE, CHARLES A. "The Early Forms of Worship in North Amer-
        ica," PAAS, new series, XXXIX (October), p. 373.
         Probably the earliest record of the order of worship
        observed by the Puritan churches is found in Cotton's
        "Questions and Answers" of 1634.

1930 A BOOKS - NONE

1930 B SHORTER WRITINGS

  1   ADAMS, JAMES TRUSLOW. "John Cotton," in Dictionary of American
        Bibliography, Vol. IV, edited by Allen Johnson and Dumas
        Malone. New York: Charles Scribner's Sons, pp. 460-62.
         Cotton was undoubtedly one of the most influential men
        of his day, but it is difficult to avoid the conclusion
        that he was more and more warped from his own nature by
        the unconscious desire to retain his prestige and influ-
        ence in the narrow and bigoted environment in which he
        had become great. He became more and more reactionary.

  2 *BACHELLER, IRVING. Candle in the Wilderness. New York:
        Bobbs.
         Cited in A. T. Dickinson, American Historical Fiction
        (3rd edition), Metuchen, N. J.: Scarecrow Press, 1971,
        p. 19 as "Boston in stern colonial days; Reverend John
        Cotton, Sir Harry Vane, and others appear."

  3   CALDER, ISABEL M. "John Cotton and the New Haven Colony,"
        NEQ, III (January), 82-94.
         A comparison between the New Haven Fundamental Orders
        of 1643 and Cotton's code of laws ("Moses his Judicials")
        shows that Cotton exerted a profound influence upon John
        Davenport and the young New Haven colony.

John Cotton: A Reference Guide

1931 A   BOOKS - NONE

1931 B   SHORTER WRITINGS

1   ANGOFF, CHARLES. A Literary History of the American People, Vol. I. New York: Alfred A. Knopf, pp. 138-43.
    After the Hutchinson uproar, Cotton, a man who otherwise might have been one of the few shining lights in early New England, succumbed to the prevailing Puritan fanaticism, lost his liberality, and became the most rabid theocrat in Massachusetts. "It was he, in fact, probably more than anybody else, who let loose the plague."

2   CALDER, ISABEL. "John Cotton's 'Moses His Judicials,'" PCSM, XXVIII (April), 86-94.
    The history of this document and critical appraisals of it: "The Cotton code was not the impracticable document that has been depicted by Gray and later writers, and deserves recognition as the earliest compilation of New England legislation."

3   PARKES, HENRY BAMFORD. "John Cotton and Roger Williams Debate Toleration," NEQ, IV (October), 735-56.
    This debate, since Cotton and Williams were equally sincere but doctrinally antithetical, gives an excellent illustration of the span of the Puritan mind. Cotton is unintelligible except to those who approach him by way of the Middle Ages, whereas Williams can only be appreciated if one looks back at him from the twentieth century. To Cotton, civil governors had to prevent spiritual error in order that the prosperity of religion might advance the prosperity of the state, a notion which is primitive as well as medieval. To Williams, if magistrates must govern men's consciences, then men's consciences must often be subject to wicked and unbelieving magistrates.

1932 A   BOOKS - NONE

1932 B   SHORTER WRITINGS

1   CALDER, ISABEL M. "The Authorship of a Discourse About Civil Government in a New Plantation Whose Design is Religion," AHR, XXXVII (January), 267-69.
    This work should indeed be attributed to Cotton and not to John Davenport. Cotton wrote the Discourse to meet objections to the fundamental principle of his code of laws, the limitation to church members of the right to vote and hold office, and gave it in manuscript to Davenport.

1932

2   LEWISOHN, LUDWIG. Expression in America. New York: Harper
         and Brothers, p. 8.
             The self-righteous authoritarianism of Winthrop is shared
         by Cotton and Hooker. "There was a touch of disease, of
         megalomania in this doctrine as held by these particular
         men.   For they were, in their time and place, the source
         of authority.... Their authoritarianism was no academic
         doctrine. The ministers came out of their studies and
         witnessed the whippings, the cuttings of ears, the boring
         of tongues with red-hot irons, the scourgings and the
         hangings which they had ordained." They had a rationali-
         zation for this sadistic power, articulated by Cotton,
         that there was only one truth, and resistance to it was
         therefore plainly wicked.

3   PARKES, HENRY BAMFORD. "The Puritan Heresy," Hound and Horn,
         II (January-March), 174.
             Except for Williams, Cotton was the only New Englander
         before Edwards with any trace of mystical feeling.

1933 A   BOOKS - NONE

1933 B   SHORTER WRITINGS

1   MILLER, PERRY. Orthodoxy in Massachusetts, 1630-1650: A
         Genetic Study. Cambridge, Massachusetts: Harvard Univer-
         sity Press, passim.
             "In the course of its researches into 'background' the
         study has offered at least one 'new' contribution to New
         England's history: it has presented a certain school of
         ecclesiastical thinkers as the specific source of the New
         England Way, and by analyzing the thought of this school
         has endeavored to depict what was the actual inheritance
         of John Cotton and his colleagues."

1935 A   BOOKS - NONE

1935 B   SHORTER WRITINGS

1   *SNEDEKER, CAROLINE. Uncharted Ways. Garden City, New York:
         Doubleday.
             Cited in A. T. Dickinson, American Historical Fiction
         (3rd edition), Metuchen, New Jersey: Scarecrow Press,
         1971, p. 30 as containing a description of Cotton's per-
         secution of the Quakers.

John Cotton: A Reference Guide

1937 A BOOKS - NONE

1937 B SHORTER WRITINGS

1 HORNBERGER, THEODORE. "Puritanism and Science: The Relationship Revealed in the Writings of John Cotton," NEQ, X (September), 503-15.
   Cotton is certainly interested in turning his knowledge of the sciences to homiletic purposes, but he is clearly familiar with Plato, Aristotle, Galen, and their medieval successors. His method (emphasis on authorities rather than observation and experience) is also clearly medieval, but, surprisingly, he shows himself already familiar with the non-scriptural arguments against the Copernican theory. Cotton shows that the Puritan was interested in the how as well as the why of natural phenomena, and makes us wonder if we know the real relation between Puritanism and later confidence in capitalistic technology.

2 MILLER, PERRY. "The Puritan Theory of the Sacraments in Seventeenth Century New England," CHR, XXII (January), 409-25.
   Cotton is mentioned throughout this discussion of Baptism and the Lord's Supper.

1938 A BOOKS - NONE

1938 B SHORTER WRITINGS

1 MERRILL, DANA K. "The First American Biography," NEQ, XI (March), 152-54.
   John Norton's life of Cotton entitled Abel being dead: "The memoir is composed of nearly equal parts of biography, eulogy, and sermon. The purely biographical portion, however, is a framework overlaid with homiletic thought and embellished with laudatory phrases."

1939 A BOOKS - NONE

1939 B SHORTER WRITINGS

1 RUSK, RALPH L. The Letters of Ralph Waldo Emerson, Vol. IV. New York: Columbia University Press, p. 486.
   Letter in which Thomas Carlyle expresses his wish to buy a volume by Cotton: "He was a man of real intelligence .... Cotton's memorial is properly the name Boston: that he carried some echo of poor old St. Botolph...across

1939

(RUSK, RALPH L.)
the Atlantic, on those surprising terms: this is the
smallest but by far the most immortal of the actions of
Cotton."

1941 A BOOKS - NONE

1941 B SHORTER WRITINGS

1   HIRSCH, ELIZABETH FEIST. "John Cotton and Roger Williams:
Their Controversy Concerning Religious Liberty," CH, X
(1941), 38-51.
   The controversy would never have been started without
Williams's participation in the debates of the Long Parlia-
ment in 1643/44. Though most of us sympathize with
Williams, Cotton's religious experience was deeper, his
Christianity more in accord with the complexity of our
lives than Williams's, and, finally, it is questionable for
us whether separation of church and state is a necessary
presupposition for liberty of conscience.

2   MILLER, PERRY. "Declension in a Bible Commonwealth," PAAS,
LI (April), 71.
   In The Way of Life Cotton composed the finest exposition
of what Max Weber has called the Protestant Ethic: man
was encouraged to make profits, but he was not expected
to succumb to the seductions of civil life. The distinctive
cast of the Puritan theory which contrasts radically with
19th century assumptions appears in the emphasis on public
good and dependence upon God's powers.

1942 A BOOKS - NONE

1942 B SHORTER WRITINGS

1   MORGAN, EDMUND S. "The Puritans and Sex," NEQ, XV (December),
592.
   Cotton's attitude toward marriage shows that he did not
ignore human nature, nor think of it as a spiritual
partnership.

1943 A BOOKS - NONE

1943 B   SHORTER WRITINGS

1   MILLER, PERRY. "Preparation for Salvation in Seventeenth
        Century New England," JHI, 4 (June), pp. 253-86, esp.
        266-76.
        What Hooker and Shepard called preparation was for
        Cotton simply the impact of grace; the prepared were al-
        ready saints. This difference was social and political
        as well as theological, and if Cotton had stood his ground
        in the Antinomian controversy he would either have had to
        flee, or the society would have been torn apart.

1944 A   BOOKS - NONE

1944 B   SHORTER WRITINGS

1   JANTZ, HAROLD S. The First Century of New England Verse.
        Worcester, Massachusetts: American Antiquarian Society,
        pp. 13, 193.
        Bibliography plus brief mention of Cotton's poetry.
        His two best poems are those preserved in Norton's biography
        (See also PAAS, LIII [October, 1943], pp. 219-508).

1945 A   BOOKS - NONE

1945 B   SHORTER WRITINGS

1   LEVY, BABETTE MAY. Preaching in the First Half Century of
        New England History. Hartford, Connecticut: The American
        Society of Church History, pp. 141-44 and passim.
        Cotton's sermons are disappointing reading, especially
        when contrasted with Hooker and Shepard, because he was a
        fanatic believer in plain sermons, because most were printed
        from short hand notes, and because his appeal may have been
        more dependent on the force of his personality. Cotton
        lacks the companionable touch with his listeners, and it
        is unfortunate that so much of his energy was given to
        denunciation.

2   WATTERS, R. E. "Biographical Technique in Cotton Mather's
        Magnalia," WMQ, series 3, II (April), 151.
        Mather's statement that Cotton was innocent of all
        responsibility in the Antinomian controversy is a deliber-
        ate perversion, since he did not wish to provide fresh fuel
        for criticism of his own political interventions.

1946

1946 A   BOOKS - NONE

1946 B   SHORTER WRITINGS

1   FROOM, LE ROY EDWIN. The Prophetic Faith of Our Fathers, Vol.
    III. Washington, D. C.: Review and Herald, pp. 33-42.
        Discussion of Cotton's prophecies in An Exposition upon
    the Thirteenth Chapter of the Revelation and The Pouring
    Out of the Seven Vials.

1948 A   BOOKS

1   WELLES, JUDITH B.   "John Cotton, 1584-1652: Churchman and
    Theologian." Unpublished Ph.D. dissertation, University
    of Edinburgh.
        Purpose is to present a thorough study of Cotton's life
    and work, and to indicate the extent of his influence out-
    side the Massachusetts Bay Colony and particularly in
    England. Ziff says this dissertation was "of special value
    to me because of her intelligent use of the English sources
    for a reconstruction of Cotton's Career" (1962.A2).

1948 B   SHORTER WRITINGS

1   EISINGER, CHESTER E.   "The Puritans' Justification For Taking
    the Land," EIHC, LXXXIV (April), 131-43.
        For Cotton, private property is created when labor is
    expended on vacant soil. Since the Indians did not occupy
    the entire country, Cotton could find divine sanction for
    both taking over the land and the institution of private
    property.

2   SPILLER, ROBERT, et al. Literary History of the United States,
    Vol. III. New York: Macmillan, pp. 455-57.
        A bibliography which contains a chronological listing
    of primary material and selected references to reprints,
    biography, criticism, and bibliography (See also the
    Bibliography Supplement, 1959, and the Bibliography Supple-
    ment II, 1972, edited by Richard M. Ludwig).

1949 A   BOOKS

1   *COME, DONALD R.   "John Cotton, Guide of the Chosen People."
    Unpublished Ph.D. dissertation, Princeton University.
        The clergy in Massachusetts loomed large in political,
    economic, and religious decision making, and Cotton "was
    rightfully recognized as being the greatest and most in-
    fluential of all the clergymen" (See DA, 15: 566-67).

1949 B SHORTER WRITINGS

1 MURDOCK, KENNETH B. Literature and Theology in Colonial
New England. Cambridge, Massachusetts: Harvard University
Press, pp. 120-27.
The purpose of Norton's Life of Cotton was to commemorate
the good deeds of a pious man so that others would seek
holiness in their turn. Norton's style is that of an eru-
dite and rhetorically precise scholar, but there are flashes
of typical Puritan diction and imagery. Cotton is more
"individual" than the heroes of most other early pious
biographies, there are hints of modern biographical techniques, and special emphasis is given to the migration
from Old England to New.

1952 A BOOKS

1 *CHRISTY, WAYNE H. "John Cotton: Convenant Theologian." Unpublished master's thesis, Duke University.
Cited in Etulain (1969.B2), Emerson (1965.A1), and Ziff
(1962.A2).

1952 B SHORTER WRITINGS - NONE

1954 A BOOKS - NONE

1954 B SHORTER WRITINGS

1 BROWN, B. KATHERINE. "A Note on the Puritan Concept of
Aristocracy," MVHR, XLI (June), 105-12.
What Cotton meant by aristocracy has a close relation
to our understanding of democracy. Cotton defined aristocracy by how many ruled, not by how those rulers came to
power, so if delegates chosen by the people governed, it
was aristocracy. In the famous letter to Lord Say and
Seal, Cotton is obviously downplaying the democratic
tendencies in Massachusetts in order to encourage the
nobleman to settle there.

1955 A BOOKS

1 ZIFF, LARZER. "John Cotton: Congregationalist, Theocrat,
Puritan." Unpublished Ph.D. dissertation, University of
Chicago.
A study which attempts to see the man behind the writings,
so as to illustrate the contrasting tensions which were

1955

(ZIFF, LARZER)
resolved into Congregationalism, the Massachusetts theocracy, and American Puritanism, and which deals more
particularly with the way he differed from the general
characteristics of his colleagues. Cotton was a with-
drawn scholar often unable to act without hesitation at
crucial moments, a man willing to compromise on outward
forms, not a leader in civil affairs. Cotton's treatises
should not be disregarded, but it is as a preacher that
he should be remembered.

1956 A   BOOKS

1   *POOLE, HARRY ALEXANDER. "The Unsettled Mr. Cotton." Unpublished Ph.D. dissertation, University of Illinois.
Based on extensive use of English manuscripts. Cotton's
seeking after divine truth led him into politically undesir-
able theological positions both in Old and New England,
and in both places he recanted (See DA, 16: 1670).

1956 B   SHORTER WRITINGS

1   HARASZTI, ZOLTAN. The Enigma of the Bay Psalm Book. Chicago:
University of Chicago Press, pp. 19-27.
Based on similarities between the draft, the preface, and
Cotton's Singing of Psalmes, as well as handwriting, Har-
aszti ascribes the preface of the Bay Psalm Book to Cotton
not Richard Mather.

2   MACLEAR, JAMES FULTON. "The Heart of New England Rent: The
Mystical Element in Early Puritan History," MVHR, XLII
(March), 621-52.
Cotton was not a spirit-mystic, but he emphasized a call
to a warmth of piety, an ardor of devotional love, an im-
mediate experience of Christ, an emphasis on the Holy
Spirit which, in the Antinomian matters, was carried fur-
ther by some of his followers.

1957 A   BOOKS - NONE

1957 B   SHORTER WRITINGS

1   TREFZ, EDWARD K. "The Puritans' View of History," BPLQ, IX
(July), 117-18.
The general lines in which the Puritan viewed history
can be seen in Cotton's Pouring Out of the Seven Vials.

2   ZIFF, LARZER.   "The Salem Puritans in the 'Free Aire of a New
        World,'" HLQ, XX (August), 373-84.
            Uses a letter of Cotton to Samuel Skelton in 1630 and
        Cotton's sermon in Salem in 1636 to argue, against Perry
        Miller, for the influence of Plymouth on Salem and,
        through Salem, on Boston and the other churches.

1958 A   BOOKS - NONE

1958 B   SHORTER WRITINGS

1   COTTON, JOHN.   Gods Mercie Mixed With His Justice, edited by
        Everett H. Emerson.   Gainesville, Florida: Scholars'
        Facsimiles and Reprints.
            Each of the six sermons reprinted here reveals an
        important aspect of Puritanism.   The first, for instance,
        uses a text frequently chosen by Puritan preachers (the
        preacher knocking on men's hearts with his sermons), is
        witty, and invites a voluntaristic approach to the con-
        version process.

1959 A   BOOKS - NONE

1959 B   SHORTER WRITINGS

1   GUMMERE, RICHARD M.   "Church, State, and Classics: The
        Cotton-Williams Debate," CJ, LIV (January), 175-83.
        See 1963.B6.

1960 A   BOOKS - NONE

1960 B   SHORTER WRITINGS

1   HASKINS, GEORGE LEE.   Law and Authority in Early Massachusetts:
        A Study in Tradition and Design.   New York: Macmillan
        Company, pp. 124-26.
            Cotton's "Moses his Judicials" is important because it is
        the first constructive effort to produce a body of laws
        to serve as a constitution, because its heavy reliance
        on scripture illustrates the religious influence on legal
        thinking, because it had enduring influence outside
        Massachusetts, and because several provisions found their
        way into the permanent laws of the colony.

1960

2   JONES, JOSEPH, et al. <u>American Literary Manuscripts: A Check-
     list of Holdings</u>. Austin, Texas: University of Texas
     Press, p. 86.

<u>1962 A   BOOKS</u>

1   *BOLAZS, MARY W. "A Critical Edition of Three Poems by John
       Cotton." Unpublished M.A. thesis, Pennsylvania State
       University.
          <u>See</u> J. A. Leo Lemay, "Additions to Seventeenth-Century
       American Poetry: A Bibliography of Scholarship, 1943 to
       1966," <u>EALN</u>, I (Winter, 1966-67), 14.

2   ZIFF, LARZER. <u>The Career of John Cotton: Puritanism and the
       American Experience</u>. Princeton, New Jersey: Princeton
       University Press.
          Ziff wishes this work to be seen as less a biography,
       less a documented life, than the story of Cotton's career,
       a sense of the world in which he lived, which can be best
       summarized as the movement through Puritanism and the
       American experience. Cotton's experience of the presence
       and the power of the Deity within him led him to accept
       the organic nature of history, to strive for the embodi-
       ment of the theocratic ideal, and to encourage the sup-
       pression of those who would ruin the chance to share in
       the divine experience. Cotton's time may be called
       "American Medieval," and pieces of the pattern he put
       together are strewn throughout the course of American
       history. The bibliographical note gives evidence for
       dating the composition of Cotton's works.

<u>1962 B   SHORTER WRITINGS</u>

1   BATTIS, EMERY. <u>Saints and Sectaries: Anne Hutchinson and
       the Antinomian Controversy in the Massachusetts Bay
       Colony</u>. Chapel Hill, North Carolina: University of North
       Carolina Press, pp. 18-36 and <u>passim</u>.
          Traces the development of Cotton's doctrine and the in-
       fluence of Richard Sibbes. Cotton established a delicate
       balance between grace and works, but Hutchinson adopted
       his doctrine of assurance with vigorous liberalism and
       pushed its logical implications to the farthermost limits.
       The desire to be understood by all was precisely Cotton's
       undoing, for in expounding doctrinal subtleties in
       language comprehensible to the meanest capacities, he
       opened perilous vistas to even the most blameless of hearers.

John Cotton: A Reference Guide

1963 A   BOOKS - NONE

1963 B   SHORTER WRITINGS

1   AHLSTROM, SYDNEY E.   Review of The Career of John Cotton by
Larzer Ziff, CH, XXXII (March), 106-8.
A fine and important book, though the distinction between profession and practice is treacherous, showing
the difficulty in describing a Puritan career without
extensive treatment of theology.

2   ANON.   Review of The Career of John Cotton by Larzer Ziff,
TLS (16 August), 622.
Ziff "gives some examples of Cotton's preaching style
and he is not likely to persuade many people today to turn
to the once great Boston doctor. But there is plenty of
evidence of the effect of these highly theological sermons
on audiences that, Professor Ziff seems to suggest, had
nothing else to do with their spare time.... It is easy to
respect John Cotton, but he is not a hero one warms to.
Indeed, one may think he has been favoured above his
deserts by finding so intelligent an apologist as Professor
Ziff."

3   CARY, JOHN.   Review of Saints and Sectaries by Emery Battis,
JMH, XXXV (December), 397-98.
Battis writes of antinomianism and of the complex char-
acter of Cotton with the complexity that both deserve.

4   DUNN, RICHARD S.   Review of Saints and Sectaries by Emery Battis,
MVHR, L (June), 105-7.
Battis is particularly good at analyzing Cotton's subtle,
equivocal theological position, though one may question
his conclusion that Cotton emerged from the Antinomian controversy with his principles unscathed.

5   EMERSON, EVERETT H.   Review of The Career of John Cotton by
Larzer Ziff, AL, XXXV (March), 91-92.
This excellent study is worthy to stand beside Morgan's
book on Winthrop as perhaps the most useful works since
Miller renewed serious interest in American Puritanism.
Because of Ziff's special interest in the relationship
of Puritanism to the American experience, he is most help-
ful on such subjects as the development of Congregationalism.

1963

6 GRABO, NORMAN S. Review of The Career of John Cotton by
    Larzer Ziff, WMQ, XX (April), 289–91.
      The subtitle is misleading; the book treats only Cotton's
    Puritanism and Cotton's experience in America. Cotton
    functions as a central consciousness through whom we see
    the activities in which he participated, but this has
    liabilities. We know Cotton only as a lens, never as a
    man, and yet none of the major issues is treated as com-
    pletely as it deserves because the point of view is
    restricted to Cotton. Still, a first rate study.

7 GUMMERE, RICHARD M. The American Colonial Mind and the
    Classical Tradition. Cambridge, Massachusetts: Harvard
    University Press, pp. 44–54.
      Effect of the classical tradition on the Cotton–Williams
    debate. Cotton abjured his training in ancient languages
    and favored a conservative theology; Williams combined
    mystical symbolism and classical illustrations to go far
    afield in linguistics, law, and diplomacy.

8 MESEROLE, H. T. Review of The Career of John Cotton by Larzer
    Ziff, SCN, XXI (Spring and Summer), 27.
      Though the era and its events are familiar, this book
    which focuses on Cotton's view of them adds a valuable
    dimension and sharpens our focus. Particularly interesting
    is the chapter on Cotton's literary theory and practice.

9 MORGAN, EDMUND S. Visible Saints: The History of a Puritan
    Idea. Ithaca, New York: Cornell University Press, pp.
    95–105.
      Cotton's position on tests of faith and church covenants.

10 _____. Review of Saints and Sectaries by Emery Battis, AN&Q,
    1 (April), 125–26.
      Battis shows how precarious was the balance between
    divine omnipotence and human will; Cotton was close to the
    complete negation of man. Hutchinson was a strong per-
    sonality, craving in Cotton an authority figure she failed
    to find in her husband.

11 NUTTALL, GEOFFREY F. Review of The Career of John Cotton by
    Larzer Ziff, Journal of Ecclesiastical History, XIV
    (October), 236–37.
      An important book, none the worse for the fact that it
    reverses no earlier judgments on Cotton's "semiseparatism,"
    and his involvements with Williams and Hutchinson.

12   SMITH, PETER H. "Politics and Sainthood: Biography by Cotton
      Mather," WMQ, XX (April), 186-206.
         The content, format, and presentation of Johannes in
      Eremo, which contains the life of Cotton, points directly
      to Mather's political interests in 1695. By pointing to
      Cotton's attachment to men of high standing in England,
      for instance, Mather was able to support his claim that
      New England had always been dedicated to Britain's royal
      interests.

13   SMYTH, CHARLES. Review of The Career of John Cotton by Larzer
      Ziff, Church Quarterly Review, CLXIV (July-September),
      386-88.
         Ziff "contributes a fascinating and suggestive, if some-
      what inconclusive, investigation of Cotton's influence on
      the formation of the New England Mind."

14   SNOOK, S. LUCIAN. Review of The Career of John Cotton by
      Larzer Ziff, CHR, XLIX (July), 242-43.
         Saturation in and by the spirit is the brighter side of
      the mind of this man with a strong but understandable anti-
      Catholic prejudice.

15   STEARNS, RAYMOND P. Review of The Career of John Cotton by
      Larzer Ziff, MVHR, L (June), 104-5.
         "This is by far the best study of John Cotton made to
      date," though the author is inclined to be over sympathetic
      to his subject, to exaggerate Cotton's importance in
      molding New England Congregationalism, and to lean too
      heavily, for example, on the works of Frances Rose-Troup.

16   WINSLOW, OLA E. Review of The Career of John Cotton by Larzer
      Ziff, NEQ, XXXVI (June), 263-65.
         This book attempts to resolve the apparent contradiction
      between Cotton's impressive stature on two continents
      during his lifetime and the completeness with which he
      soon after was forgotten, and students will find new angles
      of inquiry and new answers to old inquiry. Ziff's analy-
      sis of the Cambridge Platform is particularly original and
      brilliant.

17   WISH, HARVEY. Review of The Career of John Cotton by Larzer
      Ziff, AHR, LXVIII (April), 759-60.
         Ziff dwells primarily on Cotton's sermons, although
      he concludes that it was the changing social environment
      that rendered his theology obsolete in one generation.
      Though a more rounded biographic form might have been
      more effective in unraveling the mystery of Cotton, the
      focus here is the evolution of Cotton's non-conforming
      ideas from the influence of William Perkins in England.

1964

1964 A BOOKS - NONE

1964 B SHORTER WRITINGS

1   DAVIDSON, EDWARD H.   Review of The Career of John Cotton by
        Larzer Ziff, JEGP, LXIII (January), 183-84.
        The key to Cotton is balance, sanity, judiciousness, and
    this study which shows that even in the beginning New
    England Puritanism was directed by nearly first rate minds
    is written in a superb style.

2   MANIERRE, WILLIAM R.   Review of The Career of John Cotton by
        Larzer Ziff, MP, LXII (August), 70-72.
        Ziff's work belongs essentially to the category of
    intellectual history, seeing Cotton as exemplar of ideas
    rather than as a flesh-and-blood human being, and its
    primary contribution is the presentation of Cotton's per-
    spective on the part he played in early New England history.

3   STEARNS, RAYMOND P.   Review of Saints and Sectaries by Emery
        Battis, AHR, LXIX (April), 782-83.
        Among the book's strongest features are its treatment
    of Cotton's deviations from New England orthodoxy and of
    Hutchinson's relations with and reactions to Cotton's
    teachings.

1965 A BOOKS

1   EMERSON, EVERETT H.   John Cotton. New Haven, Connecticut:
        College and University Press (Twayne's United States
        Authors Series).
        The Puritan quality of organicism--the idea that church
    and state, law and government, manners and morals, business
    and labor all are one--is largely due to the work of Cotton.
    Though Roger Williams and Thomas Hooker may seem more
    interesting to the modern reader, an appreciation of Cot-
    ton's sense of mission gives insight into the essential
    religious nature of the Massachusetts Colony. Cotton be-
    gan as a radical and a non-conformist, but during his
    twenty years in America, and partially as a result of the
    Antinomian Controversy, his values hardened into a system.
    Full discussions of his works under such headings as "The
    Puritan Writings," "The Congregational Writings," and "The
    Controversy with Williams." Bibliography of primary and
    secondary sources.

2 *ROSENMEIER, JESPER. "The Image of Christ: The Typology of John Cotton." Unpublished Ph.D. dissertation, Harvard University.
Cited by Etulain (1969.B2).

1965 B   SHORTER WRITINGS

1 BAMBURY, EWART. Review of John Cotton by Everett H. Emerson, CH, XXXIV (December), 471–72.
"This book is a masterpiece of condensation," summarizing the main points of all Cotton's works. The fantastic nature of some of Cotton's exegesis and the often neglected eschatological side of Puritan thinking are well illustrated here.

2 GILSDORF, ALETHA. "The Puritan Apocalypse: New England Eschatology in the Seventeenth Century." Unpublished Ph.D. dissertation, Yale University, pp. 88–100.
Cotton envisioned a great period within history during which the saints would restrain evil through the righteous exercise of civil and ecclesiastical authority, a thousand year extension of the New England Way which would begin during the lifetime of the people then living.

3 HALL, DAVID D. "John Cotton's Letter to Samuel Skelton," WMQ, XXII (July), 478–85.
Reprints the letter, and introductory remarks indicate that it does not resolve the problems of Cotton's consistency or of the relationship between the Churches at Plymouth and Salem.

4 RUTMAN, DARRETT B. Winthrop's Boston: Portrait of a Puritan Town, 1630–1649. Chapel Hill, North Carolina: University of North Carolina Press, passim.
Uses Cotton's works, particularly the manuscript letters, for details of religious and social history.

1966 A   BOOKS – NONE

1966 B   SHORTER WRITINGS

1 ISRAEL, CALVIN. Review of John Cotton by Everett H. Emerson, SCN, XXIV (Summer), 29–30.
Since Emerson concentrates on Cotton as a theologian, this book is an excellent guide to the theological writings. Emerson is also successful tracing Cotton's ideas as they affected early American thinking and as they clarify first generation conflicts, but he does not evaluate Cotton as artist and writer.

1966

2   PETTIT, NORMAN. <u>The Heart Prepared: Grace and Conversion in Puritan Spiritual Life</u>. New Haven, Connecticut: Yale University Press, esp. pp. 125-57.

    While preaching in England, Cotton developed, in a sense, a concept of preparation, arguing that sinners, although utterly depraved, could still be held accountable for their failure to achieve salvation. In New England, however, Cotton denied that man could respond affectively to the external call, reasserting the doctrine of human helplessness, and refusing to allow for preparation in the sense of a personal turning toward God. But the preaching of a state of depravity from which man may be saved only by seizure could lead to antinomianism, and, after the Anne Hutchinson matter, Cotton altered his doctrine, though not in a radical way, to stress the drawing activities of the Spirit.

3   ROHMAN, D. GORDON. "Thoreau's Transcendental Stewardship," <u>ESQ</u>, XLIV (3rd Quarter), 72-77.

    Comparison of Thoreau's transcendental vocation with Cotton's Christian calling.

4   RUTMAN, DARRETT B. Review of <u>John Cotton</u> by Everett H. Emerson, <u>NEQ</u>, XXXIX (March), 112-14.

    The author, trained to deal with past literature in critical terms, ends up assessing literary merit alone, an assessment in which Cotton inevitably comes off badly. Emerson is not trained as an historian, does not sense the multi-causal structure of the past, "does not have the historian's consciousness of time which would have told him that Cotton's mind was ever evolving and that inconsistencies in part reflect the evolution and are vital evidence of it."

5   SAMPSON, GRANT. Review of <u>John Cotton</u> by Everett H. Emerson, <u>WMQ</u>, XXIII (January), 176-78.

    This is a conscientious piece of work, though, because of the amount of valuable primary material to be dealt with, the result is often confusing.

6   WINSLOW, OLA E. Review of <u>John Cotton</u> by Everett H. Emerson, <u>AL</u>, XXXVII (January), 480-81.

    Emerson omits the personal life entirely, dealing with the treatises, sermons, and controversial pamphlets that record Cotton's nonconformist views from the time he was twenty nine.

John Cotton: A Reference Guide

1967 A BOOKS

1 POLISHOOK, IRWIN H. Roger Williams, John Cotton and Religious
    Freedom: A Controversy in New and Old England. Engle-
    wood Cliffs, New Jersey: Prentice-Hall, Inc.
      Collection of original documents plus a substantial
    introduction.

1967 B SHORTER WRITINGS

1 BENTON, ROBERT M. "The American Puritan Sermon Before 1700."
    Unpublished Ph.D. dissertation, University of Colorado,
    pp. 137-43.
      "God's Promise to his Plantations" is given rhetorical
    power and a sure sense of imagery through Cotton's use
    of analogies for clarification, and his organization of
    the entire sermon around one central metaphor, and it
    shows that Cotton saw the sermon as an act rather than a
    product.

2 BERCOVITCH, SACVAN. "Typology in Puritan New England: The
    Williams-Cotton Controversy Reassessed," AQ, XIX (Summer),
    166-91.
      The controversy between Cotton and Williams reveals an
    opposition between two different typological approaches,
    the allegorical and the historical. Williams stresses
    that the spiritual progress of the church from first to
    last is figurative and allegorical, whereas Cotton stresses
    the literal-spiritual continuity between the two testa-
    ments and the colonial venture in America. Cotton's view
    is a central formulation of the colonists' mission in the
    New World, offering a summary of their first statements
    of purpose, and adumbrating, in concept and in expression,
    the later New England histories.

3 ETULAIN, RICHARD. "John Cotton and the Anne Hutchinson Con-
    troversy," Rendezvous, II (#1), 9-18.
      Cotton's part in the controversy may be summarized
    in three points: 1) he was a central figure, holding
    a doctrinal position mid-way between Winthrop and Hutch-
    inson; 2) Cotton denounced the Antinomian view as heresy
    as soon as he realized they were using his name and his
    helpful, lenient attitude to cover up their unorthodoxy;
    3) Cotton's views from 1636-38 were consistent. "Cotton
    had his faults, but his actions in the controversy demon-
    strate an honest man earnestly searching for a peaceful
    solution to a series of perplexing problems."

1968

1968 A BOOKS - NONE

1968 B SHORTER WRITINGS

1 *AKIYAMA, KEN. "The Poetry and Typology of Edward Taylor,"
      The Rising Generation [Japan], CXIV (#8), 507-9.
         Cotton's God's Promise to His Plantation is used as an
      example of early use of typology. See EAL, VIII (Spring,
      1973), 97.

2 GRABO, NORMAN S. "John Cotton's Aesthetic: A Sketch,"
      EALN, III (Spring), 4-10.
         Even a cursory review yields evidence of an aesthetic
      with literary significance. Cotton, for instance, acknow-
      ledges the power of art over the affections, and does not
      see human compositions as valueless per se; unlike the
      mechanism of Hooker, Cotton's view is insistently organic,
      and thus better accommodated to his sense of the spirit
      as inclination.

3 HALL, DAVID D. The Antinomian Controversy, 1636-38: A
      Documentary History. Middletown, Connecticut: Wesleyan
      University Press.
         In the new documents gathered here Cotton is the major
      figure. His difference of opinion with the other ministers
      is clearly at the heart of the controversy.

4 ROSENMEIER, JESPER. "The Teacher and the Witness: John
      Cotton and Roger Williams," WMQ, XXV (July), 408-31.
         The Cotton-Williams controversy about separation of
      church and state and liberty of conscience develops from
      disagreement about the meaning of Christ's incarnation.
      Both claimed that they were interpreting the types with
      literal-spiritual understanding, and both agreed that
      state and religion had been united in the Old Testament;
      but Cotton saw the incarnation as evidence of the essential
      permanence of the covenant of grace from the time of
      creation to the time of judgment, whereas Williams saw it
      as the historical moment when God had changed the nature
      of His kingdom radically. Cotton's typology becomes more
      spiritualized in the 1630's, shifting from an emphasis on
      the prophetic and the historical to an emphasis on the ex-
      emplary and eternal, as exhortation rather than attack be-
      came the central purpose.

5   ZIFF, LARZER. John Cotton on the Churches of New England.
     Cambridge, Massachusetts: The Belknap Press of Harvard
     University Press.
          Contains a valuable introduction to three Cotton works.
     In establishing Congregationalism, the Puritans had to
     steer between outright separatism and schism on the one
     hand, and a virtual Presbyterianism on the other, and
     Cotton was the chief helmsmen. The Sermon Deliver'd at
     Salem supplied scriptural justification for the polity
     Cotton found, but also established its limits. The Keys
     of the Kingdom of Heaven, with "a contemporary democratic
     strain sinewing its scriptural arguments," demonstrates
     that the church founded in apostolic times was Congrega-
     tional. The Way of Congregational Churches Cleared ex-
     plains the relationship of Congregationalism to Separatism,
     sketches the family tree of New England theory, contrasts
     life under the Bishops with life in New England, and gives
     an account of the Antinomian Controversy.

1969 A   BOOKS - NONE

1969 B   SHORTER WRITINGS

1   DAVIS, RICHARD BEALE. American Literature Through Bryant,
     1585-1830. New York: Appleton-Century-Crofts, pp. 25-26.
          Selected bibliography.

2   ETULAIN, RICHARD W. "John Cotton: A Checklist of Relevant
     Materials," EAL, IV (#1), 64-69.
          The primary sources here supplement the lists by
     Emerson (1965.A1) and Tuttle (1924.B1); some of the
     secondary sources have short annotations, and there is
     information on the manuscripts.

3   _____. Review of Roger Williams, John Cotton, and Religious
     Freedom by Irwin H. Polishook and John Cotton on the
     Churches of New England by Larzer Ziff, EAL, IV (#1),
     47-49.
          Polishook's introduction is especially useful in demon-
     strating how the conflict with Williams influenced men
     outside the New World, especially in the English Indepen-
     dent-Presbyterian ideological struggles of the 1640's.
     Most of Ziff's introductory biographical material has
     appeared before, but here he stresses the various church
     polities that confronted the Puritans and points up the
     problems that the Congregational organization left un-
     solved. Both men reflect the more sympathetic portrayal
     of Cotton appearing in the last decade.

1969

4 HABEGGER, ALFRED. "Preparing the Soul for Christ: The Contrasting Sermon Forms of John Cotton and Thomas Hooker," AL, XLI (November), 342-54.

Cotton knew the sermon itself could not bring about salvation, but he hoped he could provide a logical and deductive bridge of words between the text and his audience which God might use to convey grace. Hooker, believing that preparation must precede grace, regarded the sermon as an efficacious instrument and tried to make it as powerful and rhetorical as possible. Cotton scrupulously opens the entire text, extracting as many doctrines as necessary, even if this destroys the unity of the sermon, whereas Hooker considers only as much of the text as coincides with what he already has in mind. Hooker mingles the different parts of the sermon much more often than Cotton.

1970 A BOOKS - NONE

1970 B SHORTER WRITINGS

1 BERCOVITCH, SACVAN. "Horologicals to Chronometricals: The Rhetoric of the Jeremiad," Literary Monographs, III (1970), pp. 4-5.

Winthrop's Model of Christian Charity and Cotton's God's Promise to His Plantations embody a conflict between literal content and prophetic form. They alternate between the provisional and the predetermined, identifying the settlers at once with a fallen people and with an irreversible movement toward redemption. It is precisely the determination to impose the chronometrical (Heaven's perfect time) upon the horological (the imperfect time of mankind) which motivates their rhetoric.

2 *JONES, JAMES WILLIAM. "The Beginnings of American Theology: John Cotton, Thomas Hooker, Thomas Shepard and Peter Bulkeley." Unpublished Ph.D. dissertation, Brown University.

These men can best be understood by means of a scale of decreasing Christocentrism. Cotton, for instance, the most Christocentric, rejected the idea of preparation, that sanctification could be evidence of justification, and stressed the passivity of faith. See DAI, 31: 6703A.

3   ROSENMEIER, JESPER.   "New England's Perfection: The Image
       of Adam and the Image of Christ in the Antinomian Crisis,
       1634 to 1638," WMQ, XXVII (July), 435-59.
          Throughout the crisis, the question of Christian sancti-
       fication is primary, embracing individual salvation as
       well as redemption of the world. Those opposing Cotton
       believed that Christ enabled man to return to Adam's
       original holiness, whereas Cotton saw history as a never
       ceasing creation moving toward its culmination in the New
       Jerusalem with the image of Christ's Crucifixion and Resur-
       rection as guide. The new kingdom in America would be as
       different from the Garden of Eden as Christ's image was
       from Adam's. Thomas Shepard set forth the doctrine of re-
       newal in Adam's image which proved victorious in the
       controversy.

1972 A   BOOKS - NONE

1972 B   SHORTER WRITINGS

1   BURG, B. RICHARD.   "A Letter of Richard Mather to a Cleric in
       Old England," WMQ, XXIX (January), 81-98.
          The letter is a transitional document between Cotton's
       The True Constitution of a Particular Visible Church and
       Mather's Church-Government and Church-Covenant Discussed.

2   COLACURCIO, MICHAEL J.   "Footsteps of Anne Hutchinson: The
       Context of The Scarlet Letter," ELH, XXXIX (September),
       459-94.
          Although the portrait of Dimmesdale is unlike the one
       Hawthorne gives of Cotton in his sketch of "Mrs. Hutchin-
       son," their positions are disturbingly similar. It is
       impossible not to feel that Cotton's drastic change of
       relation to Hutchinson lies somewhere behind Dimmesdale's
       movement from partner with to judge of Hester.

3   ETULAIN, RICHARD.   "The New Puritan: Recent Views of John
       Cotton," Rendezvous, VII (#1), 39-51.
          Review of the recent books by Ziff, Battis, Emerson,
       and Rutman, to show that Cotton is no longer viewed as
       the demi-god of the pre-1900 interpreters or the villain
       of the Parrington era, but in a more balanced view as an
       otherworldly scholar, not temperamentally shaped to be a
       rebel or a dramatic innovator, more interested in being a
       teacher and writer than a leader, whose involvement in
       issues and ideas is much more complex than other writers
       have indicated.

1972

4   HALL, DAVID D.   The Faithful Shepherd: A History of the New
      England Ministry in the Seventeenth Century.   Chapel Hill,
      North Carolina: University of North Carolina Press, pp.
      93-120 and passim.
         The Cambridge Platform is a symbol of Cotton's vision
      of the kingdom Christ commanded him to build in the wilder-
      ness, and it bears the mark of his brute encounter with
      the lawless liberty of that wilderness which the Platform
      set itself against.

5   *STEVENS, DAVID MARK.   "John Cotton and Thomas Hooker: The
      Rhetoric of the Holy Spirit." Unpublished Ph.D. disserta-
      tion, University of California at Berkeley.
         Cotton and Hooker "chose a style meant to convey dialecti-
      cally and with aesthetic-felt apprehension the immediate
      presence and the practical experience of the action of the
      Holy Spirit theologically approved in Scripture texts and
      mirrored in the natural language of everyday prose."
      (See DAI, 33: 3602A.)

1973 A   BOOKS - NONE

1973 B   SHORTER WRITINGS

1   JONES, JAMES W.   The Shattered Synthesis: New England
      Puritanism Before the Great Awakening.   New Haven, Con-
      necticut: Yale University Press, pp. 3-31.
         Review of Cotton's position in the Antinomian contro-
      versy in the discussion of John Norton's The Orthodox
      Evangelist as an act of reconciliation between Cotton and
      the majority of ministers.

1974 A   BOOKS - NONE

1974 B   SHORTER WRITINGS

1   *ALPERT, HELLE M.   "Robert Keayne: Notes of Sermons by John
      Cotton and Proceedings of the First Church of Boston from
      23 November 1639 to 1 June 1640." Unpublished Ph.D.
      dissertation, Tufts University.
         Contains notes of Cotton's sermons taken by Keayne. The
      introduction discusses four themes relevant to the sermons
      (the crucifixion, resurrection, world, and spirit) and
      Cotton's preaching style, and there is a biographical
      sketch in the appendix (DAI, 35: 3667A).

2 PETTIT, NORMAN. "Hooker's Doctrine of Assurance: A Critical Phase in New England Spiritual Thought," NEQ, XLVII (December), 518-34.

  Hooker's dispute with Cotton marked a critical phase in the development of New England spiritual thought, for Cotton refused to concede that men should descend into themselves in order to gain assurance of saving grace.

1975 A BOOKS - NONE

1975 B SHORTER WRITINGS

1 MACLEAR, J. F. "New England and the Fifth Monarchy: The Quest for the Millennium in Early American Puritanism," WMQ, XXXII (April), 223-60.

  The most important expressions of the apocalyptic mood in early New England are in Cotton. His three works on Revelation were all composed between 1639 and 1641 when the Puritan mood in England lifted from despair to soaring optimism. Cotton believed the millennium would emerge by the ordinary means of propagating the gospel, and even his proposed legal code shows eschatological tendencies.

2 STOEVER, WILLIAM K. B. "Nature, Grace and John Cotton: The Theological Dimension in the New England Antinomian Controversy," CH, XLIV (March), 22-33.

  An attempt to see how Cotton's understanding of the systematic context of election differed so much from his colleagues that his approach appeared radically different, and an attempt to locate Cotton in the history of Reformed Protestantism. Whereas reformed orthodox divines insisted that men are saved by grace alone through created instruments and infused habits, Cotton excluded means for emphasis on direct action by the Spirit, and illegitimate subordination of created nature to the increated power of the Trinity. The association of Cotton and Edwards as representatives of a thorough-going Reformed Protestantism is not incorrect, but there are significant differences which qualify the relationship.

Writings About Thomas Hooker,
1695 - 1974

1695 A BOOKS - NONE

1695 B SHORTER WRITINGS

1   MATHER, COTTON. "Piscator Evangelicus. Or, the Life of Mr.
        Thomas Hooker, the Renowned, Pastor of Hartford-Church,
        and Pillar of Connecticut-Colony, in New-England."
        Published as an Appendix to Mather's Johannes in Eremo.
        Memoirs, Relating to the Lives, of...John Cotton...
        John Norton...John Wilson...John Davenport...and
        Mr. Thomas Hooker, who dyed, /d. 5m. 1647. Pastor of the
        Church at Hartford; New England. Boston: Michael Perry.
          Proclaims at the outset to the churches of Connecticut
        that "Satan alone had reigned" there "without Controul
        in all former Ages: But your incomparable Hooker" put
        him to rout. Hagiography which stresses the veneration
        in which Hooker was held by other ministers. Hooker
        devoted one day a month to fasting and quiet prayer. He
        chose to preach to the poor rather than to the great, and
        had no equal in "Treating a Troubled Soul." He avoided
        polemical divinity in his preaching, for "the very Spirit
        of his Ministry lay in the points of the most Practical
        Religion and the Grand Concerns of a Sinner's Preparation
        for...and Salvation by...Jesus Christ." His printed
        sermons were greatly useful. The venerated theologian
        William Ames echoed fully the reverent testimony of
        Hooker's followers when he stated that he had known many
        scholars in various nations, but he had "never met with
        Mr. Hooker's Equal, either for Preaching or for Disputing."

1702 A BOOKS - NONE

1702

1702 B   SHORTER WRITINGS

1   MATHER, COTTON. "The Light of the Western Churches: Or, the
    Life of Mr. Thomas Hooker, the Renowned Pastor of Hartford-
    Church, and Pillar of Connecticut-Colony, in New-England,"
    in Magnalia Christi Americana, Book III. London: Thomas
    Parkhurst, pp. 122-31.
       Except for a partial change of title, identical to
    Mather's Piscator Evangelicus, published in 1695 (1695.B1).

1825 A   BOOKS - NONE

1825 B   SHORTER WRITINGS

1   WINTHROP, JOHN. The History of New England from 1630 to 1649,
    Vol. I, edited by James Savage. Boston: Little, Brown
    and Company, pp. 88, 108, passim.
       Extensive references to Hooker. Despite his consider-
    able differences with Hooker, Winthrop sustained a deep
    respect for him and his work. His personal eulogy on the
    occasion of Hooker's death in an epidemic is quoted by many
    later commentators on Hooker: "But that which made the
    stroke [epidemic] more sensible and grievous, both to them
    and to all the country, was the death of that faithful
    servant of the Lord, Mr. Thomas Hooker...who for piety,
    prudence, wisdom, zeal, learning, and what else might make
    him serviceable in the place and time he lived in, might
    be compared with men of greatest note; and he shall need
    no other praise: the fruits of his labors in both Englands
    shall preserve an honorable and happy remembrance of him
    forever."

1846 A   BOOKS - NONE

1846 B   SHORTER WRITINGS

1   YOUNG, ALEXANDER. Chronicles of the First Planters of the
    Colony of Massachusetts Bay, from 1623 to 1636. Boston:
    Charles C. Little and James Brown, p. 512n.
       Biographical account of Hooker and his family.

1849 A   BOOKS

1   HOOKER, EDWARD W. The Life of Thomas Hooker. Boston: Massa-
    chusetts Sabbath School Society. [Vol. vi, in "Lives of
    the Chief Fathers of New England" series.]

(HOOKER, EDWARD W.)
   Consists largely of quotations from Hooker's writings
and earlier accounts of Hooker's life and work. Based
on Cotton Mather's life of Hooker in the Magnalia (1702.B1)
and on Winthrop (1825.B1).

1849 B SHORTER WRITINGS - NONE

1857 A BOOKS - NONE

1857 B SHORTER WRITINGS

   1   SPRAGUE, WILLIAM B. Annals of the American Pulpit, Vol. I.
       New York: Robert Carter and Brothers, pp. 30-37.
          Biographical sketch drawn from Cotton Mather's life of
       Hooker in the Magnalia (1702.B1) and several seventeenth-
       century sources.

1878 A BOOKS - NONE

1878 B SHORTER WRITINGS

   1   TYLER, MOSES COIT. A History of American Literature, 1607-
       1765, Vol. I. New York: G. P. Putnam's Sons, pp. 193-204.
          The seminal and monumental history to which all later
       scholars, whether sharing or disputing its judgments, re-
       main indebted. Describes the personal force and integrity
       of Hooker's character. He follows the traditional form
       of the Puritan sermon, but his language has "exceptional
       literary advantages": drama, cumulative energy, and blunt
       power. His cadenced words clearly are written for the ear
       rather than the eye and he shapes them for swift and
       practical effect on the mind and passions. His theology
       has a "fierce and menacing" side; he "right heartily"
       assures the sinner of damnation and his pages "gleam and
       blaze with the flashes of threatened hell-fire." Yet the
       concreteness of Hooker's rhetoric seeks to move the heart
       not only to the fear of God but to an awareness of Christ's
       mercy. Hooker's tone and images often have a "soothing
       tenderness." Hooker seeks to draw men to the higher
       spiritual life by the imagery of love and "utmost tender-
       ness" and to assure them that "in the grace of utter
       resignation they touch the very essence of felicity and
       victory."

1884 A BOOKS - NONE

1884

1884 B   SHORTER WRITINGS

   1   WALKER, GEORGE LEON. History of the First Church in Hartford.
          Hartford, Connecticut: Brown & Gross.
             Chapters I-VI focus on Hooker, including "Thomas Hooker
          in England and Holland," "The Church at Newtown," "The
          Transplanted Church: Early Days," and "Thomas Hooker's
          Writings" [Chapter VI]. Describes several volumes of
          Hooker's sermons, relates stories concerning the power of
          his preaching, and states that the "union of vigor and
          sincerity" which "made his utterance in the pulpit so ar-
          restive of the most wandering or antagonistic attention"
          also "makes the faded pages of his printed books frequent-
          ly so pungent and picturesque." The mass of his writings
          comprise a body "not of doctrinal, but of experimental
          divinity." Cites Cotton Mather's life in the Magnalia
          (1702.B1) to support this claim: all of Hooker's works
          relate to the "Application of Redemption; and that which
          eminently fitted him for the handling of those principles
          was, that he had been from his youth trained up in the ex-
          perience of those humiliations and consolations and sacred
          communions which belong to the New Creature." Appendix II:
          "Thomas Hooker's Will and Inventory of Estate," pp. 422-25
          (See 1891.A1). Appendix III: "Poems on the Death of
          Hooker," pp. 426-28. Appendix IV: "Notes of Mr. Hooker's
          Sermon," pp. 429-34 (not from holograph). Appendix V:
          J. Hammond Trumbull, "Thomas Hooker's Published Works,"
          pp. 435-42 (See 1891.B2).

1891 A   BOOKS

   1   WALKER, GEORGE LEON. Thomas Hooker: Preacher, Founder,
          Democrat. New York: Dodd, Mead, and Company.
             The standard biography of Hooker. Chapters on Hooker's
          birth and boyhood; education; English ministry; life in
          Holland and departure for America; ministry in Massachusetts
          and removal to Connecticut; Connecticut ministry; his
          writings. Appendix I is "Hooker's Will & Inventory"
          (See also 1884.B1). Appendix II is "Thomas Hooker's
          Published Works" (See 1891.B2). Conflicts and tensions
          between "aristocratic" Massachusetts Bay and "democratic"
          Connecticut provide a central theme. Strong emphasis on
          Hooker's democratic values. Criticizes Shepard for per-
          secuting Anne Hutchinson, then notes that in the clash
          between Winthrop and Hooker, Hooker "took, as usual, the
          democratic side." The written Constitution of Connecticut
          is thoroughly democratic and constitutes Hooker's "most

(WALKER, GEORGE LEON)
distinguishing and abiding monument." Hooker's prose,
from which long passages are quoted, is characterized by
a "wonderful variety of patterns, homely, forcible illus-
tration," and "sharp, searching, and energetic application."
Although Hooker's theology at times seems harsh or incom-
prehensible, there can be no denying the efficacy of his
preaching or his religious and political ministry: "A
son of thunder and...consolation by turns, his ministry
--whatever the defects or extravagances of his theology--
could not have been other than that which all testimony
declares it to have been, one of the most powerful of
his age."

1891 B SHORTER WRITINGS

1   TRUMBULL, JAMES HAMMOND. "Thomas Hooker's Published Works,"
     in George Leon Walker, Thomas Hooker: Preacher, Founder,
     Democrat (1891.A1), Appendix II, pp. 184-95.
        Earlier form appeared in George Leon Walker, History of
     the First Church in Hartford (1884.B1), Appendix V,
     435-42. With Babette Levy's (1945.B1), the most useful
     and, in this standard biography, accessible annotated
     checklist of Hooker's writings.

1893 A BOOKS - NONE

1893 B SHORTER WRITINGS

1   WALKER, WILLISTON. "Hooker's Summary of Congregational
     Principles, 1645," in The Creeds and Platforms of
     Congregationalism. New York: Charles Scribner's Sons,
     pp. 132-48.
        Introduces excerpts from A Survey of the Sum of Church
     Discipline with a good discussion of the forms of Congre-
     gationalism and the historical and theological situation
     in which Hooker's Survey was written. Useful notes to,
     and commentary on, the Survey itself.

1894 A BOOKS - NONE

1894

1894 B   SHORTER WRITINGS

 1 WALKER, WILLISTON. <u>A History of the Congregational Churches
   in the United States</u>. New York: The Christian Literature
   Company, pp. 92-93. 133-34, <u>passim</u>.
    Brief but useful accounts of Hooker's relationship to
   the Synod on Antinomianism, Roger Williams, and
   Hopkinsianism.

1908 A   BOOKS - NONE

1908 B   SHORTER WRITINGS

 1 GOODWIN, GORDON. "Thomas Hooker," in <u>Dictionary of National
   Biography</u>, Vol. IX, edited by Leslie Stephen and Sidney
   Lee. New York: Macmillan Company, pp. 1189-90.
    Good biographical sketch. Bibliography lists nineteen
   of Hooker's works.

1910 A   BOOKS - NONE

1910 B   SHORTER WRITINGS

 1 JOHNSON, EDWARD. <u>Wonder-Working Providence of Sions Saviour
   in New England, 1628-1651</u>, edited by J. Franklin Jameson.
   New York: Charles Scribner's Sons, pp. 87, 90, 93, <u>passim</u>.
    His hagiographical tone toward "the faithfull and labo-
   rious" emphasizes Hooker's rhetorical ability as he used
   it to further the Kingdom. His writings "are of great
   request" among the believers. Johnson's poem on Hooker
   intensifies this focus: "Thy Rhetorick shall peoples
   affections whet/Thy golden Tongue and Pen Christ caused
   to be/The blazing of his golden truths profound."

1921 A   BOOKS - NONE

1921 B   SHORTER WRITINGS

 1 ADAMS, JAMES TRUSLOW. <u>The Founding of New England</u>. Boston:
   Atlantic Monthly Press, pp. 189-93, <u>passim</u>.
    Sharp distinction between the "ethical morbidity" and
   hellfire of Hooker's sermons and the democratic government
   he advocated for Connecticut. His "democratic attitude"
   ensured that "only those elements which were of a democratic tendency" would become part of the Fundamental
   Orders and thus stand in stark contrast to the theocracy
   of Massachusetts Bay.

Thomas Hooker: A Reference Guide

1927 A   BOOKS - NONE

1927 B   SHORTER WRITINGS

  1   PARRINGTON, VERNON LOUIS. <u>Main Currents in American Thought:</u>
      <u>The Colonial Mind, 1620-1800</u>. New York: Harcourt, Brace
      and Company, pp. 53-62. Also p. 68, <u>passim</u>.
        While Roger Williams erected the democracy of Rhode
      Island, Hooker "was as busily engaged in erecting the
      democracy of Connecticut." Hooker was "the father of New
      England Congregationalism" when it became democratic rather
      than oligarchic. Hooker rejected equally the "reactionary
      theocracy" of John Cotton and the "leveling radicalism" of
      Williams. Hooker was vigorous in speech and action. His
      compelling vision of democracy and liberalism was rooted
      in the doctrines of popular sovereignty, the compact theory
      of the state, and the conception of the state as a public-
      service corporation strictly responsible to the will of
      the majority. The Fundamental Orders were pervasively
      democratic in substance and tone. "As a left-wing In-
      dependent [Hooker] would have a...popular fundamental
      law to safeguard the liberties of the people; and he saw
      to it that the new commonwealth was broadly based on the
      common will, rather than narrowly on the rule of the
      gentry." Connecticut's democratic order was "English
      Independency transplanted to the new world" by a profoundly
      liberal thinker.

1931 A   BOOKS - NONE

1931 B   SHORTER WRITINGS

  1   MILLER, PERRY. "Thomas Hooker and the Democracy of Connecticut,"
      <u>NEQ</u>, IV (October), 663-712.
        Takes sharp and sustained exception to the position held
      by Parrington and others that Hooker and seventeenth-
      century Connecticut were thoroughly or even partially
      "democratic." Such an interpretation rests on gross mis-
      readings of Hooker's <u>Survey</u> and the Fundamental Orders
      and on a kind of modern ideological wish-fulfillment.
      Hooker was a completely orthodox Puritan who rarely even
      suggested differences with the religious and political
      theory of Cotton and Massachusetts Bay. He reiterates the
      traditional claim that Congregationalism derives from the
      Word; denounces Separation as a sin; shares Cotton's con-
      ceptions of the role of elders and synods and the authority
      and duties of the magistrate and repudiates any idea of
      toleration. Hooker, like Cotton, does insist with

1931

(MILLER, PERRY)
Augustine that since the saint must believe in order to
understand, there is always the possibility that the
common man, if a believer, might understand more than the
scholar, no matter how massive the scholar's erudition.
"Some of the more extravagent claims that have been advanced for Hooker's democracy come from secularists no
longer capable of grasping this Protestant paradox." But
this is simply to say that there was an "irrepressibly
democratic dynamic in Protestant theology, though all good
Protestants strove to stifle it." In the process by which
Congregationalism inadvertently opened a bit wider a door
for the democratic propulsion, there is "no issue of
democrat versus aristocrat." Cotton and Hooker were "so
closely in step" that to apply to them the modern and
opposing usages of theocrat and democrat is to distort
their positions beyond recognition. The polity of Hooker
and Connecticut was most definitely an expression of its
age, and while "it represents another development from
the same premises upon which the Massachusetts theocracy
was erected, it was in no sense a breaking away from that
philosophy." See also 1956.B3.

1932 A   BOOKS - NONE

1932 B   SHORTER WRITINGS

1   ADAMS, JAMES TRUSLOW.   "Thomas Hooker," in Dictionary of
     American Biography, Vol. IX, edited by Dumas Malone.
     New York: Charles Scribner's Sons, pp. 199-200.
          Emphasizes Hooker's importance as the champion of de-
     mocracy in an otherwise theocratic New England.   "His main
     dispute with Winthrop was on the subject of democracy.
     Winthrop and the other Massachusetts leaders opposed de-
     mocracy tooth and nail; Hooker was a born democrat."

2   WOOLLEY, H. CLARK.   Thomas Hooker Bibliography, together with
     a Brief Sketch of His Life.   Hartford, Connecticut:
     [Hartford] Center Church Monographs, pp. 21-32.
          Everett Emerson (1971.B2) notes that this rare biblio-
     graphy is of "no great value, though it locates some
     copies of Hooker's works."

1933 A   BOOKS - NONE

1933 B   SHORTER WRITINGS

1   MILLER, PERRY. Orthodoxy in Massachusetts, 1630-1650. Cam-
    bridge, Massachusetts: Harvard University Press, pp. 107-
    11, passim.
        Discusses Hooker's prominence as a Puritan divine in
    England, the turbulence of his Dutch ministry, and his
    profound influence in New England. In no way can Hooker's
    political or ecclesiastical position during the conflicts
    within New England Congregationalism be called "democratic."
    Although he was aware of the inherent difficulties of a
    restrictive polity for church membership, for example,
    he concluded in his Survey that the principle would work
    and that any other principle would threaten the unity of
    the churches and the coherence of the New England Way.

1935 A   BOOKS - NONE

1935 B   SHORTER WRITINGS

1   MILLER, PERRY. "The Marrow of Puritan Divinity," PCSM, XXXII,
    247-300.
        Refers to Hooker throughout as a central thinker in the
    "federal" theology of Puritan New England. Hooker and
    the Puritans cannot be seen simply as "Calvinists"; they
    must rather be seen as Protestant "scholastics" who, while
    not elevating natural reason over revelation and faith,
    sought to rescue it from the "rubbish heap" where Calvin
    had cast it. Their task was to bring God to time and
    reason and confine His transcendence by a law of ethics
    without reducing His mystery and absolute power to a
    mechanism; that is, to ascertain "the reliability of human
    reason and the trustworthiness of human experience as
    measurements of the divine character." The central con-
    cern in federal theology, and therefore for Hooker, was
    the covenant. In struggling with the conception of the
    covenant, the Puritans were desperately striving on
    the one hand to subordinate humanity to God without un-
    duly abusing human values, and on the other to "vaunt
    the powers of the human intellect without losing the sense
    of divine transcendence." This was "the central problem
    of the seventeenth century as it was confronted by the
    Puritan mind." As the covenant gradually became a "con-
    tract" which viewed divine grace as man's opportunity to
    strike a bargain with God for his own salvation, such
    "preparationist" preachers as Hooker and Shepard emphasized
    the possibilities and efficacy of human activity. "If an
    individual does not close the deal when he has the chance,

1935

he certainly cannot blame God because it gets away from
him." In New England, Hooker was "clearly the most extreme" of those who emphasized the extent to which an
unregenerate man could go in the work of preparation. He
stressed man's ability to bring about the receptive frame
of mind for grace, and "dared to assert that he who could
force himself to the point of readiness would certainly
receive grace in time." The difference between Hooker and
Cotton on this crucial issue may shed light on the reasons
Hooker removed to Connecticut rather than remaining in
Massachusetts, where Cotton was the principal interpreter
of dogma. (See also 1956.B4).

1937 A BOOKS - NONE

1937 B SHORTER WRITINGS

1   MILLER, PERRY. "The Puritan Theory of the Sacraments ·in
Seventeenth-Century New England," CHR, XXII (January),
409-25.
A study of the Puritan conception of the sacraments.
Draws on Hooker's writings in addition to those of Shepard,
John Cotton, and such later divines as Cotton Mather and
Solomon Stoddard.

1939 A BOOKS - NONE

1939 B SHORTER WRITINGS

1   MILLER, PERRY. The New England Mind: The Seventeenth Century.
Cambridge, Massachusetts: Harvard University Press,
pp. 3, 14, 26, 27, passim.
Refers to Hooker throughout as a central figure in New
England Puritan history, literature, and thought. In his
discussion of the Puritan conception of Nature, Miller
stresses Hooker's literary and scientific abilities by
quoting a passage in which Hooker describes, through the
analogy of the moon drawing the tides, the necessity that
the sinful heart be acted upon and drawn by divine grace.
The significance of the passage rests not only in the way
"it illustrates how better writers and greater men than
Cotton Mather practiced the art of spiritualizing earthly
objects, but for its revelation of the scientific knowledge possessed by so capable and alert a mind as Thomas
Hooker."

2   PIERCY, JOSEPHINE K. Studies in Literary Types in Seventeenth
        Century America (1607-1710). New Haven, Connecticut:
        Yale University Press, pp. 84, 241-43, passim.
            Hooker's rhetoric and style were strongly influenced by
        the Bible, especially in its use of parallelism. Hooker's
        parallelism is effectively varied in its forms. Hooker
        is equally skillful in using analogies and parables for
        the purpose of illustration. At their best, the writings
        of Hooker, Benjamin Colman, and Roger Williams are rep-
        resentative of the early American prose most comparable
        to English prose in the seventeenth century.

1943 A BOOKS - NONE

1943 B SHORTER WRITINGS

1   WINTHROP, JOHN. Winthrop Papers, edited by Samuel Eliot
        Morison, et al. Boston: Merrymount Press, III (1631-
        1637), 60, 139, passim.
            References to Hooker's removal to Connecticut.

1944 A BOOKS - NONE

1944 B SHORTER WRITINGS

1   MORGAN, EDMUND S. The Puritan Family: Essays on Religion
        and Domestic Relations in Seventeenth-Century New England.
        Boston: Trustees of the Public Library, p. 26, passim.
            Quotes passage in which Hooker tenderly describes the
        ordinances of the church as "Christ's love-letters."
        Hooker's language makes it clear that the love between
        husband and wife was to be genuinely longed for and
        valued in the same way as that between Christ and the
        Church or soul.

2   WINTHROP, JOHN. Winthrop Papers. Edited by Samuel Eliot
        Morison, et al. Boston: Merrymount Press, IV (1638-1644),
        6, 15, 35, passim.
            Refers to Hooker in several political and personal
        contexts.

1945 A BOOKS - NONE

1945

1945 B   SHORTER WRITINGS

1   LEVY, BABETTE MAY.   Preaching in the First Half Century of
New England History.   Hartford, Connecticut: The American
Society of Church History, pp. 4, 6, 9, passim.
Fine study of New England Puritan preaching style.   Of
Hooker, Cotton, and Shepard, the three most important
pulpit leaders in early New England, Hooker was the "most
capable and forceful" in his preaching.   Most of Hooker's
works are conscientious and utilitarian in purpose, yet
at times he allows the "more spiritual and poetic side of
his nature" to shine forth in them.   He uses repetition
effectively, and elucidates and makes concrete each step
and concept of the argument by several illustrations.   He
uses a variety of analogues and, of all the ministers, has
"the greatest diversity in his use of homely imagery."
The earthy concreteness of his images is sustained and
effective; their very lack of pretension makes them ap-
pealing, and his "brief pictures, whether taken from every-
day life or from the Bible," are clear and vivid.   Hooker's
only weaknesses occur when he elaborates in too great
length and detail on his graphic descriptions, especially
of hell.   Includes a checklist of twenty-six of Hooker's
works.

1946 A   BOOKS - NONE

1946 B   SHORTER WRITINGS

1   STEWART, RANDALL.   "Puritan Literature and the Flowering of
New England," WMQ, Third Series, III (July), 319-42.
Hooker's impassioned and powerful prose exemplifies the
best qualities of the Puritans' language and imagination.
It is telling that the greatest American authors of the
nineteenth century--including Emerson, Thoreau, and
Hawthorne--were those who felt the Puritan influence most
strongly.   This "neglected continuity" is an important
aspect of the American literary tradition.   "Rarely has
the written word been used more effectively" than in
Puritan New England, or "the human spirit burned with an
intenser, brighter flame."

1949 A   BOOKS - NONE

THOMAS HOOKER: A REFERENCE GUIDE

1949 B SHORTER WRITINGS

1 MURDOCK, KENNETH B. Literature and Theology in Colonial New
   England. Cambridge, Massachusetts: Harvard University
   Press, pp. 34-35, 59-60.
      Hooker makes extensive and effective use of homely
   diction and imagery, including household images: "Sweep
   your hearts ... make roome for Christ." The value of
   Hooker's imagery lies in its earthy and concrete realism.
   Hooker argues that when divines display Latin and ornateness
   in their sermons, those who hear them are in danger of
   going to hell "hood-winckt, never awakened."

1952 A BOOKS - NONE

1952 B SHORTER WRITINGS

1 ROSSITER, CLINTON. "Thomas Hooker," NEQ, XXV (March-December),
   459-88.
      Argues for a kind of middle position between those of
   Parrington (1927.B1) and Miller (1931.B1) on the question
   of Hooker's democratic theory. Parrington sees Hartford
   as the birthplace of democracy; Miller views Hooker as
   "thoroughly orthodox" and insists that Parrington's
   interpretation "rests upon a misreading of two or three
   of Hooker's utterances." For Rossiter, Hooker was "certainly no democrat in our sense of the word, nor can we
   look upon Connecticut as a genuine democracy. On the
   other hand, he was not quite so orthodox" as Miller "would
   have us believe." As "the noblest of the New England
   Puritans," the roots of Hooker's political ideas are
   theological. They are a "transcribed ecclesiasticism"
   drawn from Augustine, Calvin, Beza, Ramus, and Ames.
   The covenant is central to his thought; it is a living
   conception underlying Hooker's political tenets, including
   such incipient or explicit democratic ideas as ecclesiastical
   equality; the individual's liberty to join or refuse the
   covenant; the explicit nature of the covenant; the resem-
   blance of the Church covenant to all other bodies politic;
   "mutual subjection" and the "good of the whole"; the
   sovereignty of the people; and limited magisterial authority. The Fundamental Orders are thus "a long and popular
   step forward" from the Massachusetts Bay Charter of 1629.
   Hooker demonstrated that New England "contained the seeds
   of its own liberation." Hooker represents "the forces of
   liberty inherent in Puritanism more dramatically than any
   colonial in the seventeenth century."

1955

1955 A   BOOKS

  1   *EMERSON, EVERETT H.   "Thomas Hooker and the Reformed Theology:
      The Relationship of Hooker's Conversion Preaching to Its
      Background." Unpublished doctoral dissertation, Louisiana
      State University. Synopsis by Emerson in CH, XXIV
      (December), 369-70.
         Though he is in the tradition of Reformed scholasticism,
      Hooker's Puritan concern for man's salvation differs from
      Calvin's emphasis on God's glory. Calvin taught the
      sacramental preaching central to Hooker, but it is not
      important to Calvin because of his lesser concern with the
      salvation process. Most important doctrine in Hooker's
      conversion teaching is the sermon as a means of grace.
      The sermon must apprehend and use psychological processes.
      Hooker's effectiveness as a preacher comes from the ability
      to analyze the "shifts and rationalizations" by which men
      avoid taking the prescribed steps for salvation. Two
      weaknesses in Hooker's thought are the somewhat ambiguous
      role of conversion and the paradox that conversion is long
      and painful, yet those who fail to attempt it are said to
      be resisting God's free grace. Cotton and Shepard are
      radically different from Hooker in their teaching on con-
      version; they belong to the Reformed theology of Calvin
      and his successors. Hooker's greatest accomplishment was
      his degree of success in reconciling predestination and
      man's responsibility; but "his effort was not sufficiently
      successful to warrant for him an important place in the
      history of seventeenth-century ideas."

1955 B   SHORTER WRITINGS - NONE

1956 A   BOOKS - NONE

1956 B   SHORTER WRITINGS

  1   EMERSON, EVERETT, ed. "Introduction," in Redemption, Three
      Sermons. Gainesville, Florida: Scholars' Facsimiles &
      Reprints, pp. vii-xvi.
         Introduction to facsimile reprintings of three of Hooker's
      sermons--The Unbeleevers Preparing for Christ (1638), The
      Application of Redemption...The Ninth and Tenth Books
      (1656), and The Soules Ingraffing into Christ (1637).
         Each sermon has a facsimile reproduction of the title
      page in which it was first included. Hooker is part of
      the Reformed tradition as it became "codified into
      Protestant scholasticism." His greatness comes from his
      abilities as "expert psychologist" and "powerful and

(EMERSON, EVERETT)
effective preacher." His preaching techniques made
possible a "bold emphasis on man's spiritual inability
and a vigorous demand that man assume responsibility for
his spiritual state." Hooker's "nervous and energetic
style" makes extensive use of analogies to the secular
world; but when the text of the sermon is in rather fig-
urative language, Hooker keeps to the figure.

2   EMERSON, EVERETT H. "Notes on the Thomas Hooker Canon,"
    AL, XXVII (January), 554-55.
       Corrects and supplements specific entries in the two
    most useful check lists of Hooker's writings--those by
    B. M. Levy (1945.B1) and Trumbull (1891.B2). It is un-
    likely that The Equall Wayes of God (1632), a treatise
    listed in Levy and Trumbull, is by Hooker. The work
    alludes consistently to classical authors, which Hooker's
    works never do, and is more theoretical than Hooker's.
    Thomas Haynes may be the author. Immortality of the Soul,
    a meditation listed in Levy and considered doubtful by
    Trumbull, is surely not by Hooker. Its style is Ciceronian
    and its point of view latitudinarian. "To the Reader,"
    an introductory epistle in the third edition of John
    Rogers, The Doctrine of Faith (1629), is signed by Hooker
    but listed only in the Hooker bibliography in the
    Dictionary of National Biography.

3   MILLER, PERRY. "Preface" to reprinting of "The Marrow of
    Puritan Divinity" (1935.B1), in Errand into the Wilder-
    ness. Cambridge, Massachusetts: Belknap Press, 48-50.
       Defends conception of New England Puritan theology and
    theologians as "federal" rather than Calvinist. But
    acknowledges more clearly than he had that the federal
    theology was deeply Calvinist; it was simply "an idiom
    in which these Protestants sought to make a bit more
    plausible the mysteries of the Protestant creed." The
    Puritan conception of man's predicament was that which all
    the Reformed churches maintained. "Were I to rework this
    piece today...I should more strongly emphasize the
    underlying connection; though even so, I should retract
    nothing from the fascinating peculiarity of the federal
    phraseology."

4   _____. "Preface" to reprinting of "Thomas Hooker and the
    Democracy of Connecticut" (1931.B1), in Errand into the
    Wilderness. Cambridge, Massachusetts: Belknap Press,
    pp. 16-18.
       In 1931, V. L. Parrington and J. T. Adams "had in effect
    conspired to present Thomas Hooker as a sort of John the

1956

(MILLER, PERRY)
Baptist to Thomas Jefferson." Miller notes that his own
essay in that year (1931.B1) has provoked a "curiously
sullen reaction" from scholars. But the intervening fifteen
years have given no reason for altering his judgment,
though he would most call into question his earlier assump-
tion that Separatist and Nonseparatist Congregationalism
should appear so closely interwined as he implied. Now
also fully persuaded that the purely personal rivalry
between Hooker and Cotton was a far more important factor
in Hooker's removal to Connecticut than he had naively
supposed. Takes to task those critics who doggedly insist,
"without offering evidence" or understanding Congregational
thought, that Connecticut was more "free" than Massachusetts. Miller's unequivocal judgments would seem directed
at, among others, Rossiter (1952.B1): "They blandly assert
that the truth lies somewhere in the 'middle,' between
Parrington and me. On this matter there is no middle.
Parrington simply did not know what he was talking about."

1958 A BOOKS

1   PELLMAN, HUBERT RAY. "Thomas Hooker, A Study in Puritan Ideals."
     Unpublished doctoral dissertation, University of Pennsyl-
     vania.
     Four ideals motivate Hooker's writing: search for, and
loyalty to, the truth; absorbing desire to know God and do
His will; sustaining of a "sharply-defined scale of values";
living for the purpose of helping his countrymen. Hooker
never fully resolved the conflict between predestination
and free will; he "held to both and urged men to be ready
to cooperate if and when He came to save them." He was
redemptive in outlook and preached the love as well as the
wrath of God. Hooker's literary theory stresses the direct
style, and his style in practice is marked by "sincerity,
liveliness, cogency, concreteness, directness, and the
controlled use of...parallelism, alliteration, cadence,
and effective tropes." Hooker's style demonstrates that
Puritan literary style differs from the Anglican not in
kind but in degree.

1958 B   SHORTER WRITINGS - NONE

1961 A   BOOKS

1   DENHOLM, ANDREW THOMAS. "Thomas Hooker: Puritan Teacher,
     1568-1647." Unpublished doctoral disseration, Hartford
     Seminary Foundation.
          Part One is biographical. Chapter I: general biography.
     II: influences of personal and educational experience
     in England and Holland, arrival at Newtown. III: removal
     to Connecticut; Hooker as leader. IV: Hooker as liberal
     but not "democrat" in the modern sense. Part Two discusses
     the form and style of Hooker's preaching. V: personal
     nature of Hooker's religious experience and writings. VI:
     delineation of Hooker's "most characteristic and most vital
     topic: The regeneration of the soul" in context of Federal
     Theology and the Covenant of Redemption. VII: ethical
     and social implications of Covenant theology. VIII:
     Hooker's plain style, especially as reflected in his similes.
     A substantial Appendix including The Wolcott Diary; The
     Thanksgiving Sermon; The Twenty Propositions; and Inven-
     tory of estates of Hooker and Stone; and, most importantly,
     the first transcription and reproduction of Miscellanea,
     Hooker's personal note-book. See also Everett Emerson,
     "Thomas Hooker Materials at the Connecticut Historical
     Society," EAL (1971.B2).

1961 B   SHORTER WRITINGS - NONE

1962 A   BOOKS - NONE

1962 B   SHORTER WRITINGS

1   BATTIS, EMERY. Saints and Sectaries: Anne Hutchinson and
     the Antinomian Controversy in the Massachusetts Bay Colony.
     Chapel Hill, North Carolina: University of North Carolina
     Press, pp. 26, 59, 95, passim.
          Clear and basically solid account of the antinomian con
     troversy and Hooker's role in it. Describes Hooker's
     anxieties over the possible suffering of accused antino-
     mians at the hands of their zealous antagonists. Hooker
     remained troubled over the process and potential outcome
     even after leaving Newtown. When he knew the trial would
     be held, he urged that it not be dragged on. He also
     exhorted Winthrop and the court to be scrupulous in their
     legal procedures: "Attend nothing for ground of deter-
     mination but that which will convey an undeniable evidence
     to an impartiall judge."

1963

1963 A   BOOKS - NONE

1963 B   SHORTER WRITINGS

1   MORGAN, EDMUND S.   Visible Saints: The History of a Puritan
        Idea.   [New York]:   New York University Press, pp. 79-80,
        95, passim.
            Hooker in his church at Hartford made some effort to
        discern faith in prospective members.   But he was far more
        charitable than the ministers of Massachusetts Bay on the
        nature and importance of the profession of faith.   "None
        was more concerned than Hooker with the generation of
        saving faith, and none preached or wrote more eloquently
        about its operation; but Hooker believed that the first
        signs of it could be detected at an early stage in the
        morphology of conversion."

1965 A   BOOKS - NONE

1965 B   SHORTER WRITINGS

1   EMERSON, EVERETT H.   John Cotton.   New York: Twayne Publishers,
        pp. 8, 17, 18, passim.
            References to Hooker's preaching relationship with
        Roger Williams, covenant theology, several works.   Cotton
        is more cautious in his preparationist exhortations than
        Hooker, who promises his hearers that "if they prepare
        for the coming of Christ, He will come and save them."

2   MORGAN, IRVONWY.   The Godly Preachers of the Elizabethan
        Church.   London: Epworth Press, pp. 126, 134.
            Hooker, among others, exemplifies the mysticism and as-
        ceticism of the Puritan divines, who in their vocation
        and practices continued to express the most substantive
        qualities and values of the medieval monks and friars.

3   ZOLLA, ELEMIRE.   "Lo stile di Thomas Hooker," Studi Americani,
        II, 43-52.
            Brief biographical information.   Hooker's style is not
        pedantic.   It avoids Ciceronian ornateness in favor of the
        essential characteristics of the plain style and such
        homely imagery as the nautical and mechanical.   His sermons
        follow the Ramist schema.   The strong language of his
        descriptions is extremely powerful and effective; its
        quality of the "sudden" and "unexpected" contributes to its
        power.   Hooker's theological knowledge and literary style,
        including his use of images drawn from commonplace experi-
        ence, may not seem immediately relevant to our times, yet
        we draw on just this past even though we may not be aware of
        it.

THOMAS HOOKER: A REFERENCE GUIDE

1966 A   BOOKS - NONE

1966 B   SHORTER WRITINGS

1   PETTIT, NORMAN. The Heart Prepared: Grace and Conversion in
       Puritan Spiritual Life. New Haven and London: Yale
       University Press, pp. 88-91, passim.
          Considers Hooker, among others, in his relationship to
       the Puritan conceptions of preparation, grace, conversion,
       and the covenant. The dilemma of covenant theology
       is that "God alone can bend the heart to grace; and that
       man must enter the covenant of his own free will." Em-
       phasizes Hooker's special concern, in speaking for the
       doctrine of preparation, that man should have his own
       part to play in the movement toward salvation. Hooker's
       conversion, like Shepard's, was long and painful. But
       where Shepard, in seeking an alternative to excessive con-
       straint, placed the efficacy of the Law at the center of
       his experience, Hooker "had emphasized personal acknowl-
       edgement of the promises."

1967 A   BOOKS - NONE

1967 B   SHORTER WRITINGS

1   EMERSON, EVERETT. "Thomas Hooker: The Puritan as Theologian,"
       Anglican Theological Review, XLIX (April), 190-203.
          Hooker's teachings, career, and interests reveal "almost
       uniquely" the nature of Puritanism in its most crucial
       years. His voluminous works are "rigorously tough-minded."
       They clearly stand in the Reformed tradition of soteriology,
       in which sin, atonement, justification, vocation, or
       "Effectual Calling," and finally sanctification define
       the movement of the converted soul. Hooker speaks little
       to the nature of the good life or the sphere of practical
       morality; doing good to all consists in moving them onto
       the path to salvation. Hooker's metaphorical language is
       homey and never contrived. His powerful images transfer
       theology into psychological terminology.

2   WILLIAMS, GEORGE H. "The Pilgrimage of Thomas Hooker (1586-
       1647) in England, The Netherlands, and New England,"
       Bulletin of the Congregational Library [Boston], XIX, No.
       1, 5-15; No. 2, 9-13.
          An account of Hooker's ministry in its three general
       phases and locations. Hooker's experience with the case
       of Mrs. Joan Drake (1968.B3) is set briefly in this larger
       biographical context.

1968

1968 A BOOKS

  1   DARROW, DIANE MARILYN. "Thomas Hooker and the Puritan Art of
        Preaching." Unpublished doctoral dissertation, Univer-
        sity of California, San Diego.
          Examines Hooker's collection of sermons, The Application
        of Redemption, in the light of Renaissance humanism,
        rhetoric, and theological and artistic concerns. The
        Puritan sermon is a human imitation of the effectual Word
        of God, and hence radically metaphorical. The sacramental
        nature of preaching validates human language. Hooker
        achieved an implicit "poetics" of the sermon by "explain-
        ing and embodying the spiritual artifice" by which the
        Puritan preacher gave his religious doctrines the necessary
        "imaginative realization" for them to move the heart and
        affections.

1968 B SHORTER WRITINGS

  1   DAVIDSON, CLIFFORD. "Thomas Hooker's First Publication?" AN&Q,
        VI (January), 69-71.
          Some Scholars continue to assume that The Soules Pre-
        paration for Christ (1632) is Hooker's first published
        work. But "The Poore Doubting Christian Drawne unto Christ,"
        a sermon, was published in 1629 as part of The Saints
        Cordials, a work generally attributed to Sibbes. Hooker's
        sermon attempts to convert the listener or reader. His
        rhetoric, like Sibbes's, is baroque, and therefore Hooker
        stands in marked contrast to Cotton, who advocates the
        plain style. A footnote indicates that Emerson (1956.B1)
        correctly identifies "The Poor Doubting Christian" as the
        first of Hooker's works to be published. Cf. Winfried
        Herget (1972.B4), who states that The Poor Doubting
        Christian has long been assumed to be Hooker's first
        published work.

  2   FREDERICK, JOHN T. "Literary Art in Thomas Hooker's The Poor
        Doubting Christian," AL (March), 1-9.
          The Poor Doubting Christian, Hooker's most popular work,
        has a definite and coherent structure. Its form, Hooker's
        virtuosity in shaping sentences, and his "extensive use of
        varied and vigorous imagery--including images drawn from
        the sea, trade, and husbandry--contribute to the work's
        power and artistry. Hooker's imagery, like that of Shep-
        ard, clearly influenced Edward Taylor's, though little
        attention has been paid to what is so obvious and impor-
        tant a relationship. Tyler's (1878.B1) characterization of
        Hooker as a preacher of hell and damnation is false: "the
        smell of brimstone is totally absent from these pages."
        Hooker sympathetically enjoins the discouraged believer to

(FREDERICK, JOHN T.)
avoid despair as well as presumption. The work demonstrates
the "rich resources of forceful style and vital imagery"
on which such later Puritan writers as Taylor and Edwards
could and did draw freely. It offers a "needed corrective"
to the distorted ideas of the exclusively "stern and haggard" (Tyler) nature of the literary expression of the
Puritans.

3   WILLIAMS, GEORGE H.   "Called by Thy Name, Leave Us Not: The
Case of Mrs. Joan Drake, A Formative Episode in the
Pastoral Career of Thomas Hooker in England," HLB, XVI
(April), 111-28; (July), 278-300.
Detailed description and interpretation of the formative
effect of Hooker's relationship to a woman he knew and
after whom he and his wife named their first daughter.   A
narrative about her--Prolonged Temptation and Mystical
Conversion of Mrs. Joan Drake 1615-1625 (London, 1654)--
described her profoundly mystical experience of conversion.
Although mysticism, with its disciplined preparation for
the divine illumination, was not an acknowledged part of
Puritan theology, her experience demonstrates the continu-
ation of the mystical impulse within a Puritan terminology
almost too dry and rigid to convey it without being
"galvanized" by its "spiritual voltage." Joan Drake was
a "belated kind of Puritan mystic whose ecstasy, interpreted as conversion or justification by faith alone, was
to become the unconscious model of what Hooker would ever
thereafter seek to have his parishoners and readers imitate
in the quest for the reformed and blessed life."

1969 A   BOOKS - NONE

1969 B   SHORTER WRITINGS

1   HABEGGER, ALFRED.   "Preparing the Soul for Christ: The Contrasting Sermon Forms of John Cotton and Thomas Hooker,"
AL, XLI (November), 342-54.
Cotton's sermons are forms that evolve from a Biblical
text; Hooker's uses the text as an occasion for "promul-
gating a message." Cotton's sermons follow Perkins in
their deductive and exegetical pattern. Hooker's follow
conventional sequence, but the doctrine and application
are taken not from the text but from a schema based on
the stages of the soul's preparation for regeneration.
Cotton reconciles the integrity of the text with the
deductive movement of the traditional Puritan sermon.
Hooker mingles the functions of the parts of the sermon

1969

(HABEGGER, ALFRED)
and hence abandons the traditional movement even while he
"continued to pay lip service to it." Although the stages
of regeneration provide the basis of Hooker's sermons, he
"pretended" to be directed by Scripture. Hooker's doctrine
of preparation marks the beginning of the end for the
Puritan sermon. Cotton knew the sermon in itself could
not cause salvation, yet he hoped God would use its logical
and deductive "bridge of words" to convey grace. But
Hooker, "believing that preparation must precede grace,
regarded the sermon as an instrument efficacious in its
own right and tried to make it as powerful and rhetorical
an instrument as possible."

1970 A BOOKS - NONE

1970 B SHORTER WRITINGS

1 JONES, JAMES WILLIAM. "The Beginnings of American Theology:
John Cotton, Thomas Hooker, Thomas Shepard and Peter
Bulkeley." Unpublished doctoral dissertation, Brown
University.
Discusses tensions in thought of four New England Puritan
theologians between the role of believer and the role of
Christ in the work of salvation. Cotton is the most
Christocentric of the four; he rejects the idea of preparation and the possibility that sanctification could be an
evidence of justification. Hooker "did not emphasize
sanctification as an evidence but he did stress the need
for preparation." On the question of whether the new
covenant is conditional, Cotton insisted that it had no
conditions, while Hooker argued that "it might have conditions but they were fulfilled only in Christ." Perry
Miller implies that the ideas of preparation and a conditional covenant moved Puritanism toward anthropocentrism;
but "the Christocentric context of their theology kept
these men from the position Miller attributed to them."
Their Christocentrism "meant that even when they suggested
that the covenant might have conditions, it was Christ and
not man who fulfilled them." Hooker, like Shepard, did
not discuss preparation in the context of the covenant,
but in the context of Christ's spirit working upon man.
Discusses the antinomian controversy from this perspective.
Suggests that it was the Christocentrism of this theology,
rather than the covenant or preparation, which moved
American Puritanism from theocentrism to anthropocentrism.

1971 A   BOOKS - NONE

1971 B   SHORTER WRITINGS

1   BUSH, SARGENT, JR. "Bosom Serpents before Hawthorne: The
         Origins of a Symbol," AL, LIII (May), 181-99.
             New England Puritanism is one of the traditions and
         sources on which Hawthorne may have drawn for his
         "Egotism; or, The Bosom Serpent." Hooker uses the image
         of the bosom serpent to dramatize sin. Since "not all
         American Puritan preachers had imaginations fertile
         enough to produce such poignantly symbolic metaphors as
         those from Hooker's writings," efforts to find similar
         passages in other Puritan writings "are by no means
         guaranteed to be successful." In any event, we must
         ultimately associate the image chiefly with Hawthorne, for
         he transformed a common idea into "a lasting literary
         symbol for the insidious and corrupting effect of sin on
         the soul of man."

2   EMERSON, EVERETT. "Thomas Hooker Materials at the Connecticut
         Historical Society," EAL, VI (Fall), 187-88.
             The Connecticut Historical Society, Hartford, is rich
         in materials on Hooker which have largely been neglected.
         It holds twenty of the twenty-three separate works ascribed
         to Hooker. Describes five additional items: 1) A volume
         of manuscript notes, in shorthand, of seventeen of Hooker's
         sermons between 1638-1641, compiled by one who heard
         Hooker preach them. The volume was transcribed in 1959
         and is also available. 2) A volume that includes fifty-six
         apparently holographical pages, with paragraphs on "Adam,"
         "Resurrection," and several other topics. 3) An apparently
         unique copy of Gods Image on Man and His Covenant (1653),
         the title page of which identifies Hooker as the author.
         Its style indicates that the work is by Hooker, though its
         content differs from that of Hooker's other works.
         4) H. Clark Woolley's bibliography of Hooker's works.
         (See 1932.B2). 5) A manuscript volume of 538 pages con-
         taining what seems to be the text of sermons by Hooker.
         The volume includes "Preparing for Christ," "The Preparation
         of the Heart," "The Soules Ingraffing," and three other
         topics.

3   MIDDLEKAUFF, ROBERT. The Mathers: Three Generations of Puritan
         Intellectuals, 1596-1728. New York: Oxford University
         Press, pp. 32, 66-67, passim.
             References to Hooker's conceptions of the will and pre-
         paration. Hooker did not attribute a prominent role to
         the affections in the process of conversion. His

1971

psychology was "oriented around the will." The will for
Hooker assumes a cast "remarkably like the reason in other
analyses--it functions as if it had intelligence and knowledge which enabled it to understand the...Gospels. Its
affective responses do not take on much importance except
when in its sin it resists the force of Christ's sacrifice."
Hooker distinguishes between "legal" and "evangelical" preparation. The law should inform the individual of all
the correct rules of morality, and simple self-examination
would produce contrition in those who deviated from those
rules. Terror, and even humility, might follow. But
evangelical preparation "carried the sinner to union with
Christ" through the movement of the Holy Spirit.

4 SHUFFLETON, FRANK C. "Thomas Prince and His Edition of Thomas
Hooker's Poor Doubting Christian, EAL, V (Winter), 68-75.
Scholars studying Hooker's works should restrict themselves to the early seventeenth-century editions. In his
1743 edition of Hooker's small treatise, The Poor Doubting
Christian, Prince twice inserts his own language to replace
or add to Hooker's. His addition of parallelisms and
parenthetical statements obscures and dilutes the forceful urgency of Hooker's original prose. Prince's stylistic
intrusions and changes, which he introduced for his own
doctrinal purposes in the context of the Great Awakening,
are constant. Certain foolishly negative judgments on the
prose style of the treatise have been made by scholars
who have assumed that the text of the 1743 edition was
"pure Hooker." But the most accurate versions are those
printed in Hooker's lifetime: the text of 1629 as printed
in The Saints Cordials, which is probably the best text,
1635, and 1638.

1972 A BOOKS

1 SHUFFLETON, CHARLES. "Light of the Western Churches: The
Career of Thomas Hooker, 1568-1647." Unpublished doctoral
dissertation, Stanford University.
A biographical account of Hooker. Chapter II treats
The Poor Doubting Christian in context of Hooker's pastoral
care; III treats The Soules Preparing for Christ in context of Hooker's preparationist theology and English
preaching career. Final chapter considers nature of
Hooker's influence through Cotton Mather and Edwards.
Writings distinguished by concern for authentic experience,
for practicalities rather than abstractions, for individual
purification, and for judging others with rational charity.

1972 B   SHORTER WRITINGS

1   BUSH, SARGENT, JR. "Thomas Hooker and the Westminster Assembly,"
    WMQ, Third Series, XXIX (April), 291-300.
       In 1642, English Puritans and members of Parliament
    invited John Davenport, John Cotton, and Hooker to represent
    New England at the Westminster Assembly. Though each man
    declined the invitation, "convincing circumstantial
    evidence" suggests that by publishing four books, three
    of which were published in London in 1645, Hooker hoped to
    influence the Assembly's deliberations on church doctrine
    in the direction of the Calvinist tenets that were central
    to the Puritan movement. The Lord's Prayer, and Hooker's
    careful theological explication of it, was the subject of
    two of the books. But the third book, a catechism--An
    Exposition of the Principles of Religion--was undoubtedly
    the most influential of the works. It probably was among
    the catechisms "known and even consulted" in the final
    processes of composing the Larger and Shorter Catechisms."
    Hooker's catechism may have contributed to the more dis-
    tinctly Calvinist tone of the final version of each
    catechism.

2   EMERSON, EVERETT, ed. "A Thomas Hooker Sermon of 1638," RALS,
    II (Spring), 75-89.
       This sermon of thanksgiving follows the conventional
    Puritan form: text, explication, doctrines, reasons, uses.
    It uses homey analogies and expresses a strong "sense of
    time and place." Although the sermon is occasionally
    obscure, it is valuable. Trumbull comments that "nothing
    of Hooker's that remains to us...brings the man so
    directly to the mind's eye, as this." Since Hooker preached
    the sermon in America, critical interest in it and in
    Hooker may be stimulated, which would only be appropriate;
    though John Cotton is studied with greater care than
    Hooker, Hooker is actually a better writer.

3   HALL, DAVID D. The Faithful Shepherd: A History of the New
    England Ministry in the Seventeenth Century. Chapel Hill,
    North Carolina: University of North Carolina Press, pp.
    47, 71, 76-78, passim.
       Hooker's relation to origins of New England Congregation-
    alism, conception of church order, evangelism. Notes
    Hooker's agreement with Shepherd's "legal" preparationist
    preaching, which emphasizes man's active role in seeking
    salvation. Hooker "called for the same preparatory
    striving in a series of sermons" he preached in the early
    1640's. Hooker feared that "many men were casting at
    Christ by the wrong 'method.' Like Shepard he responded
    to this threat by laying down rules for every would-be
    saint to follow."

1972

4   HERGET, WINFRIED. "Preaching and Publication--Chronology
     and the Style of Thomas Hooker's Sermons," HTR, LXV
     (April), 231-39.
         Outlines the formidable problems of establishing an
     accurate chronology of Hooker's works from the earliest
     one, The Poore Doubting Christian, which was originally
     included in The Saints Cordials. No holograph manuscripts
     have been found. No notes exist for the sermons Hooker
     preached in England. Since the identities of the note-
     takers and redactors of Hooker's sermons are unknown, there
     are immense difficulties in trying to determine the
     relationships between texts as Hooker wrote or spoke them
     and texts as they were printed. In light of such complex-
     ities, the task of collating variant texts in order to
     establish a text as close to Hooker's actual words as
     possible becomes arduous and even herculean. Although
     Hooker's literary style has often been praised, the con-
     ditions of its transmission in spoken, written, and tran-
     scribed forms rarely have been taken into account. "The
     consequences which the complicated history of the preach-
     ing and publication of the sermons has for our appreciation
     of Hooker await further detailed study."

5   STEVENS, DAVID MARK. "John Cotton and Thomas Hooker: The
     Rhetoric of the Holy Spirit." Unpublished doctoral disser-
     tation, University of California, Berkeley.
         Emphasizes the similarity of Cotton and Hooker's con-
     ception of the place of rhetoric in the soul's movement
     toward salvation. They "achieved their sermon style through
     a dynamic use of natural forms of logic and imagery whose
     inner force was animated by a holy person, an imago dei
     whom they considered the power behind all spiritual
     language, the implicit speaker of reformed, redeemed speech
     known to them as the Holy Ghost." Their plain style
     provided an aesthetic parallel to the "felt-apprehension
     of the divine-present in the Scripture," while their simple
     dialectical forms and images expressed the unity of the
     Trinity. Cotton and Hooker conceived of the Holy Spirit
     as a literary form, a pure act, a dynamic of persuasion
     through whom they recognized the visionary light. By an
     artful use of the plain style, they attempted to convince
     Puritan saints of the validity of their Puritan vision.

1973 A   BOOKS - NONE

Thomas Hooker: A Reference Guide

1973 B   SHORTER WRITINGS

1   BUSH, SARGENT. "The Growth of Thomas Hooker's The Poor
    Doubting Christian," EAL, VIII (Spring), 3-20.
          Early American bibliographies have never done justice to
    Hooker's writings. Few scholars are aware of widespread
    popularity of The Poor Doubting Christian in the seven-
    teenth century. Describes popularity and importance of the
    work as a Puritan handbook; gives bibliographical details
    of its publishing history; corrects several errors of
    previous scholarship, particularly with regard to editors
    of the book in seventeenth and eighteenth centuries; pro-
    vides groundwork for much-needed establishment of a more
    authoritative text than we now have. Meeting this last
    need for Hooker's works and other early American works
    will be complicated, but it must be done. Includes check-
    list of twenty-two editions of The Poor Doubting Christian.

2   SPRUNGER, KEITH L. "The Dutch Career of Thomas Hooker," NEQ,
    XLVI (March), 17-44.
          Discusses the nature and more sustained effects of
    Hooker's ministry in the Netherlands, which began in June,
    1631 and lasted at least twenty months and possibly longer.
    Hooker received and accepted a call from the English Re-
    formed Church at Amsterdam. Theological and political
    pressures came about within the Classis and were brought
    to bear on Hooker, who was disqualified from his ministry
    without a hearing. The apparent reasons for Hooker's dis-
    qualification were theological: Hooker was opposed to the
    Brownists but held that it was not a sin to hear them on
    occasion; he expressed doubts over baptizing children
    whose parents were not church members; and he contended
    that the individual congregation had full authority with-
    out regard to the Classis. The underlying reasons for
    the action by Classis and Synod, however, were clearly
    political in nature. Though a dissident group continued
    to support Hooker, he left his congregation at his dis-
    qualification and moved to Delft, where his experience
    with a Congregational-style church in the larger context
    of an English Classis was far more peaceful and satisfying.
    Any consideration of Hooker's later "democratic" sympathies
    must take into account as an influence these two experiences
    of synods and classes acting tyrannically, and more purely
    congregational forms of church government acting cooper-
    atively in good faith. It may even be that Hooker's later
    democratic seeds were first sown in the Netherlands.

1974

1974 A   BOOKS - NONE

1974 B   SHORTER WRITINGS

1   BUSH, SARGENT, JR.   "Four New Works by Thomas Hooker: Identity
        and Significance," RALS, IV (Spring), 3-26.
        Description and discussion of four newly-discovered
        works: The Sinners Salvation, The Properties of An honest
        Heart, Spirituall Thirst, and The Story of the Faithfull.
        Strong external and internal evidence points to Hooker's
        authorship.   Several of the works indicate a concern over
        the condition of church and commonwealth.   The others,
        especially Properties, deal with Hooker's most lasting
        concern: the preparation of the heart for grace and the
        experiences of assurance.   Each of the works either makes
        a "significant contribution" to our knowledge of Hooker or
        corroborates our previous knowledge with material similar
        to the extant sermons.

2   PETTIT, NORMAN.   "Hooker's Doctrine of Assurance: A Critical
        Phase in New England Spiritual Thought," NEQ, XLVII
        (March-December), 518-34.
        Hooker viewed the order of salvation, ordo salutis, as
        the central concern of the Christian life.   Eternal life
        comes not by deeds but by God's free gift, to which man
        must respond in gratitude.   Yet conversion need not be
        violent or sudden; emotions are not sufficient evidence
        of assurance.   Best evidence of assurance is "walking in
        covenant," or demonstrating faith in practice.   Such
        assurance depends in turn on what Hooker calls "the bias
        of the soul," or that which determines the direction of
        the heart in the covenant relationship.   Hooker's
        soteriology emphasizes the mixture and complexity of hope
        and fear, joy and doubt, that remain part of the believer's
        soul: "In one sense, he relied upon a clear expectation of
        grace to encourage the doubting Christian in the quest for
        salvation.   In another, he deliberately fostered an atti-
        tude of doubt, so that no man could claim to be regenerate
        without embarking on a project that was harsh, tedious,
        and long."   Truly regenerate souls must ultimately judge
        themselves not by external criteria but, in Hooker's words,
        by "experience, that which they have felt in their own
        hearts."

Writings About Edward Johnson, 1814 - 1975

1814 A   BOOKS - NONE

1814 B   SHORTER WRITINGS

1   JOHNSON, EDWARD. "A History of New England," CMHS, second
        series, II, 49-96.
            An edition of the Wonder-Working Providence by James Sav-
        age which is continued in succeeding volumes. Contains
        a short "Notice of Edward Johnson" excerpted from an 1809
        lecture in Woburn by Joseph Chickering.

1822 A   BOOKS - NONE

1822 B   SHORTER WRITINGS

1   FARMER, JOHN and JACOB B. MOORE. Collections, Topographical,
        Historical and Biographical, Relating Principally to New-
        Hampshire, Vol. I.   Concord, New Hampshire: Hill and
        Moore, pp. 252-56.
            Short memoir.   "It appears that he was distinguished for
        those principles of piety and religion which activated the
        Fathers of New-England....   His caution in his history,
        never to make a league with any of those sectaries, might
        have been better followed than the spirit of persecution."
        Originally appeared in the Columbian Centinel, June 16,
        1819.

1837 A   BOOKS - NONE

1837 B   SHORTER WRITINGS

1   ANON. "Prefatory Note" to "A Briefe Narration of the Original
        Undertakings of the Advancement of Plantations into the
        Parts of America," CMHS, third series, VI, 46.
            The ascription of the Wonder-Working Providence to Gorges
        is by singular ignorance or consummate fraud.

1843

1843 A   BOOKS - NONE

1843 B   SHORTER WRITINGS

   1   SAVAGE, JAMES. "Gleanings for New England History," <u>CMHS</u>,
          third series, VIII, pp. 276, 284, 288.
            Remark that <u>Good News from New England</u> "is much in the
          style of Johnson's Wonder-working Providences," perhaps
          the first suggestion that Johnson wrote the former work,
          evidence for dating the <u>Wonder-Working Providence</u> at 1653,
          and evidence that Johnson claimed he was a "joiner"
          when he migrated.

1847 A   BOOKS - NONE

1847 B   SHORTER WRITINGS

   1   FOLSOM, GEORGE. "Preliminary Notice" to "Brief Narration of
          the Original Undertakings of Plantations in America. By
          Sir Ferdinando Gorges," <u>Collections of the Maine Historical
          Society</u>, II, ix-x.
            Conjectures that the publisher is responsible for bind-
          ing Johnson's work in with the Gorges tracts.

1853 A   BOOKS - NONE

1853 B   SHORTER WRITINGS

   1   WINTHROP, JOHN. <u>The History of New England From 1630 to
          1649</u>, Vol. I, edited by James Savage. Boston: Little,
          Brown and Company, pp. 101, 119, 319, 358.
            Often quoted remarks about Johnson scattered throughout
          the footnotes: "There are some interesting materials
          in the work of Johnson, that can be found in no other
          place; but the style is above or below criticism"; John-
          son "shows little precision in any thing but his creed";
          Johnson "gives very unsatisfactory accounts of this earth-
          quake. He was more engaged in the shaking of the people
          out of their antinomianism"; Johnson is better acquainted
          "with the use of the sword than the Bible, though so fre-
          quently ambitious of exhibiting his dexterity in handling
          the word."

1862 A   BOOKS - NONE

1862 B   SHORTER WRITINGS

1   FELT, JOSEPH B.   The Ecclesiastical History of New England,
Vol. II.   Boston: Congregational Library Association
and the Congregational Board of Publication, p. 489.
    Though the style of Johnson's writings falls short of
that now mostly popular, "they exhibit a spirit fitted
more for communion with serious obligation than common
practice."

1866 A   BOOKS - NONE

1866 B   SHORTER WRITINGS

1   DUYCKINCK, EVERT A. and GEORGE L.   Cyclopaedia of American
Literature, Vol. I.   New York: Charles Scribner, p. 39.
    The Wonder-Working Providence is somewhat rambling
and diffuse in style and matter.

1867 A   BOOKS - NONE

1867 B   SHORTER WRITINGS

1   JOHNSON, EDWARD.   Wonder-Working Providence of Sions Saviour
in New England, edited by William Frederick Poole.
Andover, Massachusetts: Warren F. Draper, pp. i-cliv.
    Lengthy introduction contains proof for Johnson's author-
ship, a discussion of the Gorges Tracts, a discussion of
"Good News," a biographical sketch, Johnson's will, a gen-
ealogy, and much other valuable information.   The sketch,
which is the best extant, is quite complimentary, high-
lighting Johnson's participation in many important public
and political activities; but Poole is less complimentary
about Johnson's writing ability.   "Captain Johnson's merits
do not lie in the direction of literary composition.   It
is sufficient to claim that he wrote the most important
book on the Massachusetts Colony that was printed during
the first hundred years after the settlement, that he was
a man of action rather than of letters, and took a leading
part in the events he described."

2   UPHAM, CHARLES W.   Salem Witchcraft, Vol. I.   Boston: Wiggin
and Lunt, p. 425.
    Evidence that Johnson was a friend of accused witch, Ann
Hibbins.

1868

1868 A BOOKS - NONE

1868 B SHORTER WRITINGS

1   DEANE, CHARLES F. Review of Poole's Johnson's Wonder-Working
     Providence, North American Review, CVI (January), 319-30.
          Poole's edition is a worthy effort, but substantial space
     is given to refuting Poole's contention that Gorges will-
     fully passed the Wonder-Working Providence off as his own
     work. Johnson's work is forbidding; execrable; rough and
     singularly tumid in style; a mere rhapsody; a hodge-podge
     of facts and fancies, pious ejaculations, high sounding
     epithets; a poor imitation, anachronistically, of Mather
     written by an individual who sometimes sounds as if he
     fancied himself the military commander of the whole world.

2   MOORE, GEORGE H. "Work and Materials for American History,"
     Historical Magazine, second series, III (February),
     87-91.
          The section of Poole's introduction which relates to the
     Massachusetts Laws of 1648 is an extraordinary specimen
     of critical operosity, misleading the reader into the
     belief that Johnson was the master spirit of the committee
     which formulated the laws.

3   PARK, EDWARDS A. "A Layman's View of the New England Puritans,"
     Congregational Quarterly, X (January), 24-37.
          Description of Johnson's work, with lavish quotations,
     on the occasion of Poole's edition. Johnson had an active,
     but uncultivated imagination; and he was strangely fanci-
     ful in style, though energetic and judicious in action.
     One striking point is Johnson's portrayal of the great
     suffering which he experienced.

4   SEWALL, SAMUEL. The History of Woburn. Boston: Wiggin and
     Lunt, Publishers, pp. 73-76.
          Sketch of Johnson's life which focuses on his public
     employments. His history shows a mind embittered against
     the English prelates but also a sincere zeal for God and
     religion.

1877 A BOOKS - NONE

1877 B   SHORTER WRITINGS

1   WASHBURN, JOHN D.   "Report of the Council," PAAS, 1875-77
        (April), 14-32.
            Sketch of Johnson's 'life which focuses on his public
        roles, though arguing through a brief review of other
        writers that Johnson's poetry is not as bad as Poole makes
        it out to be.

1878 A   BOOKS - NONE

1878 B   SHORTER WRITINGS

1   TYLER, MOSES COIT.   A History of American Literature, 1607-1765,
        Vol. I. New York: G. P. Putnam's Sons, pp. 137-46.
            Johnson handled the pen as he did the broadaxe, to ac-
        complish something with it, in this case, to delineate the
        successive stages in a stupendous religious campaign
        inaugurated and sustained by Christ for a hallowed pur-
        pose. The value of his book is not in what we commonly
        call history; it lacks impartiality, coolness, comprehen-
        siveness, critical judgment, and sweet expression. Yet
        it is a simple, picturesque, often comic account, the
        sincere testimony of an eye-witness and an honest man,
        and its very faults render it a most authentic and priceless
        memorial of American life and character in our earliest
        period.

1881 A   BOOKS - NONE

1881 B   SHORTER WRITINGS

1   DEANE, CHARLES.   "Remarks by Mr. Deane," PMHS, XVIII (June),
        432-35.
            Gives evidence that N. Brooke, the publisher of the
        Wonder-Working Providence, and not Ferdinando Gorges was
        responsible for binding Johnson's work in with the Gorges
        Tracts.

1885 A   BOOKS - NONE

1885 B   SHORTER WRITINGS

1   CHAMBERLAIN, MELLEN.   "Samuel Maverick's House," PMHS, second
        series, I (January), 366-73.
            Cites evidence that Johnson is an untrustworthy historian
        in this and other instances.

1888

1888 A   BOOKS - NONE

1888 B   SHORTER WRITINGS

   1   ELLIS, GEORGE. The Puritan Age. New York: Houghton Mifflin
      and Co., p. 3.
       "He was a Puritan of the Puritans, historian--after a
     sketchy, uncouth, and fragmentary fashion--of affairs of
     State and Church identified with each other. His prose is
     to a degree intelligible, but his attempts at poetry are
     distressing, suggestive of cramps and dyspepsia in the
     writer."

1889 A   BOOKS - NONE

1889 B   SHORTER WRITINGS

   1   DOYLE, J. A. English Colonies in America, Vol. III. New York:
      Henry Holt and Co., pp. 78-79.
       Johnson is the same type man as Dudley and Endicott, a
     man whose hearty bigotry stems from a belief that his
     narrow system of dogma is as natural and necessary as the
     air which he breathes. His history is a triumphal hymn,
     whose imagery, though florid and inappropriate at times,
     is never trite, seldom lacking in originality, and often
     striking. With all his rhetoric, he can, like a Hebrew
     prophet, stoop to tell of plain things in plain words with
     no loss of dignity.

   2   FISKE, JOHN. The Beginnings of New England. Boston: Houghton,
      Mifflin and Company, pp. 305-9.
       The general sentiment of the early New England writers
     was like that of the Wonder-Working Providence, though
     it did not always find such rhapsodic expression. It was
     the spirit of the Wonder-Working Providence that hurled
     the tyrant from his throne at Whitehall and prepared the
     way for the emancipation of modern Europe. "With narrative,
     argument, and apologue, abounding in honesty of purpose,
     sublimity of trust, and grotesqueness of fancy, wherein
     touching tenderness is often alternated with sternness
     most grim and merciless, yet now and then relieved by a
     sudden gleam of humor--and all in a style that is unusually
     uncouth and harsh, but sometimes bursts forth in eloquence
     worthy of Bunyan," we are told of the New England Soldiers
     of Christ and their holy war.

1891 A   BOOKS - NONE

Edward Johnson: A Reference Guide

1891 B SHORTER WRITINGS

1 JAMESON, J. FRANKLIN. The History of Historical Writing in
America. Boston: Houghton, Mifflin and Company, pp.
29-40.
Johnson's work, often inaccurate, is not a historical
source of the first quality. Its value comes from the
fact that Johnson was a typical rank and file, middle
class, average Puritan. Johnson embodies the hot zeal,
the narrow partisanship, the confident dogmatism which
characterizes so much of Puritanism. The church militant
was more than just a metaphor to him; hewing Agag in
pieces before the Lord was an attractive religious duty.

1892 A BOOKS - NONE

1892 B SHORTER WRITINGS

1 WHITTIER, JOHN GREENLEAF. "Margaret Smith's Journal," in The
Prose Works of John Greenleaf Whittier, Vol. I. Boston:
Houghton, Mifflin and Company, pp. 152-55.
Johnson is given one piece of dialogue in this account
of a journey into New Hampshire to discover the source
of the Merrimac River, and Whittier includes a poem,
printed nowhere else, which he attributes to Johnson (See
1944.B1 and 1970.A1).

1899 A BOOKS - NONE

1899 B SHORTER WRITINGS

1 HOWE, DANIEL WAIT. The Puritan Republic of the Massachusetts
Bay in New England. Indianapolis, Indiana: The Bowen-
Merrill Company, p. 180.
Johnson's work consists largely of accounts of church
planting and biographical sketches of colonists "whose
names are rarely spelled correctly" and who are "embalmed
in jingling verses."

1901 A BOOKS - NONE

1901

1901 B   SHORTER WRITINGS

   1   ONDERDONK, JAMES L.   History of American Verse (1610-1897).
        Chicago: A. C. McClurg and Co., pp. 34-35.
         Johnson's chief poetic effort was "a prolonged wail
        through twenty-two stanzas of unmitigated grief at the
        degeneracy of the age."

1902 A   BOOKS - NONE

1902 B   SHORTER WRITINGS

   1   SEARS, LORENZO.   American Literature in the Colonial and
        National Periods.   Boston: Little, Brown, and Company,
        pp. 39-42.
         Johnson, in comparison with Winthrop and Morton, stands
        for the final alliance of zeal and authority. If the
        Indians could have understood his work, they would have
        instantly fled at the report of all the armies of Europe
        advancing upon them. The opening chapters resemble an
        officer's harangue to his troops, and throughout Johnson
        writes in martial and angular strains, in trumpeting prose
        with agonizing verse, a Cromwellian soldier touched with
        the poetic afflatus.

1904 A   BOOKS - NONE

1904 B   SHORTER WRITINGS

   1   EMERSON, RALPH WALDO.   The Complete Works of Ralph Waldo
        Emerson, Vol. XI, edited by Edward Waldo Emerson. Boston:
        Houghton, Mifflin and Co., pp. 32-36.
         Emerson quotes liberally from Johnson's description of
        the founding of Concord in his speech at the second cen-
        tennial celebration.

1905 A   BOOKS - NONE

1905 B   SHORTER WRITINGS

   1   JOHNSON, EDWARD FRANCIS.   "Captain Edward Johnson, of Woburn,
        Mass., and Some of His Descendants," NEHGR, LIX (January,
        April, July), 79-86, 143-53, 275-82.
         Genealogy.

Edward Johnson: A Reference Guide

1906 A   BOOKS - NONE

1906 B   SHORTER WRITINGS

1   THOREAU, HENRY DAVID. The Writings of Henry David Thoreau,
        Vol. I, II, VI. Boston: Houghton, Mifflin and Co.,
        pp. 8-9, 42-44, 198.
        Quotes liberally from Johnson's description of Concord
    and Sudbury here in the first few pages of A Week on the
    Concord and Merrimack Rivers. Also cites "Old Johnson"
    as a vivid example of the prudence of primitive necessity
    in Walden.

1909 A   BOOKS - NONE

1909 B   SHORTER WRITINGS

1   OTIS, WILLIAM BRADLEY. American Verse, 1625-1807. New York:
        Moffatt and Yard, pp. 5-8.
        "Good News" contains a sly Chaucerian humor rare in
    Puritan works, and its vivid depiction of New England
    winter antedated and finally culminated in "Snowbound."

1910 A   BOOKS - NONE

1910 B   SHORTER WRITINGS

1   JOHNSON, EDWARD. Johnson's Wonder-Working Providence, 1628-
        1651, edited by J. Franklin Jameson. New York: Charles
        Scribner's Sons, pp. 3-18.
        Johnson had a mind much inferior to Bradford and Winthrop,
    and his work is disfigured by many errors, inaccuracies,
    and confusions; yet he gives us the essential spirit of
    the rank and file in the colony. Johnson exhibits hot
    zealotry, narrow partisanship, and confident dogmatism,
    but he was a kindly man, and it is impossible not to
    admire his exaltation and fervent enthusiasm. His
    enthusiasm, however, leads him into rhetorical flights
    which, though often vigorous, manly, and imaginative, are
    mostly turgid, bombastic, and tedious.

1917 A   BOOKS - NONE

1917

1917 B   SHORTER WRITINGS

   1   TRENT, WILLIAM PETERFIELD, et al.   The Cambridge History of
       American Literature, Vol. I.   New York: G. P. Putnam's
       Sons, pp. 22–23.
         Johnson was a man of strong natural traits, self-made,
       representing the middle class, who gave loyal allegiance
       to the ministers and was dazzled by their piety and learn-
       ing. We read his work to learn to what degrees of
       credulity the early New Englanders went in their acceptance
       of the power of the supernatural over human affairs.

1920 A   BOOKS – NONE

1920 B   SHORTER WRITINGS

   1   McCUTCHEON, ROGER P.   "Americana in English Newspapers,
       1648–1660," PCSM, XX (1920), 90–91.
         Reference to the inclusion of Johnson's history in the
       Gorges Tracts.

1927 A   BOOKS – NONE

1927 B   SHORTER WRITINGS

   1   HAZARD, LUCY LOCKWOOD.   The Frontier in American Literature.
       New York: Thomas Y. Crowell Company, pp. 174–75.
         Frontier optimism swells into sweeping poems of praise,
       and Whitman's Leaves of Grass is a natural growth from
       the Wonder-Working Providence. The faint but fatal inti-
       mations of imminent decline and decay can best be realized
       if we place the rhapsodies of Whitman and Johnson together.
       In unrestrained lyrical outpouring, in passionate faith,
       in mystical conviction, these celebrations of the New
       World are very much alike, very much like the Hebrew
       Scriptures.

1928 A   BOOKS – NONE

1928 B   SHORTER WRITINGS

   1   MURDOCK, KENNETH B.   "The Puritan Tradition," in The Reinterpre-
       tation of American Literature, edited by Norman Foerster.
       New York: Harcourt, Brace and Company, pp. 107-8.
         In Bunyan's hands Johnson's allegory might have burned
       with divine fire, but he undertook more than he could
       accomplish, revealing both the vision and the blindness of
       the Puritan turned artist.

EDWARD JOHNSON: A REFERENCE GUIDE

1931 A   BOOKS - NONE

1931 B   SHORTER WRITINGS

1   ANGOFF, CHARLES. A Literary History of the American People,
    Vol. I. New York: Alfred A. Knopf, pp. 98-105.
       Like nearly all the historians of his time, Johnson
    interspersed his terrible prose with even more dreadful
    poetry. "The greater part of his book is unintelligible,
    and the little that has sense is of negligible worth
    artistically. He probably tried to imitate the sonorous
    style of the Bible, and succeeded only in being incom-
    prehensibly vehement." But the book, since Johnson is
    more typical of his time than Bradford or Winthrop, has
    great value for depicting the dominant temper of mind.

2   MURDOCK, KENNETH B. "Colonial Historians," in American
    Writers on American Literature, edited by John Macy.
    New York: Tudor Publishing Co., pp. 3-12.
       Johnson displays the dilemma of the colonial historians
    who had a great subject and were tempted to imitate other
    writers, but who of necessity were pioneers and adventurers
    rather than men of letters. Johnson is frequently
    effective, but usually he is harassed into dullness by
    importunate fact. "His ardor led him to play the sedulous
    ape to better artists and spotted his pages with travesties
    of the ornateness and elegance and pattern of prose writers
    who were bred to their art and not cramped by a frontier
    town in which one's real work must be with gun and ax."
    Even so, Johnson's work has more robust life than hundreds
    of later histories.

1933 A   BOOKS - NONE

1933 B   SHORTER WRITINGS

1   MORISON, SAMUEL ELIOT. "Edward Johnson," in Dictionary of
    American Biography, Vol. X, edited by Dumas Malone. New
    York: Charles Scribner's Sons, p. 95.
       Johnson's work is not a reliable authority in controversial
    matters, but he gives many homely facts ignored by the more
    intellectual chroniclers.

1937 A   BOOKS - NONE

1937

1937 B   SHORTER WRITINGS

   1   KRAUS, MICHAEL. A History of American History. New York:
        Farrar and Rinehart, pp. 45-49.
          See 1953.B3.

1938 A   BOOKS - NONE

1938 B   SHORTER WRITINGS

   1   MILLER, PERRY and THOMAS H. JOHNSON. The Puritans: A Source-
        book of their Writings. New York: American Book Co.,
        pp. 89-90.
          Very influential anthology. Johnson is a representative
        of the rank and file, a lesser figure than Winthrop or
        Bradford, who writes in a much more ornate, windy, and
        verbose style. "Even at his most inflated moments he is
        not without a certain charm, however, and the zest for
        living which so conspicuously marked the writings of
        Elizabethan England had not yet died out in him."

1944 A   BOOKS - NONE

1944 B   SHORTER WRITINGS

   1   JANTZ, HAROLD. The First Century of New England Verse.
        Worcester, Massachusetts: American Antiquarian Society,
        pp. 23-29, 220-24.
         Bibliography, plus evidence that Johnson wrote Good News
        from New England (1648), plus an enthusiastic appreciation
        of Johnson's style. Johnson has a true sense of the epic,
        and he. must have known Virgil, perhaps even Homer, for
        he may be the first English writer to successfully transfer
        the Homeric dactylic rhythm to our language. He has a
        charming sense of humor, a salty dash of satire, a splen-
        did human realism, and his work is a complete synthesis
        of the New England mind (See also PAAS, LIII [October,
        1943], 219-508).

1946 A   BOOKS - NONE

1946 B   SHORTER WRITINGS

   1   FROOM, LE ROY EDWIN. The Prophetic Faith of Our Fathers, Vol.
        III. Washington, D. C.: Review and Herald, pp. 92-93.
        Apocalyptic references in Johnson's work.

1948 A   BOOKS - NONE

1948 B   SHORTER WRITINGS

   1   SPILLER, ROBERT, et al.   Literary History of the United States,
       Vol. I.   New York: Macmillan Company, p. 35.
         Johnson's work is revivalistic in style, a homely record
       of workaday facts to which other chronicles are apt to
       be superior.

1949 A   BOOKS - NONE

1949 B   SHORTER WRITINGS

   1   MURDOCK, KENNETH B.   Literature and Theology in Colonial
       New England.   Cambridge, Massachusetts: Harvard University
       Press, pp. 85-90.
         Johnson reveals the intellectual and emotional belief in
       God's partnership in the colonial venture better than any-
       body else.   Johnson does not preach, argue, or document.
       His allegorical vision is simply the natural form taken
       by the spontaneous expression of a man writing from an
       attitude central to his whole life.   The writing problems
       are too much for him, but for all his stylistic faults and
       breathless confusion,   Johnson's enthusiasm shines through
       and goes far to disarm criticism of his technical defects.

1952 A   BOOKS - NONE

1952 B   SHORTER WRITINGS

   1   MORSE, JARVIS M.   American Beginnings: Highlights and Side-
       lights of the Birth of the New World.   Washington, D. C.:
       Public Affairs Press, pp. 162-65.
         Johnson wrote history from personal experience rather
       than intellectual curiosity, from a middle class point of
       view rather than a clerical one.   He may be inferior to
       Bradford or Winthrop in grandeur of spirit, but his work
       is rendered forceful by hot zeal and confident dogmatism.
       "His obtrusive bias is refreshing and easily discounted."

1953 A   BOOKS - NONE

1953

1953 B   SHORTER WRITINGS

1   FEIDELSON, CHARLES, JR.   Symbolism and American Literature.
       Chicago: University of Chicago Press, pp. 79-83.
          The symbolizing process was constantly at work in the
       Puritan minds. Johnson's examples from biblical history
       become parts of a living language through which he per-
       ceives the world, and in the reference to Anne Hutchinson,
       for instance, he produced the bare bones of a metaphysical
       conceit.

2   HEIMERT, ALAN. "Puritanism, the Wilderness, and the Frontier,"
       NEQ, XXVI (September), 361-82.
          Johnson's work is the first full exposition of the new
       interpretation of New England's mission. Instead of the
       promised land, America had become the wilderness through
       which the Chosen People must pass to reach Canaan.

3   KRAUS, MICHAEL. The Writing of American History. Norman,
       Oklahoma: University of Oklahoma Press, pp. 27-28.
          Johnson's work is burdened by frequent rhetorical and
       poetic flights, is poorly arranged, contains many errors,
       has little of Bradford's gentleness or Winthrop's culture,
       and emphasizes the routine life of the community; but it
       also has interesting material for the economic and social
       history of Massachusetts.

1955 A   BOOKS - NONE

1955 B   SHORTER WRITINGS

1   MURDOCK, KENNETH B. "Clio in the Wilderness: History and
       Biography in Puritan New England," CH, XXIV (September),
       221-38.
          Johnson's allegorical translation of the colonists into
       God's champions must have stirred the readers to renewed
       confidence in their dignity, and his apparent jumbling
       of pagan mythology, the Bible, and other scraps of learning
       is an example of the characteristic response to crisis
       situations. (Reprinted in EAL, VI [Winter, 1972], 201-19).

2   VANCURA, ZDENEK. "The Humble Song of Captain Johnson,"
       Philologica (Prague), VII (#1), 1-11.
          Johnson's purpose was to defend the New England Way
       against the criticism of English Presbyterianism, and his
       individuality rests in the unquestioning intensity of his
       belief and the symbolic presentation of contemporary
       history rather than in any individual stylistic embellish-
       ments. The whole work is an extended metaphor, impressing

(VANCURA, ZDENEK)
>the reader with an emphasis which the persuasiveness of logic could never achieve; but it fails because his art, though considerable, is incommensurate to his ambitious aims. The history reminds you of an early opera, containing a series of pathetic arias connected by spoken recitative; Johnson's verses, for instance, function as fanfare, repeating the same strain of melody again and again with slight variation.

1959 A BOOKS - NONE

1959 B SHORTER WRITINGS

1 DUNN RICHARD S. "Seventeenth Century English Historians of America," in Seventeenth-Century America: Essays in Colonial History, edited by James Morton Smith. Chapel Hill, North Carolina: University of North Carolina Press, pp. 195-225.
>Johnson's work is a militant propaganda tract announcing the erection of a model community. Johnson's style is verbose, turgid, sustained only by energy and zeal, but his history demonstrates the difference between the Pilgrim and Puritan conceptions of America better than Winthrop's.

1960 A BOOKS - NONE

1960 B SHORTER WRITINGS

1 JONES, JOSEPH, et al. American Literary Manuscripts: A Checklist of Holdings. Austin, Texas: University of Texas Press, p. 197.
>Contains several items on Johnson.

2 WISH, HARVEY. The American Historian: A Social-Intellectual History of the Writing of the American Past. New York: Oxford University Press, pp. 15-16.
>Johnson's ultra-orthodox history, written in a militant style, interlarded with poetry in the Elizabethan mode or modeled on the psalms, frequently inaccurate and biased, gives fresh illustrations for the fact that the Puritans were God's chosen people.

1961 A BOOKS - NONE

1961

1961 B   SHORTER WRITINGS

   1   SANFORD, CHARLES. The Quest for Paradise: Europe and the
        American Moral Imagination. Urbana, Illinois: University
        of Illinois Press, p. 83.
          Johnson "is better likened to the popular performer in
        a band concert. His rustic trumpet, sounding loud among
        the common folk, echoed the finer trumpets" of Cotton,
        Shepard, Hooker, Davenport, Eliot, and others.

1962 A   BOOKS - NONE

1962 B   SHORTER WRITINGS

   1   GRABO, NORMAN S. "The Veiled Vision: The Role of Aesthetics
        in Early American Intellectual History," WMQ, XIX (October),
        493-510.
          By rejecting Johnson's "special pleading" the historian
        fails to meet the colonial artist on his own terms. In
        the Hutchinson episode, for instance, the historical fact
        which Johnson is giving form to is the "spirit of giddi-
        ness" that inspired the land, but Johnson's art here is
        rarely recognized.

1963 A   BOOKS - NONE

1963 B   SHORTER WRITINGS

   1   GUMMERE, RICHARD M. The American Colonial Mind and the
        Classical Tradition. Cambridge, Massachusetts: Harvard
        University Press, p. 39.
          Johnson's use of and references to Plutarch, Ulysses,
        Caesar, Pythagoras.

1965 A   BOOKS - NONE

1965 B   SHORTER WRITINGS

   1   GILSDORF, ALETHA. "The Puritan Apocalypse: New England
        Eschatology in the Seventeenth Century." Unpublished Ph.D.
        dissertation, Yale University, pp. 117-19.
          Johnson best expresses the apocalyptic preoccupations
        of the first colonists; his history indicates the degree
        to which the apocalyptic conception of New England's des-
        tiny had taken hold of the imagination of the rank and file.

1966 A BOOKS - NONE

1966 B SHORTER WRITINGS

1   GAY, PETER. A Loss of Mastery: Puritan Historians in Colonial
     America. Berkeley, California: University of California
     Press. p. 53.
          Johnson's history is a "naive military bulletin reporting
     Christ's victories against Satan in America."

2   WALSH, THOMAS F. "Dimmesdale's Election Sermon," ESQ, XLIV
     (3rd Quarter), 64-66.
          Uses Johnson's work as a reference point for the closing
     of Dimmesdale's sermon.

1967 A BOOKS - NONE

1967 B SHORTER WRITINGS

1   NASH, RODERICK. Wilderness and the American Mind. New Haven,
     Connecticut: Yale University Press, p. 37.
          The Puritans celebrated westward expansion as one of
     their greatest achievements, and Johnson's work is an
     extended commentary on the transformation of a wild country
     into a fruitful civilization.

1968 A BOOKS - NONE

1968 B SHORTER WRITINGS

1   BERCOVITCH, SACVAN. "The Historiography of Johnson's Wonder-
     Working Providence," EIHC, CIV (April), 138-61.
          In Johnson's work the migration marks the apex of a
     foreordained movement through the Hebrews and early
     Christian Church toward the millenium, and is expressed
     in a historiography rooted in biblical exegesis, embracing
     all of history, and fundamentally derived from the prin-
     ciples of typological interpretation. Johnson's familiar-
     ity with linear typology is evident from his reference to
     typological tracts, his constant use of standard tropes
     and figures, and his use of numbers as metaphors. The
     history has more organization than previously recognized,
     moving from the divine impulse for migration, through
     building the city in the wilderness, the wars of the Lord,
     to the approaching apocalypse. The Wonder-Working
     Providence, concerned as it is with American identity,

1968

(BERCOVITCH, SACVAN)
"establishes a pattern which may be traced in secular
form through many of the subsequent urgent and obsessive
definitions of the meaning of America."

2   MESEROLE, HARRISON T.   Seventeenth-Century American Poetry.
Garden City, New York: Doubleday and Company, pp. 147-49.
It is Johnson's recognition of poetry as a means of
fixing things into permanence that motivates his verse
writing. "Johnson's verses at their worst lack taste,
balance, and sense of proportion. They jog and bounce
unmercifully. But at his best the 'Kentish Soldier' is
capable of sustaining imagery well, and of exploring with
effectiveness the subtle possibilities of language."
Agrees with Jantz that Good News from New England is
written by Johnson.

3   SILVERMAN, KENNETH.   Colonial American Poetry.   New York:
Hafner Publishing Co., p. 39.
The differences between Johnson's "brief description" in
Good News and the poem on "wonder-working providences"
from his histcry indicates what happened to the Puritan
ideal during thirty years in the New World. The assured
air of historic mission is gone. The later poem is both
the mea culpa of a personal spiritual crisis and an
unblinking, nauseated registry of New England waywardness.

4   TRIMPEY, JOHN E.   "The Poetry of Four American Puritans:
Edward Johnson, Peter Bulkeley II, Nicholas Noyes, and
John Danforth." Unpublished Ph.D. dissertation, Ohio
University.
Discussion of the form and content of the poems in the
Wonder-Working Providence with special focus on the best
poem, "The Wonder-Working Providences of Christ." Most
of the poems are testimonials which provide a model for
the reader and document God's presence on earth. Johnson
is not a major Puritan poet, but he is important because
he is groping for a literary theory, because he illustrates
the wide diffusion of a theory of words, because he illustrates the soon to disappear poetry of the common man,
and because his best poem exhibits a degree of craftsman-
ship not often found in Puritan verse.

1969 A   BOOKS - NONE

1969 B   SHORTER WRITINGS

1   BRUMM, URSULA. "Edward Johnson's Wonder-Working Providence
     and the Puritan Conception of History," JA, XIV, 140-51.
        Johnson's history is not primarily a story of past
     events, but a record of covenant duties ordered and ful-
     filled. Thus, his use of the present tense is not so
     much a means of dramatization, as a signal to the reader
     that he is going to hear something of importance. John-
     son's description of the departure, crossing, and re-
     settlement, the three archetypal stages which founded
     a new existence, stand out from the rest by their
     immediacy and emotional quality; and the keynote for all
     three is suffering, a suffering relieved by knowledge of
     its place in God's plan.

2   LYNEN, JOHN F. The Design of the Present: Essays on Time and
     Form in American Literature. New Haven, Connecticut:
     Yale University Press, pp. 55-57.
        Johnson has epic intentions, but when he descends from
     the level of vision to the level of fact the effect is
     bathetic and confusing. His theme is unsuited to his
     narrative method; emblematic episodes cannot be treated
     as events in a cause and effect sequence. His efforts to
     see narratively are always defeated by his unconscious
     preference to see typically, and the characteristic effect
     is one of petering out as the attempted narrative bogs
     down in random detail.

3   [TICHI], CECELIA L. HALBERT. "The Art of the Lords
     Remembrancers: A Study of New England Puritan Histories."
     Unpublished Ph.D. dissertation, University of California
     at Davis. Mention of Johnson passim.
        See 1971.B2.

1970 A   BOOKS

1   GALLAGHER, EDWARD J. "A Critical Study of Edward Johnson's
     Wonder-Working Providence of Sions Saviour in New England."
     Unpublished Ph.D. dissertation, Unversity of Notre Dame.
        This dissertation begins with a brief chapter devoted
     to the use, knowledge of, and critical opinion of Johnson's
     work since its publication, followed by an extensive
     examination of the 1640's, the milieu out of which the
     history was written. The immediate purpose of the history
     is polemical, and Johnson's major concern is fostering
     faith in the future of the holy commonwealth. Johnson
     fosters this faith through structures drawn from spiritual

1970

(GALLAGHER, EDWARD J.)
biography and typology, and through a variety of rhetorical
devices. The conclusion compares Johnson's history in
form and content with other first generation historical
writing, and appendices provide evidence that Johnson wrote
Good News and a list of biblical references in the history.

1970 B SHORTER WRITINGS

1 WILLIAMSON, WILLIAM LANDRAM. "An Early Use of Running Title
and Signature Evidence in Analytical Bibliography," LQ,
XL (April), 245-49.
  Poole's use of bibliographical evidence in his edition
of Johnson earns his work a modest place in the history
of analytical bibliography. Refers specifically to the
inclusion of Johnson's work in the Gorges tracts.

1971 A BOOKS - NONE

1971 B SHORTER WRITINGS

1 GALLAGHER, EDWARD J. "An Overview of Edward Johnson's Wonder-
Working Providence," EAL, V (Winter), 30-49.
  There are three basic ways through which Johnson attempts
to foster faith in the idea of a holy commonwealth. He
parallels the history to a traditional pattern of individual
spiritual history in which the elect soul moves through a
wilderness condition to heaven. He provides a typological
framework which recalls the promise of a second Exodus
and the New Jerusalem associated with the Second Coming.
He uses such rhetorical devices as the "Souldier of
Christ" metaphor, dramatization of scenes, use of dialogue,
emphasis on emotion, and the bold polarities, antitheses,
and suprises of the baroque style.

2 TICHI, CECELIA. "Spiritual Biography and the Lords
Remembrancers," WMQ, XXVIII (January), 64-85.
  The wayfaring motif of spiritual biography pervades the
histories. In Johnson the new land can only be claimed
by communal commitment to a terrible sea voyage. Similarly,
the chapter devoted to the poor soul arriving in New
England at the time of the antinomian controversy is a
cameo spiritual biography, providing cathartic effect for
the Puritan society.

146

3 _____. "The Puritan Historians and Their New Jerusalem," EAL,
VI (Fall), 143-55.
Johnson and other early historians use images of dynamic
building, constant and active construction, though they
rely on biblical familiarity for their effect and thus
the images provoke only a scripturally conditioned response.
Johnson, for example, repeatedly echoes the Old Testament
account of the building of Solomon's Temple, and his
colonists are often frequently referred to as stones or
pillars.

1972 A   BOOKS - NONE

1972 B   SHORTER WRITINGS

1 *DALY, ROBERT JAMES. "God's Altar: A Study of Puritan Poetry."
Unpublished Ph.D. dissertation, Cornell University.
Discussion of Johnson in a chapter entitled "Gnostics
and Naturalists." (See DAI, 33:5168A.)

2 STEIN, ROGER B. "Seascape and the American Imagination: The
Puritan Seventeenth Century," EAL, VII (Spring), 17-37.
In the hands of Johnson, the fragmentary and desultory
typologizing of the sea voyage by other historians and
diarists is given full imaginative shape. Johnson's con-
trolling vision obliterates the distinction between the
actual voyage and the spiritual one, fully absorbing the
world into cosmic drama. As his narrative moves beyond
the voyage, Johnson makes it even clearer that the actual
sea is not as terrifying as its typological equivalent.

1973 A   BOOKS - NONE

1973 B   SHORTER WRITINGS

1 GALLAGHER, EDWARD J. "The Case for the Wonder-Working
Providence," BNYPL, LXXVII (Autumn), 10-27.
Survey of the use of, the knowledge of, and critical
commentary on Johnson's work from time of publication to
the present; and discussion of the Wonder-Working
Providence in the context of other first generation
historiography. Johnson's history is important, not because it is a minute account of colonial affairs, but
because it is myth, history illuminated and governed by
an imaginative conception aimed at satisfying an existential
need, and because it is the first substantial attempt to
develop a native mythology.

1973

2   ZIFF, LARZER. Puritanism in America: New Culture in a New
        World. New York: Viking, pp. 126-27.
            The imaginative fusion of spirit and geography, morality
        and landscape so strong in the 19th century was a gift
        from the Puritans and is present in Johnson. The land
        does not stale for Johnson because he absorbed its features
        and made them symbols of his superior condition.

1974 A BOOKS - NONE

1974 B SHORTER WRITINGS

1   JOHNSON, EDWARD. Wonder-Working Providence of Sions Saviour
        in New England and Good News from New England. Introduc-
        tion by Edward J. Gallagher. Delmar, New York: Scholars'
        Facsimiles and Reprints.
            The introduction to the Wonder-Working Providence con-
        denses material which appeared in Gallagher (1971.B1), but
        the introduction to Good News surveys the internal and ex-
        ternal evidence for attributing authorship to Johnson.

1975 A BOOKS - NONE

1975 B SHORTER WRITINGS

1   BERCOVITCH, SACVAN. The Puritan Origins of the American Self.
        New Haven, Connecticut: Yale University Press, pp. 125-32.
            Johnson's hagiographical poems embody some of the same
        principles found in Mather's lives, but Johnson's repre-
        sentative men "turn our attention from the absolute future
        to the conditional present," and "they stand for the effort
        to fuse fact and promise." Johnson's sense of urgency and
        immediacy contrasts vividly with Mather's assured retro-
        spective tone. Johnson's lives, then, emphasize "the enor-
        mous labor that still is not done," and remind us how much
        depends on human events.

2   GALLAGHER, EDWARD J. "The Wonder Working Providence as
        Spiritual Biography," EAL, X (Spring), 75-87.
            Johnson's history signifies that New England is an apt
        land in which to prepare for individual salvation, and
        that New England should be seen, imaginatively, as if it
        were an elect individual working out its own salvation.
        Johnson's colonists, though endangered by the world, the
        flesh, and the devil, can be confident of salvation if
        they remain Soldiers of Christ. The structure of the
        history, moreover, based in the opening proclamation which
        is a correlative for the Covenant, corresponds to a pat-
        tern of election, sanctification, and glorification, sug-
        gesting that the American wilderness is gradually recon-
        stituted as a fruitful land.

Writings About Richard Mather,
1670 - 1972

1670 A   BOOKS

1   MATHER, INCREASE. The Life and Death of That Reverend Man of
       GOD, Mr. Richard Mather, Teacher of the Church in Dor-
       chester in New-England. Cambridge, Massachusetts: Printed
       by S. J. and M. J.
          The source for such later accounts of Mather as those
       by Samuel Clarke (1683.B1) and Cotton Mather (1702.B1).
       Its hagiographical tone emphasizes Mather's persevering
       holiness in his life and in his writings. Mather ful-
       fills the most demanding expectations brought to bear on
       the priestly vocation by the Reformation: "It is a true
       Observation which many from Luther have taken up, viz.
       That three things make up an able Divine. 1. Meditatio;
       Study. 2. Oratio; Prayer. 3. Tentatio; Temptation.
       Christ in wilderness." His style was plain, searching,
       and consistently efficacious: "The Lord gave him an
       excellent faculty in making abstruse things plain, that
       in handling the deepest Mysteries he would accommodate
       himself to Vulgar Capacities, that even the meanest might
       learn something." Quotes a passage from Augustine which
       Mather "much approved" in order to emphasize the impor-
       tance Mather gave to clarity in his preaching: "If...I
       preach Learnedly, then onely the Learned and not the Un-
       learned can understand and profit by me; but if I preach
       plainly, then Learned and Unlearned can understand, so I
       may profit all." Mather's doctrine was rooted in Scrip-
       ture; Thomas Hooker's praise is most just: "He was
       Mighty in the Scriptures: Whence Mr. Hooker would say of
       him, My brother Mather is a mighty man."

1670 B   SHORTER WRITINGS - NONE

1683 A   BOOKS - NONE

1683

1683 B   SHORTER WRITINGS

   1   CLARKE, SAMUEL. "Richard Mather," in The Lives of sundry
       Eminent Persons in this later age. London: Thomas
       Simmons, pp. 126-37.
         Follows quite closely the spirit and substance of In-
       crease Mather's Life and Death of...Mr. Richard Mather
       (1670.A1).

1702 A   BOOKS - NONE

1702 B   SHORTER WRITINGS

   1   MATHER, COTTON. "The Life of Mr. Richard Mather," in Magnalia
       Christi Americana, Book III. London: Thomas Parkhurst,
       pp. 122-31.
         Follows hagiographic form of lives in Book III of
       Magnalia. Based largely on Increase Mathers's Life...
       of ... Mr. Richard Mather (1670.A1). Mather made ex-
       cellent and effective use of the plain style and embodied
       in his life as well as in his writings a luminous and
       exemplary piety. His preaching ministry, like his voice,
       was extraordinarily powerful. The Wise Men followed the
       Star in the East: "But I am now to add, that in all Ages,
       there have been Stars to lead men unto the Lord Jesus
       Christ: Angelical Men employ'd in the Ministry of our
       Lord, have been those happy Stars; and we in the West,
       have been so happy, as to see some of the first Magnitude;
       among which one was Mr. Richard Mather."

1846 A   BOOKS - NONE

1846 B   SHORTER WRITINGS

   1   YOUNG, ALEXANDER. Chronicles of the First Planters of the
       Colony of Massachusetts Bay, from 1623 to 1636. Boston:
       Charles C. Little and James Brown, pp. 480-81n.
         Biographical account of Mather and his family.

1857 A   BOOKS - NONE

1857 B   SHORTER WRITINGS

   1   SPRAGUE, WILLIAM B. Annals of the American Pulpit, Vol. I.
       New York: Robert Carter and Brothers, pp. 75-79.
         Biographical sketch based on Cotton Mather's life of
       Mather in the Magnalia (1702.B1).

Richard Mather: A Reference Guide

1870 A BOOKS - NONE

1870 B SHORTER WRITINGS

1   POOLE, W. F. "The Mather Bibliography," <u>Boston Daily</u>
        <u>Advertiser</u>, 15 August.
            Describes several works by Cotton and Increase Mather
        and states that there is "no family in this country upon
        whose writings so much labor and money have been spent
        by antiquaries and collectors as the Mather family."

1878 A BOOKS - NONE

1878 B SHORTER WRITINGS

1   TYLER, MOSES COIT. <u>A History of American Literature, 1607-1765</u>.
        New York: G. P. Putnam's Sons, I, pp. 99, 275; II, pp.
        64-67.
            The seminal and monumental history to which all later
        scholars, whether sharing or disputing its judgments,
        remain indebted. Notes Mather's scholarship, his part in
        composing the Bay Psalm Book, and his power as preacher
        and writer. His writings have considerable literary merit.

1884 A BOOKS - NONE

1884 B SHORTER WRITINGS

1   *DAVIS, VALENTINE D. "Richard Mather's Voyage to America,"
        <u>Unitarian Herald</u>, 15, 22, 29 August. Cited in Alexander
        Gordon, "Richard Mather," <u>Dictionary of National Biography</u>
        (1894.B1).
            In <u>Some Account of the Ancient Chapel of Toxteth Park</u>
        (1884.B2), Davis states that Mather's <u>Journal</u> of his voyage
        to America is among the most interesting of his journals.

2   _____. <u>Some Account of the Ancient Chapel of Toxteth Park,</u>
        <u>Liverpool from the year 1618 to 1883, And of Its Ministers,</u>
        <u>especially of Richard Mather, The First Minister</u>. Liver-
        pool: H. Young.
            Chapters on Mather's early life; his teaching at a school
        of Toxteth Park, Liverpool, of which he became schoolmaster
        at the age of fifteen; his ministry in New England; his
        character and style. Emphasizes Mather's excellence as a
        teacher even as he continued his own studies in logic,
        rhetoric, and theology. The people at Toxteth were reluc-
        tant to have him respond favorably to the letters from
        Cotton and Hooker encouraging him to come to America, but

1884

(DAVIS, VALENTINE D.)
Mather was compelled to do so by his call to the ministry.
Notes Mather's importance to New England, his perseverance
--he preached every Sunday for fifty years--and his ability to give "valuable service" through his writings. His
Journal of his voyage to America is among the most inter-
esting of his journals. His doctrine was orthodox; Scripture was his final authority; his language was clear,
powerful, and totally devoid of any form of obscurity.

1891 A   BOOKS - NONE

1891 B   SHORTER WRITINGS

1   MERRIAM, JOHN M.   "Historic Burial-Places of Boston and
        Vicinity," PAAS, New Series, VII (October), 381-417.
        Notes the location of Mather's grave and gives other
    burial information, including Mather's epitaph.

1892 A   BOOKS - NONE

1892 B   SHORTER WRITINGS

1   WALKER, WILLISTON.   "The Services of the Mathers in New
        England Religious Development," Papers of The American
        Society of Church History, V, 59-85.
        Good general account of Mather's relationship to New
    England church polity and the importance of his Answer....
    "While Mather wrote throughout the tract as if speaking
    in the name of the ministers of the infant colonies, the
    work was wholly his own; but it set forth, better even
    than the later treatises of Cotton and Hooker, the actual
    practice of New England during the first decade of the
    Puritan settlement and was doubtless...formative in
    its influence. Like most of the writings of Richard
    Mather, the Answer to the Thirty-two Questions is marked
    by simplicity, directness, and common-sense, and an entire
    absence of that literary pedantry which is so conspicuous
    a feature of the work of his grandson Cotton."

1893 A   BOOKS - NONE

1893 B   SHORTER WRITINGS

1   WALKER, WILLISTON. "The Cambridge Synod and Platform, 1646–
    1648," in The Creeds and Platforms of Congregationalism.
    New York: Charles Scribner's Sons, pp. 157–237.
       Clear discussion of the preface to, and text of, the
    Cambridge Platform, the theological issues confronted by
    the Synod, Mather's relationship to the Synod and Plat-
    form, and his advocacy of the Half-Way Covenant.

1894 A   BOOKS – NONE

1894 B   SHORTER WRITINGS

1   WALKER, WILLISTON. A History of the Congregational Churches
    in the United States. New York: The Christian Literature
    Company, pp. 137–38, 154–55, passim.
       Brief but useful descriptions of Mather and the settle-
    ment, his writings, especially the Cambridge Platform,
    and his position on the Half-Way Covenant.

1901 A   BOOKS – NONE

1901 B   SHORTER WRITINGS

1   WALKER, WILLISTON. Ten New England Leaders. New York: Silver,
    Burdett and Company, pp. 97–134.
       Fine sympathetic and knowledgeable study of Mather,
    whose wisdom, skill, and shrewd yet kindly leadership
    "give him rank, if not as the first, yet among the first
    four or five in eminence of the ministerial founders of
    New England." Emphasizes Mather's important place in the
    difficult doctrinal conflicts within Congregationalism
    over such questions of polity as baptism and church mem-
    bership. Though Mather was not so brilliant as Cotton
    or Hooker, "he was a strong, learned, simple, practical,
    impressive man, a good companion, a helpful associate,
    and above all a lover of Congregationalism, because he
    believed it the way of the Scriptures." Kenneth B.
    Murdock called this essay the "best modern study" of
    Mather (See 1933.B3).

1903 A   BOOKS – NONE

1903

1903 B   SHORTER WRITINGS

   1   GREEN, SAMUEL ABBOTT. "Some engraved portraits of the Mather
       Family," in Ten Facsimile Reproductions Relating to
       Various Subjects. Boston: University Press: John Wilson
       and Son, Cambridge, Massachusetts, pp. 1-[10].
         Reproduces plates of two similar engraved portraits of
       Mather, who holds his glasses in right hand, a Bible in
       left. Engraving was frontispiece for Increase Mather's
       Life and Death of...Richard Mather (1670.A1). Original
       portrait a woodcut (c.1668) given to Massachusetts His-
       torical Society, which "specimen of an engraved portrait
       is the earliest one extant that was made in this country."
       The first and earlier of the two engravings has on it
       "Mr. Richard Mather"; the second, "Richardus Mather"
       above the portrait and "Johannes Foster sculpist" below.
       The engraving in each of its forms is almost surely the
       work of John Foster, the first printer in Boston and first
       engraver in the English colonies of America.

1909 A   BOOKS - NONE

1909 B   SHORTER WRITINGS

   1   GORDON, ALEXANDER. "Richard Mather," in Dictionary of
       National Biography, Vol. XIII, edited by Sidney Lee. New
       York: Macmillan Company, pp. 29-30.
        Sound biographical sketch. Lists fifteen of Mather's
       works.

1910 A   BOOKS - NONE

1910 B   SHORTER WRITINGS

   1   JOHNSON, EDWARD. Wonder-Working Providence of Sions Saviour
       in New England, 1628-1651, edited by J. Franklin Jameson.
       New York: Charles Scribner's Sons, pp. 104-5, 215.
        Calls Mather a "Sage, grave, reverend and faithful ser-
       vant of Christ" who was "indued by the Lord with many
       Heavenly gifts, of a plaine and upright spirit, apt to
       teach, full of gratious expressions, and Resolvedly bent
       to follow the truth, as it is in Jesus."

RICHARD MATHER: A REFERENCE GUIDE

2   TUTTLE, JULIUS HERBERT. "The Libraries of the Mathers," <u>PAAS</u>,
        New Series, XX (April), 268-356.
            Detailed account of the history of the libraries of the
        Mather family from 1610, when Mather began collecting books
        for his library, through Samuel Mather and Mather Byles,
        to 1814, when the so-called "remains of the old Library
        of the Mathers" were given to the American Antiquarian
        Society. Refers to Mather and his books throughout.

<u>1923 A BOOKS - NONE</u>

<u>1923 B SHORTER WRITINGS</u>

1   HOLMES, THOMAS J. "Notes on Richard Mather's 'Church Govern-
        ment,' London, 1643," <u>PAAS</u>, New Series, XXXIII (April-
        October), 291-96.
            Describes and interprets Mather's <u>Church Government and</u>
        <u>Church Covenant discussed in an Answer to two and thirty</u>
        <u>questions</u>...in its immediate historical setting. Gives
        an account of its printing history and the number of extant
        copies. Notes those copies that are currently for sale.

<u>1924 A BOOKS - NONE</u>

<u>1924 B SHORTER WRITINGS</u>

1   MURDOCK, KENNETH B. "Richard Mather," <u>Old Time New England</u>,
        XV (October), 51-57.
            Sympathetic consideration of Mather's life and contri-
        butions to early New England Puritanism. Tone and emphasis
        similar to those in biographical sketch of Mather (1933.B3).

<u>1927 A BOOKS - NONE</u>

<u>1927 B SHORTER WRITINGS</u>

1   HOLMES, THOMAS J. "Richard Mather defines the church polity
        of New England," in <u>The Mather Literature</u>. Cleveland,
        Ohio: Privately printed for WGM [William Gwinn Mather],
        pp. 26-32.
            The writings of the Mathers are the "outcome of an
        intensely passionate religious movement" whose spirit and
        doctrines Mather exemplifies. His <u>Platform</u> was adopted
        and recommended to the New England churches when the Con-
        vention of 1648 met at Cambridge. His <u>Answer</u>...is also
        a seminal document in Puritan history, thought, and church
        polity. Notes William Gwinn Mather's desire for a

1927

(HOLMES, THOMAS J.)
six-volume bibliography of the writings of the Mathers,
which would include "a full-size reproduction of the title-
page of every known Mather work, together with a description
of the book and a census of the known copies." The writings of the "minor" Mathers would be an important part of
the project (1940.B2).

2   PARRINGTON, VERNON LOUIS. Main Currents in American Thought:
The Colonial Mind, 1620-1800. New York: Harcourt, Brace
and Company, pp. 60, 99.
Refers only twice to Mather, first as an apologist for
orthodoxy, second as a part of that dominant family which
was "certain to have a finger in every pie baking in the
theocratic oven." In this second context, the tone and
implications of the following statements are noteworthy:
the Mather family, "from the emigrant Richard with the
great voice, chief architect of the Cambridge Platform,
to the provincial Cotton," strongly affected New England
history.

1933 A   BOOKS - NONE

1933 B   SHORTER WRITINGS

1   HOLMES, THOMAS J. "The Mather Collection at Cleveland," The
Colophon: A Book Collectors' Quarterly, Part 14, No. 3.
[Later "Reissued in a few copies by permission of The
Colophon...Part Fourteen, 1933." New York. 12 pp.].
The translation by Mather, Welde, Eliot, and others of
The Whole Booke of Psalmes...into English Metre (1640)
was printed in some fifty-seven editions (26 or 27 at
Boston or Cambridge, Mass.; 21 at London or Cambridge,
Eng.; 7 at Edinburgh; 2 at Glasgow). Library at Gwinn,
the Cleveland repository of the collection of William
Gwinn Mather, contains fifteen editions, though not the
rare first edition. Mather's Cambridge Platform was
printed some thirty times. Gwinn collection includes
those printed at Cambridge, 1649 (the first edition);
London, 1653; Cambridge, 1671; and Boston, 1680. Repro-
duces title-pages of Bay Psalm Book and Cambridge
Platform.

2   MILLER, PERRY. Orthodoxy in Massachusetts, 1630-1650. Cambridge, Massachusetts: Harvard University Press, pp. 120,
148, 155, passim.
Cites Mather throughout as one of the strongest apologists
for the orthodox order of first-generation Puritanism.

1933

(MILLER, PERRY)
Mather insisted that "the Discipline appointed by Jesus
Christ for his Churches is not arbitrary" but the same
for all churches, and that since the Congregational way
"which we here practice, be (as we are perswaded of it)
the same which Christ hath appointed, and therefore un-
alterable," no other form of church government can be law-
ful in New England. Mather's exultant statement, made
less than a decade after the founding of the religious and
social order he represented, that "there is no materiall
point, either in constitution, or government," in which
the New England churches "do not observe the same course,"
epitomized--at least for the moment--the Puritans' sense
that their experiment had come to fruition and could be
sustained.

3   MURDOCK, KENNETH B.   "Richard Mather," in Dictionary of
     American Biography, Vol. XII, edited by Dumas Malone.
     New York: Charles Scribner's Sons, pp. 394-95.
        A sympathetic sketch which concludes by citing Cotton
     Mather's praise of the efficacy of Mather's sermons and
     ministry: "His voice was loud and big, and uttered with
     a deliberate vehemency, it procured unto his ministry an
     awful and very taking majesty; nevertheless, the substan-
     tial and rational matter delivered by him, caused his
     ministry to take yet more." The eulogies of Mather by
     his descendants stress Mather's diligence, patience, and
     zeal for learning.

1937 A   BOOKS - NONE

1937 B   SHORTER WRITINGS

1   HOLMES, THOMAS J.   "The Mather Bibliography," PBSA, XXXI (Part
     I), 57-76.
        Descriptions and locations of works by the Mather family
     and attendant problems in seeking to work accurately and
     methodically with them. Cites Worthington C. Ford's
     admonition: "Mr. Holmes, you are getting into that Mather
     bog. I warn you, you will never get out of it again."
     Sets tentative number of writings of Mather and "male off-
     spring" at six hundred and twenty-one--including eleven
     by Mather and four hundred and forty-four by Cotton Mather.

1939 A   BOOKS - NONE

1939

1939 B   SHORTER WRITINGS

1   MILLER, PERRY. The New England Mind: The Seventeenth
         Century. Cambridge, Massachusetts: Harvard University
         Press, pp. 415, 435-38, passim.
           Mather exemplifies the federal theology of the Puritans
         in his use of the Judean compact between God and Israel
         as the model for the theocratic social compact of New
         England. The people were to be dedicated in the one com-
         pact both to theological and social duties. Mather's
         reasoning "exposes completely the workings of the New
         England mind; the theorists read their Bibles in the light
         of the federal theology, and from their readings arrived
         at a political philosophy."

2   PIERCY, JOSEPHINE K. Studies in Literary Types in Seventeenth
         Century America (1607-1710). New Haven, Connecticut: Yale
         University Press, pp. 107-10.
           Since "poetry must be free and unhampered by dogma,"
         Calvinist doctrine in New England was discouraging to
         literature. But Mather's "Preface" to the Bay Psalm
         Book (1956.B1) demonstrates a real awareness of literary
         expression and such principles as English metre and rhyme.
         Mather explains "with painstaking care" the necessary
         exceptions to the authors' goal of translating the Psalms
         with literal exactness. The "Preface" is, in essence,
         literary criticism. "Perhaps, after all, the author's
         failure to write good verse came not from a lack of knowl-
         edge or of literary background, but from a too conscien-
         tious purpose."

1940 A   BOOKS - NONE

1940 B   SHORTER WRITINGS

1   CADBURY, HENRY JOEL. "Harvard College Library and the Libraries
         of the Mathers," PAAS, L (April), 20-48.
           Traces exchanges of books between private libraries of
         the Mathers and Harvard College. Harvard sold many of its
         duplicate works to the Mather family, while the Mathers
         gave many books from their libraries to Harvard. Both
         Part I ("From Harvard to the Mathers," 21-27) and Part
         II ("From the Mathers to Harvard," 28-48) provide many
         references to particular works and thinkers (Thomas Aquinas,
         Augustine, Duns Scotus, Cicero, Ames) central to Puritan
         thought and rhetoric in the seventeenth and eighteenth
         centuries.

2   HOLMES, THOMAS J.   "Richard Mather, 1596-1669," in The Minor
    Mathers: A List of their Works. Cambridge, Massachusetts:
    Harvard University Press, pp. 51-107.
        Compared with separate bibliographies of Cotton and In-
    crease Mather, insists Holmes, this is a list. Mather
    published twenty-one works, two of which are fragmentary.
    Reproduces many title-pages and provides extremely detailed
    bibliograhical description. Includes Mather's will. An
    Appendix by W. S. Piper to The Minor Mathers--"Manuscripts
    of the Minor Mathers, Including Letters, Volumes, Sermons"
    (1940.B3)--is an important part of the work. Holmes notes
    that "The works...have not been analyzed here, though
    that would have been a fascinating and fruitful enterprise,
    especially in the case of the works of Richard."

3   PIPER, WILLIAM SANFORD.   "Richard Mather," in "Manuscripts of
    the Minor Mathers...," in Thomas J. Holmes The Minor
    Mathers...(1940.B2), pp. 191-204.
        Annotated compilation of Mather's extant mss. Detailed
    descriptions of nature and state of individual mss.

1945 A   BOOKS - NONE

1945 B   SHORTER WRITINGS

1   LEVY, BABETTE MAY.   Preaching in the First Half Century of New
    England History. Hartford, Connecticut: The American
    Society of Church History, pp. 10, 29, 30, 31, passim.
        Fine study of New England Puritan preaching style. Cites
    Mather on Christ's sufferings, Covenant of Grace, justifi-
    cation, degeneracy of the times. Notes Mather's direct
    vitality of mind and the simplicity and clarity of his
    style. He avoids obscurity, Latin expressions, and
    pedantry, in order to reach and move his listeners and
    readers. Mather was a better preacher than Increase or
    Cotton Mather because of his ability to elucidate the tenets
    of his belief so all could understand them. He achieved
    this lucidity "not so much by exemplification of his ideas,
    as by clarity and organization in his thinking, plus
    remarkable skill in the use of apropos Biblical citations."
    Includes checklist of two of Mather's works.

1949 A   BOOKS - NONE

1949

1949 B   SHORTER WRITINGS

   1   MURDOCK, KENNETH B.   Literature and Theology in Colonial New
        England.   Cambridge, Massachusetts: Harvard University
        Press, pp. 35, 45, 65.
          Notes Mather's concern for preaching plainly to his
        listeners.   He avoids pedantry and those tricks of rhet-
        oric which are useless and improper "in a Popular Auditory."
        Quotes Increase Mather's (1670.A1) characterization of
        Mather as one who desired to drive home a "lively and
        affectionate" sense of the divine by shooting "rhetorical
        arrows" not "over his people's heads, but into their
        Hearts."

1955 A   BOOKS - NONE

1955 B   SHORTER WRITINGS

   1   GRIFFIN, GILLETT.   "John Foster's Woodcut of Richard Mather,"
        Painting and Graphic Arts, VII, 1-19.
          Detailed discussion of the artistic qualities of the
        Foster woodcut.   Includes facsimile.

1956 A   BOOKS - NONE

1956 B   SHORTER WRITINGS

   1   HARASZTI, ZOLTAN.   "John Cotton -- Not Richard Mather," in The
        Enigma of the Bay Psalm Book.   Chicago: University of
        Chicago Press, pp. 19-27.
          Contends that John Cotton, not Mather, wrote the original
        draft of the Preface to the Bay Psalm Book.   Cites as
        internal evidence their respective prose styles and the
        form of their use of specific quotations, and as external
        evidence handwriting samples and comparisons.   Shepard
        probably added a section to the original draft and "may
        have done the final editing--not to the advantage of the
        piece...for the draft lost its spontaneity in the con-
        densation and, at times, even its lucidity."   The final
        paragraph of the Preface may also be by Cotton.

1963 A   BOOKS - NONE

1963 B   SHORTER WRITINGS

1   MORGAN, EDMUND S.   Visible Saints: The History of a Puritan
    Idea. [New York]: New York University Press, pp. 100,
    110, passim.
        Refers to Mather and the church at Dorchester and his
    advocacy of the Half-Way Covenant.

1965 A   BOOKS - NONE

1965 B   SHORTER WRITINGS

1   EMERSON, EVERETT H.   John Cotton. New York: Twayne Publishers,
    pp. 78-79, 156.
        Notes that Mather drew heavily on Cotton's works in
    writing the Cambridge Platform. Suggests the extent of
    Mather's borrowing by brief parallel passages from the
    Platform and Cotton's The Keyes Of the Kingdom.

1967 A   BOOKS

1   BURG, BARRY RICHARD.   "Richard Mather (1596-1669): The Life
    and Work of a Puritan Cleric in New England." Unpublished
    doctoral dissertation, University of Colorado.
        Detailed and thorough relation of Mather's life, with
    attention to his views on church polity especially as
    they were addressed to, and hence strongly influenced,
    the Synods of 1648 and 1662.

1967 B   SHORTER WRITINGS - NONE

1968 A   BOOKS - NONE

1968 B   SHORTER WRITINGS

1   HAMILTON, SINCLAIR.   "Portrait of a Puritan, John Foster's
    Woodcut of Richard Mather," PULC, XVIII (Winter), 43-48.
        Describes circumstances of presentation of woodcut to
    Princeton. Cut is rare; six impressions were made, only
    five have been located. The cut may have been used for
    the first American book illustration. Mather holds book
    in left hand, "absurdly diminutive" pair of eye glasses
    in right. Mather was described as a solid man of "gravity,
    grace, and wisdom," and Foster also portrays him this way.
    Cut reveals Mather as a bearded and grave man, severe but
    just, intolerant of heresy but tolerant of human weakness;
    one who loved learning, hated deceit, and walked humbly with
    God.

1969

1969 A   BOOKS - NONE

1969 B   SHORTER WRITINGS

   1   POPE, ROBERT G. The Half-Way Covenant: Church Membership in
Puritan New England. Princeton, New Jersey: Princeton
University Press, pp. 14, 19-20, 21-26, passim.
     Most complete account of Mather's central role in the
doctrinal conflicts over baptism and the Half-Way Covenant.
In 1645, Mather's pleas for a more inclusive polity on
baptism were ignored, and in 1648 the synod omitted this
same recommendation from the "Model of Church Government."
In the decade after the Cambridge Synod, Mather "provided
the leadership and the rallying point for the revisionist
ministers."

1970 A   BOOKS - NONE

1970 B   SHORTER WRITINGS

   1   BURG, B. RICHARD. "The Record of an Early Seventeenth Century
Atlantic Crossing," The Husson Review, IV (#1), 72-77.
     Straightforward summary of Mather's trip to New England,
drawn largely from Mather's Journal.

1971 A   BOOKS - NONE

1971 B   SHORTER WRITINGS

   1   MIDDLEKAUFF, ROBERT. "Richard Mather (1596-1669): History,"
in The Mathers: Three Generations of Puritan Intellectuals,
1596-1728. New York: Oxford University Press, pp. 3-75.
See also pp. 80-81, 83, passim.
     Lucid critical discussion of Mather's life and ideas on
covenant, church polity, soteriology, preparation, and the
psychology of religious experience. Deals with Mather not
simply as part of the Mather family but as a preacher and
thinker in his own right. Divides "History" into four main
sections: "The Founder"; "The Antichrist"; "The Church";
"The Word." Explores Mather's attempts to answer the
agony of man's uncertainty over his salvation. How Mather
conceived of "the affective disposition of the faculties"
largely determined his answer. Conversion "began in the
affections" and "true belief in Christ was as much an
emotional disposition as it was intellectual." The psy-
chological and moral sensitivity of Mather's conception
of religious experience comes from his insistence on the

(MIDDLEKAUFF, ROBERT)
wholeness of the mind and his analysis of motive. Sympathetic descriptions of Mather's perseverance and piety.
Kept his eyes fixed on the Church above all things. The
minister must constantly pass on to his people the reality
of Christ: "the full explication of the meaning of His
birth and death, His sacrifice and miracles, and finally
the news of the imminence of His Glorious return." In his
defense of the Half-Way Covenant, Mather made the "sad
concession to reality" that grace did not inevitably show
itself. But his preaching "does not seem ever to have
accommodated this reality." Like his generation of Puritan
divines, Mather "continued to urge men to strive after God
while he insisted that only God could draw them. And he
continued to urge them to beg for the return of Christ
even while he assured them that the Lord could not be
coerced or even persuaded."

1972 A   BOOKS - NONE

1972 B   SHORTER WRITINGS

1   BURG, B. RICHARD. "A Letter of Richard Mather to a Cleric in
     Old England." WMQ, Third Series, XXIX (January) 81-98.
       Deals briefly in an introductory comment with the
     doctrinal background of Mather's letter, which he wrote
     in 1636. The letter is valuable for two reasons: it is
     one of the Massachusetts Bay Colony's "first complete
     statements of ecclesiastical doctrine and polity," and,
     as a "transitional document," it defines more clearly the
     nature of the changes in New England church polity be-
     tween 1634 (John Cotton's True Constitution of a Particular
     Visible Church) and 1639 (Mather's own Church-Government
     and Church-Covenant Discussed).

2   HALL, DAVID D. The Faithful Shepherd: A History of the New
     England Ministry in the Seventeenth Century. Chapel Hill,
     North Carolina: University of North Carolina, pp. 80,
     86, passim.
       References to Mather's role in forming early Congrega-
     tional polity and writing Cambridge Platform. His view of
     church government held that the divines of New England
     needed and deserved the power to surmount majority rule,
     yet that church elders and ministers were "servants" and
     would not indulge in "Lordly and Princely rule."

Writings About Thomas Shepard, 1702 - 1974

1702 A BOOKS - NONE

1702 B SHORTER WRITINGS

1   MATHER, COTTON. "Pastor Evangelicus. The Life of Mr. Thomas
        Shepard," in Magnalia Christi Americana, Book III. London:
        Thomas Parkhurst, pp. 84-93.
            Hagiography which declares that Shepard was "as great a
        converter of souls as has ordinarily been known in our
        days." Shepard's individual writings combine, with the
        greatest effectiveness, doctrinal and practical divinity.
        Describes several works, including The Sincere Convert
        and The Sound Beleever. Quotes from Shepard's meditations
        in order to indicate the consistently "affective" quality
        and tone of Shepard's religious experiences. The character
        of Shepard's daily conversation was "a trembling walk with
        God." Quotes approvingly from Bulkeley's funeral elegy
        on Shepard and calls it a comprehesive epitaph: "Nominis
        Officiia; fuit Concordia Dulcis;/ Officio Pastor Nomine
        Pastor erat" ["Fitly his name and office were the same:
        Shepherd by office -Shepherd, too, by name"].

1846 A BOOKS - NONE

1846 B SHORTER WRITINGS

1   YOUNG, ALEXANDER. Chronicles of the First Planters of the
        Colony of Massachusetts Bay, from 1623 to 1636. Boston:
        Charles C. Little and James Brown, p. 558n.
            Biographical account of Shepard and his family.

1847 A BOOKS

1   ALBRO, JOHN A. The Life of Thomas Shepard. Boston: Massa-
        chusetts Sabbath School Society [Vol. IV, in "Lives of
        the Chief Fathers of New England" series].

1847

    (ALBRO, JOHN A.)
      The best and most thorough biography of Shepard. Its
tone is hagiographical yet restrained and judicious.
Twelve chapters, which begin with Shepard's English ministry and conclude with a general consideration of Shepard's
writings, the judgments of several divines with regard
to the writings, and Shepard's "personal religion." Albro's
high respect for Shepard suffuses the work, and his clarity,
intelligent emphases, and sensitivity to historical and
religious concerns give it distinction as a biographical
and interpretative study.

1847 B   SHORTER WRITINGS - NONE

1857 A   BOOKS - NONE

1857 B   SHORTER WRITINGS

   1   SPRAGUE, WILLIAM B. Annals of the American Pulpit, Vol. I.
      New York: Robert Carter and Brothers, pp. 59-68.
       Biographical sketch based on Cotton Mather's life of
Shepard in the Magnalia (1702.B1) and several seventeenth-
century sources.

1878 A   BOOKS - NONE

1878 B   SHORTER WRITINGS

   1   TYLER, MOSES COIT. A History of American Literature, 1607-1765,
      Vol. I. New York: G. P. Putnam's Sons, pp. 204-10.
       The seminal and monumental history to which all later
scholars, whether sharing or disputing its judgments,
remain indebted. Describes Shepard's confrontation with
Laud, his "subtile and commanding intellect," and influence
on Edwards. Sets out sharp distinction between Shepard's
profound mind and rhetorical ability, including his clear,
terse, energetic style ("the charm of his diction was en-
hanced by the manner of his speech, which was almost match-
less for its sweet and lofty grace, its pathos," and its
intensity) and the vengeful theology in whose service he
used them. Shepard's theology, like that of all the
Puritans, is "harsh, dark, inexorable" in its stark emphasis on man's depravity and God's wrath. Souls are
consigned to the devil with "marvellous alacrity." For
Tyler, Shepard's unrelenting conception of divine justice
is not balanced or redeemed by any such corresponding sense
of grace or mercy as is found in Hooker.

Thomas Shepard: A Reference Guide

1908 A   BOOKS - NONE

1908 B   SHORTER WRITINGS

1   DAVIS, ANDREW McFARLAND. "A Few Words About the Writings of
      Thomas Shepard," Publications of the Cambridge Historical
      Society, III, 79-89.
        Shepard's continued stature and influence is confirmed
      by the repeated republication of his works to the present
      time. Shepard's language is often technical and obscure
      to modern readers; but his contemporaries praised its
      effectiveness. Shepard's sermons are rather "strict" and
      "legal," which may prove a "stumbling block to some." He
      reveals in his works some of the customs of his times as
      well as the tenor of life in Cambridge. In Theses Sab-
      baticae, for example, Shepard indicates how he expects his
      listeners to observe the Sabbath, and from such indications
      the modern reader is able to imagine and apprehend some
      sense of the actual time and place.

1909 A   BOOKS

1   WHYTE, ALEXANDER. Thomas Shepard: Pilgrim Father and Founder
      of Harvard, His Spiritual Experience and Experimental
      Preaching. Edinburgh and London: Oliphant and Ferrier.
        An intensely personal and evangelical work. Quotes long
      passages of "soul-saving religion" from Shepard, the "so
      excellent and so venerable Pilgrim Father"--the descrip-
      tions, as Whyte notes, are David Brainerd's--and echoes
      their exhortations. Emphasizes Shepard as an "affective"
      and "experimental" preacher, and concentrates throughout
      on the power of words as referential and efficacious:
      "'Read,' so the fine aphorism runs, 'Read always with your
      eye on the object.' That is to say, read not so much with
      your eye on the words as on the things." Shepard's vital
      imagery and rhetorical power make him "the pungentest of
      preachers." Though certain of Shepard's books are "badly
      written" and at times use an English that is "all but un-
      recognizable," their language is heartfelt, experiential,
      and affecting.

1909 B   SHORTER WRITINGS

1   CAIRNS, WILLIAM B., ed. "Thomas Shepard," in Selections from
      Early American Writers, 1607-1800. New York: Macmillan
      and Company, pp. 125-33.
        Brief selections from Shepard, including a passage from
      The Sincere Convert, are preceded by a sketch. Shepard's

1909

(CAIRNS, WILLIAM B.)
style is at times "unusually modern, and he is more read-
able than many of his contemporaries, but none of his work
stands out with especial distinction."

2   COOPER, THOMPSON. "Thomas Shepard," in Dictionary of National
Biography, Vol. XVIII, edited by Sidney Lee. New York:
Macmillan Company, pp. 50-51.
Sketch notes Shepard's right rank among Puritan divines
as a writer and lists fifteen of his works.

1910 A   BOOKS- NONE

1910 B   SHORTER WRITINGS

1   JOHNSON, EDWARD. Wonder-Working Providence of Sions Saviour
in New England, 1628-1651, edited by J. Franklin Jameson.
New York: Charles Scribner's Sons, pp. 9, 103, passim.
Even given Johnson's sustained tone of veneration and
praise for other ministers among the first-generation
Puritans, his tributes to Shepard are especially rhapsodic.
Shepard is twice called a "soul ravishing Minister." He
is "a man of a thousand, indued with abundance of true
saving knowledge for himselfe and others." Shepard himself is "Heavenly minded" and his ways of moving others
to salvation "sweet-affecting."

1911 A   BOOKS - NONE

1911 B   SHORTER WRITINGS

1   DAVIS, ANDREW McFARLAND. "Hints of Contemporary Life in the
Writings of Thomas Shepard," PCSM, XII, 136-62.
For Shepard, all laws derive from Scripture; he is
clearly sympathetic to the theocratic polity of John
Cotton. But one also finds in Shepard an "unexpected
liberality of thought." Although Shepard reflects the
Puritan tendency to use as illustrations, or metaphors,
Biblical texts and analogies, there are in Shepard's works
some suggestions of the nature of daily life. Davis
arranges these references under separate headings, including "Nautical" (Shepard uses sea imagery extensively,
though it always refers to sailor and ship; he never refers
to the sea's monstrous waves or cruelty); "Sleeping in
Church"; "Housework"; "Sickness"; "Gardening"; "English
History" (references extremely rare); "Children's Manners"

(DAVIS, ANDREW McFARLAND)
("What little hope of a happy generation after us, when many among us scarce know how to teach their children manners?"); "Football" (Shepard images Satan as a kicker in echoing the older form of rugby, to which kicking was central); "Physics"; "Archaic Expressions"; and "Humor" (Shepard appreciated satire and humor; many of his pithy statements are humorously satiric). The extracts throw some light on colonial life, but may be of more interest to the topical student than to the general reader. Nonetheless, "they reveal to us that our ancestors were human." (Also see p. 163.)

1921 A   BOOKS - NONE

1921 B   SHORTER WRITINGS

1   ADAMS, JAMES TRUSLOW.   The Founding of New England.   Boston: Atlantic Monthly Press, pp. 372-73.
     Shepard's wrathful sermons denouncing the natural man reveal the "ethical morbidity" of the New England conscience. His constant focus on the problems of election and damnation indicates a pathological concern that ended only when civil, good men not of the elect refused to acknowledge the truth of the condemnations he--and the old order--hurled at them.

1930 A   BOOKS - NONE

1930 B   SHORTER WRITINGS

1   MORISON, SAMUEL ELIOT.   "Master Thomas Shepard," in Builders of the Bay Colony.   Boston: Houghton, Mifflin Company, pp. 105-34.
     A lively, sympathetic, and judicious portrayal. Even Whyte (1909.A1), Shepard's most fervent apologist, admits that Shepard's prose is often "atrocious." But such roughness stems not from Shepard, but from his hearers' note-taking and the subsequent process by which the sermon notes were published. Though it may seem difficult to read Shepard with understanding and sensitivity, "as you read his sermons...the pages worn at the edges and soiled with the loving hands that in other days turned them seeking light and truth; and when you think of Shepard preaching them in the primitive meeting-house at Cambridge, of his high sincerity and his intense rapport with his congregation; you begin to feel [his] extraordinary

1930

(MORISON, SAMUEL ELIOT)
power." Takes sharp issue with Tyler's analysis (1878.B1)
of the extent to which God's unrelenting wrath and judgment
pervades Shepard's writings. Shepard's focus on the terrors
of hell and damnation is "occasional"; Tyler distorts his
emphasis. Love and grace are the "words and thoughts
endlessly repeated" in Shepard's sermons. Shepard quotes
Bellarmine, the Jesuit theologian, more than he does Calvin.
Shepard preaches "a gospel of love, of infinite compassion."

1932 A BOOKS - NONE

1932 B SHORTER WRITINGS

1   ANON. "Introduction" and "A 'Trial' Shepard Bibliography,"
     PCSM, XXVII, 345-51.
        Precedes a reprinting of Shepard's Autobiography. Bib-
     liography is divided into sections on unpublished manu-
     scripts; individual published works, numbering twenty-one,
     the editions of which are noted, located, and often
     annotated further; prefaces to other writings; the Autobi-
     ography;collected works; letters; biographies. Although
     the bibliography suggests its tentative nature in its
     own title, it is very helpful. The attitude toward Puri-
     tanism held by its anonymous authors and researchers is
     expressed in the concluding sentence of the "Introduction":
     "Certain episodes and phrases in Shepard's Autobiography
     reveal Puritan attitudes which are repulsive or incompre-
     hensible to moderns; but taken as a whole, there emerges
     a personality that goes far to explain the authority
     exercised by the New England clergy; and to support one
     writer who ventures the position that the secret of their
     power 'was their character, and the love that they bore
     to their people and their God.'"

1933 A BOOKS - NONE

1933 B SHORTER WRITINGS

1   MILLER, PERRY. Orthodoxy in Massachusetts, 1630-1650. Cam-
     bridge, Massachusetts: Harvard University Press, pp.
     99-100, passim.
        Shepard's "Preface" to A Defence of the Answer (1648)
     provided one of the strongest justifications for the Great
     Migration. Shepard remained opposed to civil and religious
     innovation in New England and supported the founding
     orthodoxy with zeal and eloquence.

1935 A   BOOKS - NONE

1935 B   SHORTER WRITINGS

1   DEWEY, EDWARD H. "Thomas Shepard," in <u>Dictionary of American Biography</u>, Vol. XVII, edited by Dumas Malone. New York: Charles Scribner's Sons, pp. 75-76.

    Though certain of his works can "scarcely interest" the modern student, Shepard's writings always reveal his learning and his careful method. As preacher and worker, Shepard was tireless. Cites Samuel Mather's description of Shepard's preaching as "close and searching with abundance of affection and compassion to his hearers." In his sermons, Shepard dwells "at too great length" on the utter worthlessness and sinfulness of men, yet he does so without contempt. "He was of humble mind and had the Puritan willingness to submit himself completely to the Divine Will."

2   MILLER, PERRY. "The Marrow of Puritan Divinity," <u>PCSM</u>, XXXII, 247-300.

    Refers to Shepard throughout as a central thinker in the "federal" theology of Puritan New England. Shepard and the Puritans cannot be seen simply as "Calvinists"; they must rather be seen as Protestant "scholastics" who, while not elevating natural reason over revelation and faith, sought to rescue it from the "rubbish heap" where Calvin had cast it. Their task was to bring God to time and reason and confine His transcendence by a law of ethics without reducing His mystery and absolute power to a mechanism; that is, to ascertain "the reliability of human reason and the trustworthiness of human experience as measurements of the divine character." The central concern in federal theology, and therefore for Shepard, was the covenant. In struggling with the conception of the covenant, the Puritans were desperately striving on the one hand to subordinate humanity to God without unduly abusing human values, and on the other to "vaunt the powers of the human intellect without losing the sense of divine transcendence." This was "the central problem of the seventeenth century as it was confronted by the Puritan mind." As the covenant gradually became a "contract" which viewed divine grace as man's opportunity to strike a bargain with God for his own salvation, such "preparationist" preachers as Shepard and Hooker emphasized the possibilities and efficacy of human activity. "If an individual does not close the deal when he has the chance, he certainly cannot blame God because it gets away from him." In New England, Hooker was "clearly the most extreme" of

1935

(MILLER, PERRY)
those who emphasized the extent to which an unregenerate
man could go in the work of preparation. He stressed
man's ability to bring about the receptive frame of mind
for grace, and "dared to assert that he who could force
himself to the point of readiness would certainly receive
grace in time." Shepard's position on this crucial issue
agreed completely with that of Hooker; his The Sincere
Convert was attacked by Giles Firmin for its preparationist emphasis--that is, for demanding too much of the
natural man before grace. (See also 1956.B2.)

3 MORISON, SAMUEL ELIOT. The Founding of Harvard College. Cambridge, Massachusetts: Harvard University Press, pp. 92,
99, 103, 182-83, passim.
  Shepard's sustained role in founding Harvard, choosing
its location, planning for its library needs and scholar-
ships for needy students. Cites descriptions in Cotton
Mather and Edward Johnson of Shepard's formative influence
in this process, and praises the "puritan simplicity" of
John Harvard's epitaph, which was written by Shepard: "The
man was a Scholler and pious in his life and enlarged toward the cuntry and the good of it in life and death."
Includes brief biographical outline of Shepard.

1937 A BOOKS - NONE

1937 B SHORTER WRITINGS

1 MILLER, PERRY. "The Puritan Theory of the Sacraments in
Seventeenth-Century New England," CHR, XXII (January),
409-25.
  A study of the Puritan conception of the sacraments.
Makes use of Shepard's writings and those of such contemporaries as Hooker and John Cotton, as well as the works
of such later divines as Cotton Mather and Solomon Stoddard.

1939 A BOOKS - NONE

1939 B SHORTER WRITINGS

1 JOHNSON, THOMAS H., ed. The Poetical Works of Edward Taylor.
New York: Rockland Editions, p. 19ln.
  The imagery and tone of Taylor's "Preface" to Gods
Determinations...seem to echo directly the beginning
of Shepard's The Sincere Convert, in which Shepard also
uses rhetorical questions and vivid tropes. In this

(JOHNSON, THOMAS H.)

"theater of Heaven," Shepard asks, "Who set out those candles, those torches of haven on the table? Who hung out those Lanthorns in heaven to enlighten a dark world?" The influence is probable because Shepard's writings were among the most widely read of any seventeenth-century Puritan divine.

2   MILLER, PERRY. The New England Mind: The Seventeenth Century. Cambridge, Massachusetts: Harvard University Press, pp. 11, 44, 52, 62, passim.

Refers to Shepard throughout as a central figure in New England Puritan history, literature, and thought. His conviction and formulation of the close relationship between natural law and moral law is especially important. Shepard's position rejects the voluntarism of Scotus and adheres to a more classical, even Thomistic view: God's laws are not good simply because He commands them, but He commands them because they are good. This doctrine as it was maintained in New England is "best expressed" in Shepard's writings.

3   PIERCY, JOSEPHINE K. Studies in Literary Types in Seventeenth Century America (1607-1710). New Haven, Connecticut: Yale University Press, pp. 82, 88, 250, 252, passim.

Cites Shepard's exhortations on the need to be exact in oration. Shepard considers memoria, the necessary link in classical rhetoric between inventione and elocutione, to be of special importance: "Mark every mans Disputations and Conferences, and study to gett some good by every thing: and if your memory be not very strong, committ every notion this way gained unto Paper as soon as you gett into your Study."

1943 A   BOOKS - NONE

1943 B   SHORTER WRITINGS

1   WINTHROP, JOHN. Winthrop Papers. Edited by Samuel Eliot Morison, et al. Boston: Merrymount Press, III (1631-1637), 59, 60 passim.

Recounts Shepard's confrontation with Laud.

1944 A   BOOKS - NONE

1944

1944 B   SHORTER WRITINGS

   1   MORGAN, EDMUND S. The Puritan Family: Essays on Religion
      and Domestic Relations in Seventeenth-Century New England.
      Boston: Trustees of the Public Library, p. 19, passim.
        Refers to Shepard on marriage, the profound differences
      between civil, external virtue and experiential faith,
      and other social and religious topics.

   2   WINTHROP, JOHN. Winthrop Papers, edited by Samuel Eliot
      Morison, et al. Boston: Merrymount Press, IV (1638-
      1644), 99, 136, passim.
        Refers to Shepard in several political and personal
      contexts.

1945 A   BOOKS - NONE

1945 B   SHORTER WRITINGS

   1   LEVY, BABETTE MAY. Preaching in the First Half Century of
      New England History. Hartford, Connecticut: The American
      Society of Church History, pp. 6, 9, 10, 12, passim.
        Fine study of New England Puritan preaching style. Cites
      Shepard on many theological, political, and domestic con-
      cerns. As a preacher "Shepard alone truly survived his
      own time, to be loved and read for three centuries."
      Describes Shepard as a "gentle mystic" who also "knew in-
      stinctively how to be one with his audience." His imagery,
      including a consistent use of domestic similes immediately
      recognizable to all, is an important part of the strength
      of his prose style. Such "vital questions as Christian
      duty, forgiveness, and faithfulness are expressed in terms
      of marital difficulties and joys," and "children and the
      parental relationship provided him with many of his most
      apt illustrations." Shepard's homely and moving images
      are among the finest in Puritan prose. Includes checklist
      of eight of Shepard's works.

1946 A   BOOKS - NONE

1946 B   SHORTER WRITINGS

   1   STEWART, RANDALL. "Puritan Literature and the Flowering of
      New England," WMQ, Third Series, III (July), 319-42.
        Shepard's powerful imagery, like Hooker's, expresses the
      finest qualities of the Puritans' imagination and language.
      Edward Johnson's (1910.B1) description of Shepard as a

(STEWART, RANDALL)
"soule ravishing Minister" is fully understandable in the
light of Shepard's moving and effective prose. The "neglected continuity" between Puritan literature and later
American literature is a striking continuity. The most
important nineteenth-century authors--including Hawthorne,
Emerson, and Thoreau--were those who felt the Puritan influence most strongly. "Rarely has the written word been
used more effectively" or "the human spirit burned with
an intenser, brighter flame" than in Puritan New England.

1947 A BOOKS - NONE

1947 B SHORTER WRITINGS

1   WINTHROP, JOHN. Winthrop Papers, edited by Samuel Eliot
    Morison, et al. Boston: Merrymount Press, V (1645-1649),
    44, 74, passim.
        Refers to Shepard in several political and personal
    contexts.

1948 A BOOKS

1   OLSSON, KARL ARTHUR. "Theology and Rhetoric in the Writings
    of Thomas Shepard." Unpublished doctoral dissertation,
    University of Chicago.
        Chapter I: Shepard's writings as conventional rhetoric;
    II: Rhetorical procedure; III-V: Framework of topics;
    VI: Diction. Fine, careful, and lucid study of Shepard's
    writings in light of Aristotelian categories and Christian
    doctrine. Sustains cogently the necessary distinctions
    between classical and Christian assumptions concerning
    the nature of God, man, and language. When using the
    analytical categories of Aristotle to Shepard's works and
    style, terms such as "speaker," "argument," and "audience"
    expand and change their meanings, for "no finite means
    can be measured in terms of its true usefulness." Style,
    argument, and even the totality of the rhetorical work
    itself are not truly effective "unless they point beyond
    themselves to the infinite efficiency which empowers and
    the infinite end which directs their activity."

1948 B SHORTER WRITINGS - NONE

1949 A BOOKS - NONE

1949

1949 B   SHORTER WRITINGS

   1   MURDOCK, KENNETH B.   Literature and Theology in Colonial New
      England. Cambridge, Massachusetts: Harvard University
      Press, pp. 58, 62–63, 65, passim.
         Discusses unity and ideas of the Autobiography. Praises
      the imagery in Shepard's writings. Shepard is direct and
      pungent, as when he states, in referring to the page-turn-
      ing habits of possibly disinterested readers, "Jesus Christ
      is not got with a wet finger." Quotes paragraph from The
      Sincere Convert in which Shepard uses images of sweetness,
      clothing, and light to portray the world's striving for
      Christ's peace. The images––and "above all the sharp
      picture of a world tiring itself out in its search for
      rest"––give life to the abstract idea because "they are
      drawn freshly from experience." So far as a single para-
      graph can, Shepard's "illustrates the best qualities of
      Puritan prose" and reveals the process of a "definite
      literary theory" which "gave plenty of scope for an artist
      to write with imaginative force."

1955 A   BOOKS – NONE

1955 B   SHORTER WRITINGS

   1   EMERSON, EVERETT H.   "Thomas Hooker and the Reformed Theology:
      The Relationship of Hooker's Conversion Preaching to Its
      Background," CH, XXIV (December), 369–70. Synopsis of
      unpublished doctoral dissertation, Louisiana State Univer-
      sity.
         Shepard's teaching on conversion, like that of Cotton,
      differs so considerably from Hooker's teaching that the
      three men cannot be called a "school." Shepard belongs
      to the Reformed tradition of Calvin and his successors.

1956 A   BOOKS – NONE

1956 B   SHORTER WRITINGS

   1   HARASZTI, ZOLTAN.   "The Jingle of Thomas Shepard," in The
      Enigma of the Bay Psalm Book. Chicago: University of
      Chicago Press, pp. 12–18.
         In the Magnalia, Cotton Mather quotes a humorous quatrain
      Shepard had addressed to the divines who were to compose
      the translations for the Bay Psalm Book. Shepard's
      "jingle," as well as Cotton Mather's subsequent mention
      of Welde, Eliot, and Mather as the three divines Shepard

1956

(HARASZTI, ZOLTAN)
meant when he referred to the towns of Roxbury and Dor-
chester in the quatrain, have led critics to identify this
triumverate as the authors of the Bay Psalm Book. But
Cotton Mather notes their names and then speaks of "the
rest" of the authors, who in fact included, among others,
Cotton, Ward, John Wilson, Samuel Whiting, and Francis
Quarles.

2   MILLER, PERRY. "Preface" to reprinting of "The Marrow of
Puritan Divinity" (1935.B2), in Errand into the Wilderness.
Cambridge, Massachusetts: Belknap Press, pp. 48-50.
Defends the conception of New England Puritan theology
and theologians as "federal" rather than Calvinist. But
acknowledges more clearly than he had that the federal
theology was deeply Calvinist; it was simply "an idiom
in which these Protestants sought to make a bit more plau-
sible the mysteries of the Protestant creed." The Puritan
conception of man's predicament was that which all the
Reformed churches maintained. "Were I to rework this piece
today...I should more strongly emphasize the underlying
connection; though even so, I should retract nothing from
the fascinating peculiarity of the federal phraseology."

1962 A   BOOKS - NONE

1962 B   SHORTER WRITINGS

1   BATTIS, EMERY. Saints and Sectaries: Anne Hutchinson and the
Antinomian Controversy in the Massachusetts Bay Colony.
Chapel Hill, North Carolina: University of North Carolina
Press, pp. 26, 119, 190, passim.
Clear and basically solid account of the antinomian con-
troversy and Shepard's role it it. Negative tone toward
Shepard in that role also comes to extend to other aspects
of Shepard, including his "ponderous" humor.

1963 A   BOOKS - NONE

1963 B   SHORTER WRITINGS

1   MORGAN, EDMUND S. Visible Saints: The History of a Puritan
Idea. [New York]: New York University Press, pp. 92, 100,
114, 134.
Shepard admitted that the "visible" churches of New
England included hypocrites as well as saints, but insisted
that they would not be knowingly tolerated. Later in his

1963

(MORGAN, EDMUND S.)
ministry, however, he argued that a "federal" rather than
a "real" holiness was sufficient for church membership and
acknowledged that hypocrites could never be kept away
from even the most "freshly gathered" congregation of visible saints.

1964 A   BOOKS

1   HASLER, RICHARD.   "Thomas Shepard: Pastor-Evangelist (1605-
    1649), A Study in the New England Puritan Ministry." Un-
    published doctoral dissertation, Hartford Seminary Founda-
    tion.
        Part One is biographical. Chapter I: Shepard's early
    ministry. II: New England ministry. Part Two analyzes
    Shepard's covenant ecclesiology. III: Puritan interpre-
    tation of nature and implications of Covenant of Grace.
    IV: Non-Separating Congregationalist's view of the church.
    Part Three, Hasler's major focus, discusses the evangelical
    task of ministry. V: Shepard's evangelical theology, in
    which Shepard places "enormous emphasis upon man's respon-
    sibility to respond to God's grace." VI: Shepard's
    devotional life. VII: Shepard's preaching of the Word.
    VIII: Influence of Shepard's written ministry as it af-
    fected Edwards, Brainerd, nineteenth-century evangelism.
    Unmistakable signs within Shepard's own ministry adumbrate
    the time when the strong evangelical drive would be severed
    from the "New England Way" and result in the individualistic
    evangelism of American frontier. Appendix A: photostat
    of a manuscript transcribed and identified for first time
    as "Advertisements to the Reader" from Shepard's The
    Defence of the Answer (1648). Appendix B discusses plain
    style and includes Shepard's sermon, Of the Plentiful
    Dispensing of Grace in the Gospel Ministry, in which Shep-
    ard expresses his evangelical view of the ministry.

1964 B   SHORTER WRITINGS - NONE

1965 A   BOOKS - NONE

1965 B   SHORTER WRITINGS

1   EMERSON, EVERETT H.   John Cotton. New York: Twayne Publishers,
    pp. 8, 18, 27, passim.
        References to Shepard's preaching, collaboration with
    Cotton on Singing of Psalmes a Gospel-Ordinance, conceptions
    of conversion and the promises.

Thomas Shepard: A Reference Guide

1966 A   BOOKS - NONE

1966 B   SHORTER WRITINGS

  1   PETTIT, NORMAN.   The Heart Prepared: Grace and Conversion
      in Puritan Spiritual Life.   New Haven and London: Yale
      University Press, pp. 86, 87, 89, passim.
        Considers Shepard, among others, in his relationship to
      the Puritan conceptions of preparation, grace, conversion,
      and the covenant.   Shepard, "more than any other prepara-
      tionist, either in England or in America," was caught up
      in "the dilemma of covenant theology" that God alone can
      bend the heart to grace; and that man must enter the cov-
      enant of his own free will.   Shepard's conversion, like
      Hooker's, was long and painful.   But where Hooker in
      seeking an alternative to excessive constraint had em-
      phasized "personal acknowledgment of the promises," Shep-
      ard "put the efficacy of the Law at the center of his
      experience."

1967 A   BOOKS

  1   HUMPHREY, RICHARD ALAN.   "The Concept of Conversion in the
      Theology of Thomas Shepard (1605-1649)."   Unpublished
      doctoral dissertation, Drew University.
        Emphasizes central place of Holy Spirit in Shepard's
      theology.   Chapter I: Modern evaluations of Shepard's
      thought.   II: Shepard's life and times.   III: Shepard's
      theology is not an intellectual system, but experiential
      and rooted in kerygma.   IV: Shepard's preparationism
      seeks to make use of the church and its ordinaries, as in
      covenant theology, but no movement toward grace can be
      self-initiating.   Shepard's doctrine of the church is
      identical to that of John Owen, Hooker, Cambridge Plat-
      form.   V: More detailed analysis of conversion process
      and work of Holy Spirit.   Concludes that Shepard furnishes
      a bridge between Calvin and Edwards.   The "one distinctive
      feature of Shepard's theology" scholars have not emphasized
      sufficiently is his "all-inclusive doctrine of the Holy
      Spirit."   Although "the promise, the atonement, and grace
      are made available to man," it is "the work of the Holy
      Spirit that makes Christ's work efficacious."

1967 B   SHORTER WRITINGS - NONE

1968

1968 A   BOOKS

   1   STROTHER, BONNIE LEW. "The Imagery in the Sermons of Thomas
       Shepard." Unpublished doctoral dissertation, University
       of Tennessee.
         Sermons written in the plain style. Shepard avoids
       elaborate conceits and uses homely similitudes, traditional
       patterns of images, and more novel images based on
       scientific discoveries. Shepard's imagery helps to reveal
       the mind of the Puritan as he sets forth to erect the New
       Jerusalem in the Massachusetts Bay Colony.

1968 B   SHORTER WRITINGS

   1   FREDERICK, JOHN T. "Literary Art in Thomas Shepard's 'The
       Parable of the Ten Virgins,'" SCN, XXVI (Spring), 4-6.
         The general structure of Shepard's Parable is simple:
       the virgins of the New Testament parable are the New
       England churches and faithful, and the approaching wedding
       is the Second Coming. The first twenty-two sermons empha-
       size the sin of hypocrisy, while the remaining nineteen
       focus on the Second Coming and the nature and evidences
       of the gift of grace. The imaginative force and literary
       artistry of the work are seen especially in Shepard's
       skilful shaping of sentences and fresh and vigorous imagery.
       The vitality and accessibility of Shepard's prose indicate
       that the Parable was composed for the ear of the hearer
       rather than for the eye of a reader. Shepard often uses
       parallelism and antithesis for a special emphasis. Shep-
       ard's images are homely: maritime, business, landscape,
       household life. The prevailing tone is one of gentle
       persuasion. God's love and mercy, not wrath, dominate.
       Tyler's (1878.B1) stress on Shepard's harsh and unrelenting
       concern with damnation is a distortion. The tone expresses
       grief for sin rather than condemnation, hope, the love of
       Christ as God. In this emphasis it is similar to Hooker's
       The Poor Doubting Christian and "with that work offers a
       needed corrective" to the common misjudgments about Puritan
       writings.

   2   HALL, DAVID D., ed. The Antinomian Controversy, 1636-1638:
       A Documentary History. Middletown, Connecticut: Wesleyan
       University Press, pp. 14-15, 18-20, passim.
         Introduction and notes, Shepard's letters, and other
       primary sources provide a clear account of Shepard's
       crucial role in the struggle between orthodoxy and Anti-
       nomianism in the Massachusetts Bay Colony.

3 SHEA, DANIEL B., JR. Spiritual Autobiography in Early
America. Princeton, New Jersey: Princeton University
Press, pp. 105, 139-51, 155, passim.
Discusses Shepard's Autobiography as composite of three
forms of personal writing: ministerial labors and suffer-
ings, salvation narrative, declaration of providences
granted to author and colony. The work does not fully
achieve the reconciliation to the way of Providence it
strongly proclaims. Yet Shepard's "immoderately loving
memorial" to Joanna, his second wife--Hooker's eldest
daughter--"constitutes a reconciliation beyond the ade-
quacy of formula." In writing the Autobiography, Shepard
experiences once again her piety and love.

1970 A BOOKS - NONE

1970 B SHORTER WRITINGS

1 JONES, JAMES WILLIAM. "The Beginnings of American Theology:
John Cotton, Thomas Hooker, Thomas Shepard and Peter
Bulkeley." Unpublished doctoral dissertation, Brown University.
Discusses tensions in thought of four New England Puritan
theologians between role of believer and role of Christ
in work of salvation. Cotton most Christocentric of four;
he rejects the idea of preparation and the possibility
that sanctification could be evidence of justification.
Shepard "attributed the highest potency" to the law and
to preparation. On the question of whether the new covenant is conditional, Cotton insisted that it had no conditions, while Shepard argued that "it probably had
conditions which were fulfilled by Christ." Perry Miller
implies that the ideas of preparation and a conditional
covenant moved Puritanism toward anthropocentrism; but
"the Christocentric context of their theology kept these
men from the position Miller attributed to them." Their
Christocentrism "meant that even when they suggested that
the covenant might have conditions, it was Christ and not
man who fulfilled them." Shepard, like Hooker, did not
discuss preparation in the context of the covenant, but
in the context of Christ's spirit working upon man. Discusses the Antinomian controversy from this perspective.
Suggests that it was the Christocentrism of this theology,
rather than the covenant or preparation, which moved
American Puritanism from theocentrism to anthropocentrism.

1970

2   ROSENMEIER, JESPER. "New England's Perfection: The Image of
Adam and the Image of Christ in the Antinomian Crisis,
1634 to 1638," WMQ, Third Series, XXVII, 435-59.
   During the Antinomian controversy, both Cotton and Shepard, who next to Cotton was "the finest theologian and
most effective preacher in the Bay," were preoccupied with
questions of justification and sanctification. Both also
viewed the individual's salvation as a microcosm of the
redemption of the world. But their conceptions of soterio-
logical and eschatological time, with respect to the individual soul and America, differ sharply. Cotton sees a
new kingdom of Christ coming into being in America in a
future time; Shepard hopes that Adam's lost Paradise may
be regained, but rejects Cotton's futuristic vision of
Christ's new kingdom in America or the soul. Shepard
believed that "God intended man to accept Christ's Passion
as a past event, not as a recurring moment in the lives
of believers. This 'joyning the soul immediately to
[Christ] and filling it with himself,..we cannot enjoy
yet.'" Although the sinner cannot participate formally
and dramatically in Christ's Crucifixion and Resurrection,
he has available "an inexhaustible bank account of grace,
which redeems his sins, and enables him to do works as
holy as Adam's." Shepard's conception is not a form of
Arminianism. But it emphasizes a recurring stasis in man's
moral experience that stands in contrast to Cotton's
vision of the realization of Christ's kingdom on earth--
and in New England--in the present moment or in some
recognizable future time.

1971 A BOOKS - NONE

1971 B SHORTER WRITINGS

1   MIDDLEKAUFF, ROBERT. The Mathers: Three Generations of Puritan
Intellectuals, 1596-1728. New York: Oxford University
Press, pp. 51, 66, 233, 245.
   References to Shepard's preparationism and conception
of desire. Shepard and Hooker are the two most important
preparationists among the Puritan founders. But Shepard,
unlike Hooker, "did not attribute a rational power
to the will. Yet his conception of the process of conversion resembles Hooker's more closely than it does
[Richard] Mather's; for, like Hooker, Shepard did not
attribute a prominent role to the affections." In trying
to assess the character of man's desire in the work of
salvation, Shepard "left the door ajar for earnest desire
to enter as reputable evidence" of grace.

Thomas Shepard: A Reference Guide

1972 A BOOKS

1   McGIFFERT, MICHAEL, ed. "Introduction," in God's Plot: The
    Paradoxes of Puritan Piety, Being the Autobiography &
    Journal of Thomas Shepard. [Amherst, Massachusetts]:
    University of Massachusetts Press, pp. 3-32, [239-241].
       Good analysis of Shepard's life, thought, and prose
    style. Discusses Shepard's relationship to such basic Pu-
    ritan concerns as the Covenant, assurance, and soteriology.
    In England, Shepard had "forged his sermons in the burning
    pit of Hell" and in so doing anticipated the subject and
    rhetoric of similar sermons by Edwards. But in the American
    sermons ten years later, "one encounters only an occasional
    brand from this old burning." Although he continued to
    preach the fear of the Lord as a spur to saintly striving,
    he had renounced completely the "homiletics of hellfire"
    by the 1640's. Shepard preached both the law and the
    gospel--"the law to 'set out man's sin,' the gospel to 'set
    out God's love'"--but his heart was "far more deeply en-
    gaged" in the second part of this dialectic. Shepard
    sought to communicate above all "the sweetness of grace,
    the tenderness of Christ." Includes a list of secondary
    readings, each briefly described, on pp. 239-241.

1972 B   SHORTER WRITINGS

1   HALL, DAVID D. The Faithful Shepherd: A History of the New
    England Ministry in the Seventeenth Century. Chapel Hill,
    North Carolina: University of North Carolina Press, pp.
    50, 80, 89, passim.
       Shepard's relation to origins of New England Congrega-
    tionalism, conceptions of church government and ministry,
    evangelism, role in Antinomian controversy. Confronted
    by the indifference of their people, "Shepard and his
    generation took on as their final task the shaping of a
    myth that justified their disappointing life as shepherds
    in the wilderness." Shepard's evangelism stressed the
    need for men to seek Christ with all their power. As the
    quintessential "legal" preacher, Shepard "invoked the
    doctrine of the means, together with the full array of
    scholastic doctrines and distinctions, to justify man's
    active role in salvation. The same distinctions served
    to buttress Shepard's legalistic doctrine of preparation
    for salvation. Writing from within the tradition of
    'precise' evangelism, he declared that a complex and ex-
    tended process of repentance must precede the moment of
    conversion."

1973

1973 A BOOKS - NONE

1973 B SHORTER WRITINGS

  1 WOOLLEY, BRUCE CHAPMAN. "Reverend Thomas Shepard's Cambridge
     Church Members 1636-1649: A Socio-Economic Analysis."
     Unpublished doctoral dissertation, University of Rochester.
       Part II is a transcription of a "major Shepard document"
     --"The Confessions of Divers Propounded to Be Received and
     Were Entertayned as Members," which contains the confessions
     of faith of fifty applicants for membership in Shepard's
     church c. 1638-1645. Part I interprets the document in
     light of Shepard's covenant theology. None of the fifty
     seems to have been denied church membership. No direct
     correlation established between worldly estate and visible
     sainthood.

1974 A BOOKS - NONE

1974 B SHORTER WRITINGS

  1 WERGE, THOMAS. "Thomas Shepard and Crevecoeur: Two Uses of
     the Image of the Bosom Serpent before Hawthorne,"
     Nathaniel Hawthorne Journal, IV, 236-39.
       Bush (H-1971.B1) argues that one of the traditions and
     sources on which Hawthorne may have drawn for his "Egotism;
     or, The Bosom Serpent," was New England Puritanism, and
     notes Hooker's possibly unique use of the image of the
     bosom serpent to personify sin. Shepard, in The Sincere
     Convert, uses the same image in an extremely graphic way.
     The unregenerate and "poysonful" heart "contains, breeds,
     brings forth, suckles all the litter" of actual sins.
     Although "thou feelest not all these [sins] stirring in
     thee at one time, they are in thee like a nest of Snakes
     in an old hedge. Although they break not out in thy life
     they lie lurking in thy heart." For Shepard and Hawthorne,
     physical symbol and moral state are organically related.
     The bosom serpent is an important image in the Puritan
     tradition, and remains important for Hawthorne for the
     way it embodies and reveals a constant dimension of man's
     moral experience.

Index

The letters before the date reference refer to the last name of the
author in whose section the item is located.

(Cotton, John)
--The Way of Congregational
    Churches Cleared, C-1968.B5,
--Way of Life, C-1941.B2,
--will, C-1851.B1
"The Cotton Family," C-1847.B1
Cowie, Alexander, B-1962.B3
The Creeds and Platforms of
    Congregationalism, M-1893.B1,
    H-1893.B1
Crevecoeur, Hector St. Jean de,
    S-1974.B1
"A Critical Edition of Three
    Poems by John Cotton,"
    C-1962.A1
"A Critical Study of Edward John-
    son's Wonder-Working Provi-
    dence of Sions Saviour in
    New England," J-1970.A1
Cromwell, Oliver, C-1861.B1
The Cultural Life of the American
    Colonies, 1607-1763,
    B-1957.B1
Cyclopaedia of American Liter-
    ature, J-1866.B1,
    C-1866.B1, B-1866.B2

Daly, Robert James, J-1972.B1,
    B-1973.B2
Darrow, Diane Marilyn, H-1968.A1
"The Date of Governor Bradford's
    Passenger List," B-1899.B2
Davenport, John, J-1961.B1,
    C-1658.A1, C-1930.B3,
    C-1932.B1, H-1972.B1
Davidson, Clifford, H-1968.B1
Davidson, Edward H., C-1964.B1
Davis, Andrew McFarland,
    S-1908.B1, S-1911.B1
Davis, J., B-1822.B1
Davis, Richard Beale, C-1969.B1,
    B3
Davis, Valentine D., M-1884.B1-B2
Davis, William T., B-1883.B3,
    B-1885.B1, B-1903,B1,
    B-1908.B1
Deane, Charles,F., J-1868.B1,
    J-1881.B1, B-1855.B1,B4,
    B-1856.B1,B3, B-1871.B1-B2,
    B-1879.B1
"Declension in a Bible Common-
    wealth," C-1941.B2

DeFoe, Daniel, B-1939.B1,
    B-1972.B1
democracy, H-1849.A1, H-1891.A1,
    H-1921.B1, H-1927.B1,
    H-1931.B1, H-1932.B1,
    H-1933.B1, H-1952.B1,
    H-1956.B4, H-1961.A1,
    H-1962.B1
Denholm, Andrew Thomas, H-1961.A1
"The Departure of the Pilgrims,"
    B-1900.A1
The Derby School Register, 1570-
    1901, C-1902.B2
The Descendants of William Brad-
    ford, B-1951.A1
The Design of the Present: Essays
    on Time and Form in American
    Literature, J-1969.B2,
    B-1969.B8
--reviews of, B-1970.B1
Desprez, May McClellan, B-1920.B1
Dewey, Edward H., S-1935.B1
Dexter, Franklin B., B-1884.B1
Dexter, Henry Martyn, B-1856.B1,
    B-1905.B3
Dexter, Morton, B-1894.B1
Dickinson, A. T., C-1930.B2,
    C-1935.B1, B-1961.B2
Dictionary of American Biography,
    J-1933.B1, C-1930.B1,
    B-1929.B2, M-1933.B3,
    S-1935.B1, H-1932.B1
Dictionary of National Biography,
    B-1908.B2, C-1909.B1,
    M-1909.B1, S-1909.B2,
    H-1908.B1
"Die Ankunft in der neuen Welt:
    Epische and Lyrische Ges-
    taltung einer Kolonialen
    Grundsituation bei William
    Bradford und Thomas Tillam,"
    B-1964.B3, B-1968.B3
Diman, Rev. J. Lewis, C-1867.B1
Dimmesdale, Arthur, C-1972.B2
"Dimmesdale's Election Sermon,"
    J-1966.B2
Discourse about Civil Govern-
    ment, C-1932.B1
"Discovery of Gov. Bradford's
    History," B-1857.B1

INDEX

The Godly Preachers of the
    Elizabethan Church,
    H-1965.B2
"God's Altar: A Study of Puritan
    Poetry," J-1972.B1
God's Plot: The Paradoxes of
    Puritan Piety, S-1972.A1
Gomes, Peter J., B-1975.B2
"Good News from New England,"
    B-1975.B2
Goodwin, Gordon, H-1908.B1
Goodwin, John A., B-1888.B1
Gordon, Alexander, C-1909.B1,
    M-1909.B1
Gorges, Ferdinando, J-1837.B1,
    J-1847.B1, J-1867.B1,
    J-1868.B1, J-1881.B1,
    J-1920.B1, J-1970.B1
Gott, Charles, B-1930.B1
"Governor Bradford's 'Breeches'
    Bible," B-1903.B1
"Governor Bradford's Journal,"
    B-1906.B1
"Governor Bradford's List of the
    Mayflower Passengers,"
    B-1899.B1
Governor William Bradford, and His
    Son Major William Bradford,
    B-1900.A1
"Governor William Bradford's Will
    and Inventory," B-1900.B1
Grabo, Norman S., J-1962.B1,
    C-1963.B6, C-1968.B2,
    B-1969.B5
Gray, F. C., C-1843.B1, C-1931.B2
Green, Samuel Abbott, M-1903.B1
Greenough, Chester N., C-1918.B1
Griffin, Gillett, M-1955.B1
Griffin, John, B-1972.B1
Griffis, William Elliot, B-1920.B2
"The Growth of Thomas Hooker's
    The Poor Doubting Christian,"
    H-1973.B1
Guild, Reuben Aldridge, C-1866.B2
Gummere, Richard M., J-1963.B1,
    C-1959.B1, C-1963.B7,
    B-1963.B1

Habegger, Alfred, C-1969.B4,
    H-1969.B1
Halbert, Cecelia C. See Tichi

The Half-Way Covenant: Church
    Membership in Puritan New
    England, M-1969.B1
Hall, David D., C-1965.B3,
    C-1968.B3, C-1972.B4,
    M-1972.B2, S-1968.B2,
    S-1972.B1, H-1972.B3
Hall, Ruth Gardiner, B-1951.A1
Haller, William, B-1938.B1
Hamilton, Sinclair, M-1968.B1
Handlin, Oscar, B-1956.B1
Haraszti, Zoltan, C-1956.B1,
    M-1956.B1, S-1956.B1
Harris, J. Rendel, B-1920.B3
Hart, Albert Bushnell, B-1927.B1
Harvard, John, S-1935.B3
"Harvard College Library and the
    Libraries of the Mathers,"
    M-1940.B1
Haskins, George Lee, C-1960.B1
Hasler, Richard, S-1964.A1
Hawthorne, Nathaniel, J-1966.B2,
    C-1972.B2, B-1938.B3,
    B-1963.B4,B6,
    B-1965.B1, S-1946.B1,
    S-1974.B1, H-1946.B1,
    H-1971.B1
"Hawthorne and 'The Maypole of
    Merrymount,'" B-1938.B3
Haxtun, Annie Arnoux, B-1897.B5
Haynes, Thomas, H-1956.B2
Hazard, Lucy Lockwood, J-1927.B1,
    B-1927.B2
"The Heart of New England Rent:
    The Mystical Element in
    Early Puritan History,"
    C-1956.B2
The Heart Prepared: Grace and
    Conversion in Puritan Spiri-
    tual Life, C-1966.B2,
    S-1966.B1, H-1966.B1
Heath, Dwight, B-1963.B2
"The Hebrew Exercises of Governor
    William Bradford," B-1971.B2
"Hebrew Learning Among the
    Puritans of New England
    Prior to 1700," B-1911.B1
"The Hebrew Preface to Bradford's
    History of the Plymouth
    Plantation," B-1949.B1

193

INDEX

INDEX

"The Pilgrim Church and Plymouth
Colony," B-1884.Bl
The Pilgrim Fathers from a Dutch
Point of View, B-1932.Bl
The Pilgrim Fathers of New Eng-
land and their Puritan
Successors, C-1895.Bl,
B-1895.B2
The Pilgrim Fathers,or, The
Founders of New England,
B-1853.Bl
The Pilgrim Spirit, B-1921.B2
"The Pilgrimage of Thomas Hooker
(1586-1647) in England, The
Netherlands, and New England,"
H-1967.B2
The Pilgrims and their History,
B-1918.B2
The Pilgrims of Plymouth,
B-1921.B3
Piper, William Sanford,
M-1940.B2-B3
"Piscator Evangelicus, Or, The
Life of Mr. Thomas Hooker,"
H-1695.Dl
Place, Charles A., C-1929.Bl
Plato, C-1937.Bl
Plooij, D., B-1920.B3, B-1932.Bl
Plumb, Albert H., B-1920.Al
Plumstead, A. W., B-1963.B6
Plutarch, J-1963.Bl
The Plymouth Adventure, B-1950.Bl
The Plymouth Republic: An His-
torical Review of the Colony
of New Plymouth, B-1888.Bl
The Poetical Works of Edward
Taylor, S-1939.Bl,
"The Poetry of Four American
Puritans," J-1968.B4
"The Poetry of William Bradford:
An Annotated Edition with
Essays Introductory to the
Poems," B-1970.Al
Polishook, Irwin H., C-1967.Al,
C-1969.B3
"Politics and Sainthood:
Biography by Cotton Mather,"
C-1963.B12
Pond, Enoch, C-1834.Al,Bl
Pool, Rev. D. de Sola, B-1911.Bl
Poole, Harry Alexander, C-1956.Al
Poole, William Frederick,
J-1867.Bl, J-1868.Bl-3,

(Poole, William Frederick)
J-1877.Bl, J-1970.Bl,
M-1870.Bl
Pope, Robert G., M-1969.Bl
"Portrait of a Puritan, John
Foster's Woodcut of Richard
Mather," M-1968.Bl
"Preaching and Publication--
Chronology and the Style of
Thomas Hooker's Sermons,"
H-1972.B4
Preaching in the First Half
Century of New England
History, C-1945.Bl,
M-1945.Bl, S-1945.Bl,
H-1945.Bl
"A Precious Relic," B-1865.B2
"Preparation for Salvation in
Seventeenth Century New
England," C-1943.Bl
"Preparing the Soul for Christ:
The Contrasting Sermon Forms
of John Cotton and Thomas
Hooker," C-1969.B4, H-1969.Bl
Prince, Thomas, B-1848.B2,
B-1879.Bl, H-1971.B4
"The Printing of Old Manuscripts,"
B-1883.B2
The Prophetic Faith of Our
Fathers, J-1946.Bl, C-1946.Bl
Prynne, Hester, C-1972.B2
The Puritan Age, J-1888.Bl
"The Puritan Apocalypse: New
England Eschatology in the
Seventeenth Century,"
J-1965.Bl, C-1965.B2
The Puritan Family, S-1944.Bl,
H-1944.Bl
"The Puritan Heresy," C-1932.B3
The Puritan Heritage: America's
Roots in the Bible, B-1964.B2
"The Puritan Historians and their
New Jerusalem," J-1971.B3
"Puritan Literature and the
Flowering of New England,"
B-1946.Bl, S-1946.Bl,
H-1946.Bl
The Puritan Mind, B-1930.Bl
The Puritan Oligarchy: The
Founding of American Civili-
zation, B-1947.Bl
The Puritan Origins of the Ameri-
can Self, B-1975.Bl, J-1975.Bl

201

INDEX

(Rosenmeier, Jesper)
  B-1972.B3, B-1973.B3,
  B-1975.B1, S-1970.B2
Rose-Troup, Frances, C-1963.B15
Rossiter, Clinton, H-1952.B1,
  H-1956.B4
"Round About Scrooby," B-1889.B1
Rourke, Constance, B-1931.B4
Runyan, Michael G., B-1948.B3,
  B-1970.A1, B-1975.A1
Rusk, Ralph L., C-1939.B1
Rutman, Darrett B., C-1965.B4,
  C-1966.B4, C-1972.B3

Saint Paul, B-1970.B5
Saints and Sectaries, C-1962.B1,
  S-1962.B1, H-1962.B1
--reviews of, C-1963.B3-B4,B10,
  C-1964.B3, C-1972.B3
Saints and Strangers, B-1945.B1
"The Salem Puritans in the 'Free
  Aire of a New World,'"
  C-1957.B2
Salem Witchcraft, J-1867.B2
Sampson, Grant, C-1966.B5
"Samuel Maverick's House,"
  J-1885.B1
Sanford, Charles, J-1961.B1,
  B-1961.B4
Savage, James, J-1814.B1,
  J-1843.B1, J-1853.B1,
  B-1843.B1, H-1825.B1
The Scarlet Letter, C-1972.B2,
  B-1965.B1
Schoick, William J., B-1974.B1
Schneider, Herbert W., B-1930.B1
Schoff, S., B-1835.B1
Sears, Lorenzo, J-1902.B1
"Seascape and the American Imagi-
  nation: The Puritan Seven-
  teenth Century," J-1972.B2,
  B-1972.B4
Selections from Early American
  Writers, 1607-1800, S-1909.B1
"The Sensibility and Conscious
  Style of William Bradford,"
  B-1969.B4
"The Services of the Mathers in
  New England Religious
  Development," M-1892.B1
Seventeenth Century American
  Poetry, J-1968.B2

Seventeenth-Century America:
  Essays in Colonial History,
  J-1959.B1, B-1959.B1
"Seventeenth-Century English His-
  torians of America,"
  B-1959.B1, J-1959.B1
Sewall, Samuel, J-1868.B4
Shakespeare, William, B-1921.B3
The Shattered Synthesis,
  C-1973.B1
Shea, Daniel B., Jr., S-1968.B3
Shepard, James, B-1900.A1
Shepard, Thomas, J-1961.B1,
  C-1918.B1, C-1943.B1,
  C-1945.B1, C-1970.B2-B3,
  H-1891.A1, H-1935.B1,
  H-1937.B1, H-1945.B1,
  H-1955.A1, H-1966.B1,
  H-1968.B2, H-1970.B1,
  H-1972.B3, M-1956.B1
--Autobiography, S-1949.B1,
  S-1968.B3, S-1972.A1
--bibliography, S-1898.B1,
  S-1932.B1, S-1945.B1,
  S-1964.A1, S-1973.B1
--biography, S-1702.B1,
  S-1846,B1, S-1847.A1,
  S-1857.B1, S-1898.B1,
  S-1930.B1, S-1935.B3,
  S-1943,B1, S-1944.B2,
  S-1947.B1, S-1964.A1,
  S-1967.A1, S-1968.B2,
  S-1972.A1, S-1973.B1
--Journal, S-1702.B1, S-1972.A1
--Parable of the Ten Virgins,
  S-1968.B1
Shuffleton, Charles, H-1972.A1
Shuffleton, Frank C., H-1971.B4
Shurtleff, Nathaniel B.,
  B-1855.B5
Sibbes, Richard, C-1962.B1,
  H-1968.B1
Siegel, Ben, B-1964.B2
Signers of the Mayflower Compact,
  B-1897.B5
Silverman, Kenneth, J-1968.B3
Simpson, Alan, B-1955.B2
Skelton, Samuel, C-1957.B2
"Sketches of the Governors and
  Chief Magistrates of New
  England, from 1620 to 1820,"
  B-1841.B1

203